Legacies, Legends & Lies

Also by Joan Finnigan

Books

Giants of Canada's Ottawa Valley
Some of the Stories I Told You Were True
Look! The Land is Growing Giants
Laughing All the Way Home
The Best Damn Fiddler from Calabogie to Kaladar (screenplay)

Legacies, Legends & Lies

JOAN FINNIGAN

Quarry Press

Quarry Press
221 King Street East
Kingston, Ontario

ISBN 919627-62-5

Revised edition 1987

*"The intellect of man is forced
to choose perfection of the life
or of the work."*
                              –Yeats

CONTENTS

ACKNOWLEDGMENTS

This book would not have been possible without the help of two very special women: Betty Corson of Kingston, my editor; and Joan Litke of Burnstown, my transcriptionist-typist. I should also like to express my gratitude to the following resource people: Tim Gordon, Burnstown; Larry Gaffney, Deep River; Carl Jennings, Sheenboro; Ross Finnigan, Mayfred Horner, Marie and Frank Finnigan, Jr., Shawville; Hal Anthony, Lowell Green, Hon. Lloyd Francis, Ottawa; Gail and Chalmers Adams, Toronto. I should also like to acknowledge here the part my children, Jonathan, Roderick and Martha, have always played in my work. They have contributed practical advice, ongoing support, encouragement when times were tough, and real pride in my goals.

This book would not have been possible either without the financial aid of the Ontario Arts Council, the Historical Society of the Gatineau and the Finnigan Foundation for Irish Writers.

Introduction

It is almost three years to the day since historian Arthur Lower said to me, "The unique nature of the Valley is hardly understood elsewhere in Canada."

And it must be eight years ago that I completed my first Ottawa Valley taped interviews, phoned an influential friend of mine in Toronto (who naturally came from the Valley as well), and said to her, "I have done some work on my oral history of the Valley. Now I want you to send me to the best publisher for it." She promptly gave me the name of a friend of hers, a senior editor with a major publishing firm. When I reached the Toronto editor I said, "My name is Joan Finnigan and I am calling you about a book I am working on about the Ottawa Valley —". There was a long pause and then the voice exclaimed, "The Ottawa Valley! Where the hell is that?"

Now, five books, 300 tapes, 272,000 kilometres and eight years later I like to think that things have changed and that my work has been part of that change.

I like to think of how far we have come in the last ten or fifteen years. It is told that approximately fifteen years ago a young history undergraduate made history when he requested permission to do his Ph.D. thesis on the history of the Ottawa Valley, and was denied it on the grounds that there was not sufficient depth and substance in history of the Ottawa Valley to merit a doctoral thesis. Yet a few years later things had changed so much that permission was granted by the University of Ottawa for a thesis on a subject so much more narrow and insular — the politics of Pontiac County!

Unquestionably, the Ottawa Valley is a jewel in the "Canadian Mosaic" revealing itself as colourful and profound, multi-faceted and beautiful as any other part of the country. It is differentiated from all other parts of the country by its geography — it is the watershed of one of the mightiest rivers of the world fed by its twenty-six tributaries — by its accent and idiom emerging from its predominantly Irish origins, by its lumbering saga and subsequent economic history, by its story, song, dance, music, folklore, legend, humour.

The Ottawa Valley is further differentiated from other parts of Canada by the fact that it is the only regional entity which, like the Colossus at Rhodes, straddles two provinces, Ontario and Quebec, with a foot on each side of the Ottawa River. In the Valley, the flow of goods, services, people, ideas and art is not only vertical, down-river, but also distinctly horizontal — much of the historical and cultural development, social interchange and ethnography is cross-river. There continues to be an inter-provincial sharing and influence which not only makes the Valley peerless, but also enriches life there. Joseph Montferrand, the famous French-Canadian riverman from Quebec who worked in the Scottish timber baron's lumber camps in Ontario, becomes a unifying legendary symbol of the two side of the Ottawa River Valley.

My earlier book, **Giants of Canada's Ottawa Valley** began the process of relating "the tales of the people before they are forgotten" — to pass from oral to written tradition some of the heroes of the Valley, to add new stories and to document further, those who are already well known i.e. (Joseph Montferrand, the Last Laird MacNab). I hoped furthermore to save from oblivion those who had been almost lost in the oral tradition (Mountain Jack Thomson of Portage-du-Fort and Alexander MacDonnell of Sand Point) and to record for the first time those whose full story is yet to be told (Harry McLean of Merrickville and Rory MacLennan of Glengarry).

Some of the Stories I Told You Were True, my first oral history of the Valley, explored the history of roots and remains a landmark in my struggle to define the valley as unique. The second oral history, **Laughing All the Way Home,** concentrated on recording one of the Valley's outstanding characteristics — its humour. Paraxodically, by narrowing the range of emphasis, the focus was widened. **Legacies, Legends and Lies** continues the exploration of the universality of the Valley humour, and extends further into our own times with the inclusion of Harry McLean the construction genius, Mayor Charlotte Whitton of Ottawa and Pierre, Jean-Paul and Hank, three young story-tellers who carry into the present day the oral traditions of their ancestors.

Many more marvellous characters are assembled here in **Legacies, Legends and Lies**; Taddy Haggerty of the Opeongo Line whose repertoire still lives on forty years after his death; Charlie "Chain-Saw" Channigan, the sociopathic builder and developer; Nellie Finnuken and her necessarily pseudonymed very naughty nurse-in-training stories; Ed Hubert, The Great Exaggerator; Alphonse Clouthier and Ivery Newton with their wonderful collections of hunting and fishing tall tales; and Billy James whose stories have been gathered from ninety years of lumbering and farming in the Valley.

All three oral histories use a new technique, whereby, individual story-telling characters are examined in depth and distilled as in a short story. As early as in **Some of the Stories I Told You Were True** this technique was manifesting itself — Tom Murray of Barry's Bay, Winnie Inderwick of Perth, Phoebe McCord of Shawville, all emerge through their story-telling as real flesh and blood people, often unforgettable.

In all three books, characters range on the social scale from low man on the totem pole to national achiever, from Madawaska Valley singer to wife of the timber baron. And in all of them, the humour runs the gamut from low-life slapstick, raunchy, racy and irreverent, through the characteristic valley tall tales, legends and folklore, to the ultimate indigenous humour arising out of the real event, the real character, or the legitimate combination of both.

As North Americans we hold a sense of humour in the highest esteem. In every large public library on the continent the humour section is not only freighted with books that make us laugh but with a goodly sprinkling of books about *what* makes us laugh. And the indexes in psychology and medical libraries contain long lists of investigative papers about the mysteries of laughter and humour; "National Differences in Sense of Humour," "A Statistical Study of Crowd Laughter," "The Relation of Humour to Masochism," "The Effect of Laughter on Muscle Tone," "Laughing and Crying in Pre-School Children," "Sense of Humour and its Relationship to Personality, Scholastic Aptitude, Emotional Maturity, Height and Weight."

In his book *Laughter and Liberation* Harney Mindess, an American psychologist who has made a lifelong study of humour, postulates that laughter is always associated with our human struggle for freedom. We laugh or smile, or snicker, he argues, or hoot, howl, or belly-laugh at different forms of humour because they provide us with freedom from conformity, inferiority, morality, reason, language, naiveté, redundancy, seriousness and egotism.

"Within a few months after birth," writes Mindess, "all healthy infants laugh easily. Among the earliest laughter-provoking stimuli, two appear to be predominant. They are, first, mother (or any other familiar or comforting person), making an unusual face and, second, parents (or persons the child relies upon for security), tossing the baby in the air and catching him in their arms."

Mindess infers from this observation that both the face-making and the tossing-in-the-air are disruptions of the cozy life of the infant.

They upset his stability, jolt him out of his little rut, and he delights in them as long as they are mild enough for him to tolerate. Now the intriguing analogue is this; disruption, distortion, the jolt — the experience of being jerked out of a rut — is an integral aspect of all types of humour. From Twain to Thurber to Feiffer to Perelman, from Laurel and Hardy to Laugh-in, the comic spirit is an embodiment of the spirit of disruption. It breaks us free from the ruts of our minds, inviting us to enjoy the exhileration of escape.

But the most important aspect of Mindess's theory of humour is that our sense of humour in its maturest form eventually ranges beyond jokes, beyond wit, beyond pun, beyond laughter itself. Full-flowered humour, he states, must be fed with an awareness of the eternal human comedy, of the paradoxes of human behaviour. Humour, Mindess believes, like love, courage, understanding, is one of the attributes that can sustain us through the worst. "In its lesser manifestations it can lighten the load of our daily cares; at its peak it can enable us to live joyous lives in the midst of all our

Mature sense of humour includes the ability to laugh at oneself. And Mindess tells a wonderful story about a patient of his who came in for her session, told her long tale of woe and finished off by saying, "My problem's simple. I'm a total mess." Her candid assessment of herself broke them both up and the therapeutic session became relaxed and easy. In the psychology of humour this ability to take an objective, indifferent perspective on one's human predicament has been felicitously called the "God's eye View."

Another American expert writing on "what

tickles our ribs", Albert Rapp, in his book *Origins of Wit and Humour* states categorically that a sense of humour is born out of hatred, aggressiveness and hostility. It is basically savage and primitive in its sources, according to Rapp.

But paradoxically according to his theories, this is exactly what makes humour so therapeutic. He eulogizes "Doctors" Hope, Benny, Allen, Burns, Durante and McGee as "effective and painless physicians, providing us with the therapy of entertainment and relaxation." Rapp then continues; "Laughter is healthful because it calls off those impulses which arise out of anger and hatred and fear, impulses which are injurious to us if they are long retained; and it primes and stimulates and starts back into action those impulses which belong to normal activity and normal living." Rapp quotes studies done on constipation, ulcers, digestive problems, muscle tone, to say nothing of the psychiatric problems, which have been eased or cured by the magic concoctions of laughter. "The great majority of people, especially after middle life, do not laugh nearly enough for the good of their hearts."

Laughter as healing and therapeutic is being hailed on the continent on a much wider base now than the doctor-patient relationship. Over the past five years major conferences on the healing power of laughter have been held in New York City, Washington, the Hawaiian Islands, Toronto and this year in Cork, Ireland, with such prestigious participants and leaders as Peter Alsop, Ashley Montagu, Gerald Piaget, Joel Goodman, the Amazing Jonathan, Stepehen Vizzard.

Many centuries ago in ancient Egypt a very wise king named Amasis created the perfect metaphor for the healing power of laughter. Every day Amasis rose early, worked very hard, and called an end to it at noon. Then everyone was gathered about him in a kind of symposium, a feast of food, drink, story, creative ideas. But there was criticism amongst his subjects about his routine, unorthodox and hedonistic as it appeared to be. So one day one of his closest advisors took him aside and explained to him that, what a travelling salesman may get away with, a king may not.

And King Amasis replied, "Listen. When an archer goes into battle he strings his bow until it is taut. When the shooting is over, he unstrings it again. If he didn't unstring it, it would lose its snap and be no good to him when he needed it."

Many people tell me that they find my transition from poet to oral-historian-folklorist mysterious and curious. Many people ask why I began taping the old-timers of the valley. Some of the answers I do not

have. But I do know that my work in oral history was born of the empty-nest syndrome. When my children were at home their presence in the house with all its incumbent chaos, problems, grief, joy and love was an intrinsic *raison d'etre* for me. When they flew the nest I was left with myself, empty rooms and a typewriter sitting alone on a desk. My survival instinct dictated that I find something "beyond myself." The next stage of my life necessitated an external landscape.

And what were the motives beyond this? As a poet I wanted to preserve the language. As a screenplay writer and a dramatic poet, I wanted to record the dialogue of the story and the creative drama of history, the art of repertoire and the many expressions of impressionistic truth. As a lover of the Valley I wanted to preserve the people.

Every work of every writer is a kind of psycho-analysis. The subconscious motivations for my work in oral history are in some part as mysterious to me as they are to others. And, certainly the conscious purposes and goals of my work are as complex as they are manifold. But one chief objective remains clear; it is to stress the need for the recording of more community history in every region of the country as a safeguard against our rapidly disappearing Canadian heritage. People the likes of which we shall not see again are passing from the scene every day. I want my children and your children to know about them.

"For there are only two lasting bequests we can hope to give our children. One of these is roots, the other, wings." I should like to add to Hodding Carter's quote, that without roots, one does not have wings.

Joan Finnigan,
Hartington,
Ontario

1. *Taddy Haggerty, the Champion Wit of the Opeongo, in his later years, seated in front of the family homestead.*

1

Yours half truly

TADDY HAGGERTY OF THE OPEONGO LINE.

Nineteen-seventy-eight to nineteen-eighty-five. It is hard for me to believe that I have been taping the old-timers of the Ottawa Valley for seven years now. Like Dinny O'Brien of the Burnt Lands of Huntley, Taddy Haggerty of Brudenell is another one of those exceptional Ottawa Valley characters whose legend began to sift in to me, almost incidentally, as I was taping in his area around Brudenell, Killaloe, Eganville, and along the Opeongo Line. Just as people would ask me, "Say, did you ever hear of Philomene Bergeron?" or, "Has anybody ever told you about Sophie O'Hare?" so they would often declare, "Now, I'll tell you a story about Taddy Haggerty of the Opeongo Line." Gradually, through such incidents and such tellings, I began to realize that here was another Ottawa Valley humorist whose lines had lived long past his leave-taking from this earth. Even today in Quinn's Hotel in Killaloe, the old-timers sometimes amuse themselves, given the right mood, by retelling their repertoire of Taddy Haggerty stories.

Taddy Haggerty was born on the old Haggerty Farm at Brudenell in 1864, a second generation of the Irish Catholics who came up the Opeongo Line from Farrell's Landing on the Ottawa River in the 1850s and settled in the Opeongo Hills. He died in 1969 and is buried in the old graveyard at Brudenell. Except for one Indian chief, the graveyard is 100 percent Irish. It is said that Taddy Haggerty's father was a poet.

The Haggertys were famous as fiddlers and were known as the Fiddlin' Haggertys. The old log Haggerty homestead and outbuildings still stand at Brudenell, preserved and restored by log house builder Jan Steenberg.

Over the past three years I have collected Taddy Haggerty stories from many people along the Opeongo Line: the Sheridans, the Jessops, the Heinemans, the Walthers, Father John Haas of Eganville, and finally from people who phoned in to the open-line programme conducted by Lowell Green, particularly Mrs. June Winiarski of Quadville.

My name is Father John Haas, I had a classmate, Tom May, who was a nephew of Taddy Haggerty's and he told me a story about him that I believe is true. We were going to the seminary and it was during the Depression and we always came home in June for holidays. Now in those days you didn't have Gladstones or fancy soft-sided bags and suitcases; you had a square trunk with straps on it. And Tom landed in at the station at Killaloe and his family weren't rich or anything and he was worried about how he was going to get up home to Brudenell. He hadn't sent word about what time he was going to be arriving or anything. So there was no one to meet him. He had just got off the train when he spies his uncle Taddy Haggerty.

"Oh, Uncle Taddy," says Tom, "you're just the man I wanted to see. Are you going up home?"

"Yes," says Taddy.

"Can I get a chance home with you?" Tom asks.

"Of course," Taddy says, "but you'll have to wait a while. I have some shopping to do and I have to go over to the hotel. But I'll be back here in an hour or so."

So Tom settled down to wait and Taddy came back in an hour or so. And Tom had his big square trunk ready and he says to Taddy, "Well, where's your horse and buggy?"

"Oh," says Taddy, "I'm walking."

There had been an awful dry spell along the Opeongo Line and the priest at St. Mary's Church at Brudenell called a special service to pray for rain. All the parish turned out to pray except Taddy Haggerty. Taddy didn't go, so the next day the priest called in at his house.

1

"Taddy," he said, "everybody in the parish was at the special service yesterday. Why weren't you there?"

"Agh," said Taddy, "sure, I don't have an umbrella and I didn't want to get wet on the way home."

The lads were in Quinn's Hotel at Killaloe having a quart and everyone was talking about the dry spell. Oh, it was terrible dry! The grass was burning brown and the leaves were curling and the wells were going dry and the cattle were bawling at night. And Taddy listened to all this and then he said, "Well, it may be dry at your places, but not near as dry as at mine."

"How's that?" they asked.

"Neither the spring ducks nor the frogs on my place have learned to swim yet," he replied.

The following September the lads were all in Quinn's Hotel in Killaloe having a quart. They were still talking about the dry summer.

"Yes," exclaimed Taddy, "we'll all remember this summer! Sure it was so dry at my place the grasshoppers had to take along a lunch to cross the fields."

It was during the hard times in the twenties that Taddy's son, Tommy, left home to go to the United States to look for work. And one day Taddy was in Quinn's Hotel in Killaloe having a quart and he heard in the bar that this other fellow was going over to the States to find work. So Taddy went up to him and said, "I hear you're going to the States?" And the lad said, "Yes, I have to find work there." And Taddy said, "You'll see my son Tommy over there." And the lad said, "Well, yes, if I can find him, I'll see him."

So the lad went over to the States and he couldn't find any work over there and, after a while, he came back to the Opeongo Line and he was in the Hotel at Killaloe having a quart when Taddy came in.

"Aha," said Taddy, "you went to the States?"

"Yes," said the lad, "I've been in the States."

"Then you saw Tommy," said Taddy.

"No, I'm sorry," the lad said, "I didn't see Tommy."

"Then you weren't in the States!"

Taddy's son, Jim Haggerty, had a Model T Ford, the older kind with lanterns hanging on the outside. And Taddy's son, Tom, who went to the United States, did get a job over there, and did well, and came up to visit the folks at Brudenell in a brand-new Chevvy. So after they had all had a visit they decided to go to Quinn's Hotel in Killaloe and have a quart or two. Taddy got in the old

Model-T Ford with his son Jim. He said he was afraid of that damn newfangled thing that Tom had brought up from a foreign country, and he wanted to see it in motion for a while before he trusted himself inside it. So the two cars started up the Opeongo Line towards Killaloe and, of course, the two brothers gave each other the nod and began to race each other into town. And afterwards in the hotel over a quart Taddy said, "Yes sirree, I thought Tom was really showing off in that new car of his. But Jim showed him a trick or two with the old Model-T. He went so fast that you'd think the telephone poles were teeth in a fine-comb."

Martin Walsh was a neighbour of Taddy's and they used to josh each other and joke together all the time. One day Taddy met Martin coming down the big hill at Brudenell with a load of grain, drawing it to the mill at Killaloe. They drew in to talk to each other.

"You know, Martin," Taddy said, "you should buy Tom Mulvihill's place and you wouldn't have so far to draw your grain."

"I wouldn't have so much to draw either," said Martin.

Taddy's daughter, Florence, married Joe Colton from the Opeongo Line. And Taddy was not enamoured of his son-in-law. After the big wedding at St. Mary's, somebody met him in Brudenell and said, "Taddy, I hear you gave your daughter away this morning."

"Wrong," said Taddy, "I threw her away!"

No, Taddy didn't think much of his son-in-law. One time when he was with the lads in Quinn's Hotel at Killaloe having a quart or two he said, "Oh, that Joe Colton! He has a great big barn, 48 by 48 — and nothing in it but swallows!"

Now Colton's father was Abe Colton and Abe Colton was very, very, very thin; he was the thinnest man that ever lived along the Opeongo Line. So anyhow, one time the Haggertys had a great big party and some of the guests stayed overnight including Taddy's daughter, Florence, her husband, Joe, and her father-in-law, Abe Colton, who was bedded down on the sofa in the living room. In the morning when Taddy got up, he said to his daughter, "Well, Florence, I see Abe Colton left his umbrella on the sofa. You'd better go in and wake it up."

One year there was a terrible potato famine on the Opeongo Line. And after the bad crop was in in the fall the lads were sitting in the hotel at Killaloe having a quart or two and talking over the bad situation about potatoes.

"Yes sirree," said Taddy, "when you have a year with a good crop of potatoes, when you put

Taddy's son, Jim Haggerty, had a Model T Ford like this one with lanterns hanging on the outside. This Ford *was photographed in front of "the big tree", Stanley Park, Vancouver, B. C.*

them on to boil you can hear them saying to each other, 'Move over. Move over.' But this year was the worst I've ever seen."

"Tell us, Taddy, how bad was it this year?" asked some of the lads around the table.

"Well, I'll tell ye," said Taddy. "In this year's crop of potatoes there were the ones the size of marbles. And then there were the ones the size of peas. And then there were the small ones."

There used to be two old Irish bachelors around Brudenell by the name of Dooner. And any time there was a threshing or a barn-raising bee or a dance or a wake, they'd be there pushing into the table. They were no good to work but they'd get to the table and fill themselves, and they were always everywhere that you could go uninvited.

Well, anyhow, they were going to bury somebody at Brudenell and there's two graveyards there. One is the Old Graveyard and one is the New Graveyard. And at the time this dead person had requested to be buried in the Old Graveyard alongside so many of his forefathers. But when they went over there digging, every place they dug they came

on to somebody lying there already. They thought and thought until finally someone wise said, "Go over and find Taddy Haggerty. He'll know if there's anyplace at all we can dig. He'll find a place."

So they went up to his farm and they got him and he trotted all over the graveyard until finally he said, "Dig there. There's nobody there." So they dug and just when they were about deep enough down, they struck somebody. And Taddy got jumping mad and he said, "Jaipers, go ahead! Go ahead and dig! It's one of those damn Dooners. They're always stuck in the road someplace!"

They say that in the old days they always talked about the swiftness of their horses, eh? Well, they always gathered at St. Mary's Church at Brudenell and the talk was always outside the door before they went into Mass in the morning. So one Sunday there had been an awful thunderstorm during the week and Taddy Haggerty, he went out to an auction that day at Round Lake and he bought a calf and he was coming home from the sale when he got caught in the awful thunderstorm. Someone was asking him about how his ride home was through all the rain and thunder and lightning, and so on, and he said, "Well, I saw the storm coming, you know, and I touched up my horse and he got home so fast he never got a drop on him. But the calf was drowned in the back of the buggy."

Every Sunday morning Taddy Haggerty was always keeping them outside telling stories at the church door and they'd never get in for the Rosary. He'd be telling them stories on the outside when people should have been inside saying the Rosary. This day the priest came around from the sacristy to the front of the church and he says to Taddy, "Well! Here you are again telling stories when you should be in saying the Rosary. I bet if I asked you a question out of the catechism, you couldn't give the right answer."

"Try me, Father," said Taddy.

"Tell me now, Mr. Haggerty: What is baptism?" the priest asked. And Taddy said, "By God, Father, it was a dollar before you come here, and now it's two!"

One year along the Opeongo Line there was a terrible grasshopper plague. And the lads were in Quinn's Hotel in Killaloe having a quart or two and talking about the blight of grasshoppers and all the damage they had done to the crops.

One lad said, "They cut down all the oats at my place."

And another lad said, "They ruined my five-acre field of hay this year."

"Oh, God!" said Taddy. "That's nothing! They cut through all the wire fences at my place."

One really hot day in summertime a bunch of the lads from Brudenell and other places around about were in Quinn's Hotel at Killaloe having a quart or two. And it was such a hot day they fell to arguing about the hottest day on record. One said it was July 3, 1897, when it was 101 degrees in the shade and another said no, his father told him it was August 12, 1854, when it was 103 degrees in the shade, and so on and so on. And Taddy listened for a while and then he said, "No, July 24, 1937, was the hottest day on record around here."

"Well, what was the temperature that day?" the lads asked him.

"I don't remember the temperature," Taddy said, "but I'll tell you this much. There was two young pigs in the barn and I heard them squealing and roaring and dying of thirst. And I run up to the barn and grabbed one of them under each arm and ran for the creek as fast as I could. But before I got there sure they were both fried pork greeads[3] in my arms."

Taddy had this neighbour named Mick Dillon and one time Mick took a fit of trading horses. And every horse he brought home Taddy claimed he knew him, knew the horse, knew what he was bred from, knew who had owned him, knew where he came from. So Mick got fed up with this and he thought he'd get a horse that Taddy wouldn't know anything about at all. So he went away back to Combermere or Breeches Lake or somewhere, and he got an old grey and he brought him home.

So the next time Taddy came by, Mick said to him, "Come on in and see my new horse."

"You got a new horse?" Taddy said. "Now that's a wonder."

So they went into Mick's stable and Taddy took a walk around the grey, and then he went around again.

And Mick said to Taddy, "Do you know him?"

"Well, I don't know yet," Taddy said. "Where'd you get him?"

"I got him in Toronto," Mick said.

Taddy took another walk around the grey.

"Eaton's or Simpson's?" he asked.

In August, 1983, I received a phone call from Father Tom May of Vinton. He was calling to tell me that he had heard me on Lowell Green's open-line programme in the spring of the year and that he had collected some stories from and about Taddy Haggerty of the Opeongo Line. It was September before I finally got to visit him in his old parish in western Quebec where he presented me with his collection of Taddy Haggerty stories. They were an exciting surprise, for Father May had written out the stories in the language of the tarty-tongued old Irishman as the priest himself remembered it all from his childhood as a neighbour of the Haggertys. Moreover, Father May had written out the stories as though they were being told by Taddy Haggerty himself, in his very own Irish. With some slight editing, here is Father May's contribution to the history of the humour of the Ottawa Valley.

THE TALES OF TADDY HAGGERTY

(*pronounced Taydee, short for Ted*)
Opeongo Champion of Wit

Why did so many people come to Brudenell in pioneer days? It was rich settlement land as long as the timber lasted. But after that, farming was not very good because of the poor, stony land that lay, for the most part, along the Opeongo Line. Some very industrious settlers cleared the stones off; Luloff's stone fence between Brudenell and Raglan was three miles long. Also, there was a sign at the mouth of the Bonnechere River[1] which read, "Brudenell — sixty miles."[2] Those who could read came ahead. But the rest scattered over the Ottawa Valley.

When we could afford it we sent many boys to college to become lawyers, judges, engineers and priests. I sent my son Thomas[3] to high school. He learned several languages there and it was wonderful to hear him reading them off the Royal Yeast Cake boxes.

When Tam was big enough he went to the shanty. He went up for Booth. I took him to Killaloe to catch the train. We were real early and the people of the town were not yet up. Finally a fellow staggered out of the hotel. He looked at me and said, "Where in Hell did I see you before?" And I said, "What part of Hell do you come from?" But he didn't say.

We had to buy clothes and things for Tam to go to the shanty. So we went to the stores, Tam lugging his knapsack on his shoulder. So I had to tell everybody, "Tam is going up for Booth today."

When the train was leaving I carried his knapsack and parcels to the foot of the steps of the train. He stood on the steps and shouted, "Give me my stuff now, Pa." All the while the conductor was impatiently calling out, "'Board, 'board, 'board." But I said to him, "Take your time, take your time. Hold your iron horse a minute now. My boy is starting out in the world and I have to give him some advice." So I said, "Tam, always say your morning and evening prayers; on a load of logs always keep the binding-pole tight; and above all, always treat in your turn. Good-bye now."

We were blessed with great priests in Brudenell. Father James McCormac came out from Ireland about 1860. His brother, Father John, was sent to Mount St. Patrick and was drowned there. When Father James went out on a sick call, he wanted the whole community to go to the house, too, especially if the person was dying. And if you weren't there with him, the next Sunday he was liable to call out

your name in front of everybody. He took up the collection himself in his hat. If you put in a bill he would hand you back some change. He was a good hunter, especially of bears. He used to make fine bear-rug mats and give them to the people.

After him there were many fine priests like Father Frank Hogan. I remember the day when Father Hogan was giving Mrs. Whelan the last rites. He was buzzing it all off in Latin and looking at the little table to see if everything was ready for the anointing. And he stopped and said, "Maggie, get the wadding."

Once on the Sunday after the Giant Picnic, Father Hogan thanked the people for working so hard. "But," he said, "I am sorry to have to tell you all there is a big bean pot missing and the one who has it has to bring it back." But the next Sunday the bean pot was still not back. Father Hogan really scolded this time. Then he started to walk down the pulpit steps. But he suddenly popped back up and said, "If you won't bring back the bean pot, then have the decency to come and get the cover."

Father Hogan knew human nature pretty well. He always used to say, "Ten o'clock Mass always starts sharp at ten minutes after ten."

He was a great deer hunter. One Sunday in the hunting season he said Mass real early for a few of the hunters. He told them to go down to Hartney's Lake and start a chase to pass by Brudenell church just as he would be finished up with ten o'clock Mass. So they did. And just about three minutes after ten everyone in the church heard the deer hounds coming close. Father Hogan put his hand to his ear and said, "There will be no sermon today."

We all cried when he left Brudenell.

In the spring at sowing time we used to bring a small handful of seeds to church to get them blessed as prayer for good crops. One year we had a very good crop on the Haggerty farm. But all the neighbours around had very poor ones. One evening when I came home from the threshing at a neighbour's farm, my wife asked me if they had threshed much grain. And I had to say, "Sure I've often taken more in my hand to the church to get blessed."

I was never sick very much in my lifetime. But one time I got a dose of pneumonia. I had to go to the hospital in Pembroke. They put me in a room with a man who was just at his last. He died during the night. But I didn't know it. In the morning I tried to waken him by calling like I always did at home, "Tom, Tom, get up. Breakfast will soon be coming." I found out later that I could have called him Tom all day long, but he wouldn't have

5

answered because his name was John.

Most people sign off a letter with such things as Yours Truly, Sincerely Yours, Please Excuse the Bad Writing, and so forth. But for the sake of honesty I always signed Yours Half-Truly.

My son Jim went to Renfrew to work. Got married. Did real well. Built himself a real fancy house. During the Depression even the people in Renfrew suffered. One morning I took the train to Renfrew. It was cold, clear, twenty below, January. The train got in about nine o'clock. And sure things were so bad there there was only smoke coming from two chimneys — M. J. O'Brien's[4] and my son Jim's.

My son Jim was always good with money. When we would be going to the church picnic every summer, I used to share out the money to each of the children: so much for dinner, so much for candies, so much for sody-pop. When Jim ran out of money he began looking around for lost money on the ground. Finally he spied a nickel. He got his feet on top of it, but there was such a crowd packed together listening to the political speeches that he couldn't reach down. When John Carty, U.F.O. member of the Legislature, finished his speech,

everyone rushed over to shake his hand and talk to him. So Jim had room to reach down and get his nickel. Later on he told me at home, "Pa, the soles of my shoes are so thin that, while I was standing on that nickel listening to John Carty, I could tell if it was heads or tails."

We did most of our buying at the store at Brudenell Corners but, after the railroad came in, we often went to Killaloe. One time I was coming home with a bag of flour and other groceries in the back of the buggy when a really bad-looking storm suddenly came up. I whipped up the team. They galloped so hard that, although the rain hit the rear tailgate, the bag of flour and myself never got a drop. I wish that Frank Ryan could have seen that team go![1]

One time when I had gone to Killaloe and got everything on the list for the house, I decided to get the youngsters a special treat, so I bought them a pail of honey. When I got home they came out to the buggy and took the parcels into the house while I put the horses in the stable. As I started in to the house I saw one of the bairns going to the well to get a pail of water with the already-empty honey pail.

Not much is left at the once thriving Brudenell corner's of Taddy Haggerty's time — a couple of houses, the remains of Cooey Costello's grand hotel, and this deserted store with the boom-town front. The building actually goes much further back than boom-town times; underneath the insul brick is square timber.

6

There was a great tailor in Killaloe. As a young man he had lost a leg in the lumber camp by a falling tree. Instead of getting a wooden leg, he got a cork one. It was real handy in his tailor work. He would stick the needles, pins, awls, jackknife, and so on in his cork leg where they were in handy reach. But strangers and children went goggle-eyed when they first saw him do it.

I'm forgetting to tell you his name. John D. Fleming. He was also an expert horseman. He made lots of money breaking in hard-to-handle horses. Once he was taking a horse-and-buggy ride up by Brudenell and Rockingham. He bought a calf there and tied it in the back of the buggy with a good strong rope. He stopped at the store at Brudenell Corners and while he was in the store some wags cut the rope. He never found the calf. But he kept his ears open and formed a good idea about who had done the trick. A few years later the man brought in a tanned deerskin to be made into moccasins and mitts. Which John D. Fleming did. When the man came to get his fine mitts and moccasins and pay for them, J.D. said to him, "Here is the scraps left over from your deerskin. I have made them into one small pair of mitts. There was not enough to put thumbs in them. But they might be real good to wear when cutting rope off a calf."

My son Tom married a fine girl from Pakenham country by the name of Jordan. When Mrs. Jordan died at Pakenham, Mr. Jordan came to live with us at Brudenell. He was a fine, cultured, well-read, edjicated man. At first things went fine, but after a while his clear, logical mind prompted him to often try to trip me up and make me stick to the truth. It got so bad that, when the neighbours would come to me to ask at what phase of the moon to kill a pig, or when to sow the potatoes, I would just point a curved thumb at him and say, "Ask Jordan over there. He knows everything." He was always reading from an astronomy book given to him by one of the college students. He could explain all about the eclipses and the speed of stars and light. But I ask ye what has that got to do with good pork or good potatoes?

At home in Brudenell we always used to watch the sun going down in the west over the Polish Hills past Wilno there — a beautiful sight to behold. I always used to tell the youngsters that the sun might get caught on one of the peaks some evening and that we always had to be ready to go up and let it down with ropes.[5] But Mr. Jordan stopped all that fanciful "nonsense."

The sixteenth concession was to the west too. The Costellos lived on one side of the road and the O'Gradys on the other. (You have heard of Father Costello of the Flying Fathers hockey fame? He was from there.) There was a death on the sixteen concession in a real stormy time in the middle of winter. The roads were badly blocked even for horses. So the neighbours decided to carry the corpse to the church the day before the funeral. The pallbearers were three O'Gradys on one side and three Costellos on the other — the continuation of an old feud brought over from Ireland. When they got too cold in the hands they put the coffin down in the snow and boxed and fought until they got warm again. It took them all night to get the body from the house to the church. But now the old feuds are healed by time and marriage.

Our worst storms generally came from the southwest. We could tell the day before by the wind coming over the hills from the Comberemere and Rockingham side. We called it "the mountain roaring." One summer evening there was a really bad storm. The house was shaking and all the children crying. Ma calmed things down by getting us all on our knees praying, and she was sprinkling holy water all over us and towards every streak of chain lightning. She was quicker than the chain lightning. Finally I stopped her by saying, "Ma, lay off the holy water for a while so we can tell if the roof is leaking or not."

On St. Patrick's Day we would generally have a special preacher. Once we had a great orator. But the biggest part of his sermon or speech was extolling the virtues of our forefathers. When asked what I thought about it, I replied, "His politics seemed good, but I would like to hear him on religion some time."

One time a friend of ours came up from Killaloe to tell us his sad plight. His wife had left him again. Mr. Jordan chimed in very quickly to tell him to get Father Reynolds, the priest in Killaloe, to go and get her and bring her home. But the poor friend answered, "Father Reynolds has already worn out three sets of rubber tires off his buggy wheels from bringing her home."

John Carty entered politics, as I remember it, at one of Father George's picnics. I saw Carty and some other lads in a whispered conversation and I said to myself, "Something is up." He walked up on the platform carrying a wagon tire. When his turn came, he threw the tire into the centre of the platform and said, "I'm entering the ring." Then he threw his sailor hat in the tire. Carty's first election promise was to build a good road from Killaloe to his own gate, thereby, as he put it, "helping all the voters along the way." For many terms of office he was unbeatable, and whenever Mitch Hepburn wanted to take a vacation he always handed over the reins of government to John Carty of Brudenell.

When I was about ninety I got very stooped. I went up to North Bay to see some of our family there. When I came back people were all asking me how I liked North Bay. But I had to tell them that I didn't see very much of it — except the sidewalks.

When Mr. Jordon died it was rather sad because of the small wake and funeral. There was no all-night wake for him. Everybody went home at ten o'clock and we opened up again the next afternoon. And, for the funeral, we had to hire pallbearers. Different for Haggerty wakes, I tell ye! For them we always had to tear down the fences to make room for the teams. And hundreds wanted to be pall-bearers.

Now I'm dead and gone. Buried in the holy soil of Brudenell graveyard these twenty years. I didn't have as big a funeral as I expected. But pretty fair. Anyway, that is always the penalty for living to be too old; most of your friends are dead and gone before you. As I climb up the long hill towards Heaven I look up and see many of my friends there already. I can see that Mr. Jordan is in his right place — away up with the great saints and scholars. I'll be thankful to get in with just the ordinary saints. Maybe we can found a place in Heaven something like old Brudenell.

In March, 1984, following my afternoon in Palmer's Rapids with those two inimitable Franco-Irish, Willie Madigan and P. J. Ryan, still feeling myself intuitively to be on a "winning streak," I decided it was time to get to Mrs. June Winiarski of Quadville. A year or so prior to this time, I had been on radio asking for stories from the Valley when Mrs. Winiarski phoned in with a story about Taddy Haggerty. Upon hearing the strength of her voice and the Irish of her accent, I knew that someday I would find my way to her door. And that I did in March 1984. As an oral historian-folklorist of some experience now, I would say that my afternoon with Mrs. Winiarski in a house trailer on a farm back of nowhere was one of the most enjoyable I have ever spent. I did indeed "laugh until the tears ran down my cheeks." And I did, indeed, upon leaving the Winiarski place at Quadville find myself "laughing all the way home."

A woman of some fifty years, Mrs. Winiarski was born June Dupuis, daughter of the late Sam Dupuis, a riverman for McCrea Lumber Company on the Madawaska, and his first wife, Sara Gallagher. June Winiarski's great grandfather, John Gallagher, came out from Letterkenny in Ireland and settled in the area also named Letterkenny. He married Annie Turner from Eganville, a very long courting distance away in those early

A Haggerty clan gathering taken in front of the homestead house during the 1920s. There are four generations posed here. The log house has been preserved and *authentically restored by log-builder Jan Steinberg who has been responsible for many of the restorations and preservations along the Opeongo Line.*

days. Mrs. Winiarski's husband came out from Poland after the Second World War. A veteran of every campaign in that bloody war, as the row of medals on his wall in the kitchen attests, he made his way to Sam Dupuis's farm back of Quadville, went to work and found romance — one that still flourishes today.

Although a relatively young woman, Mrs. Winiarski as a storyteller is an interesting link in the oral history of the Valley because she is one of those people who has retained stories going back two or three generations. Her reach back into the early history and settlement of the Opeongo Line is invaluable. In her own words:

"I think the Kinnellys were the first people along the Opeongo Line. The Morriaritys and the Gallaghers were very early, too. My great grand-father, John Gallagher — and this story has come down the line for generations — he was out hunt-ing one day and he saw another man's track in the bush and he followed the track in to the Morriari-tys, and he found there was somebody else in the area besides himself. Imagine how he felt! And they got together, the Morriaritys and the Gallaghers, and have been friends all through the generations. And then the Heinzes came here. They came down from Sebastapol and they drove a herd of sheep up through the bush, and they didn't know anybody was here at all. And the Kinnellys were in by that time, and they lived on two farms across the way from here, and they heard sheep baaing and they knew somebody else must be in. So they came down and they met old Heinz. He was, of course, German from Germany and he couldn't speak a word of English. And they were neighbours and friends and worked together from then on. And old Mr. Heinz, until the day he died, spoke English with an Irish accent because he learned it all from old Mr. Kinnelly. All the German people here have an Irish accent, and a lot of the French who settled here, like my father, learned bits and pieces of English that comes out Irish."

Mrs. Winiarski was proudly and profoundly Irish, part of the Irish clans that came up the Opeongo Line out of the potato famine in Ireland in the 1840s. But hers was not a complete Irish enclave like that of Sheenboro, Quebec. The Opeongo Line was an ethnic melting pot of German, Polish, French and Irish. Besides all the Irish

friends and neighbours, the O'Briens, the Haggertys, the Morriaritys, the Kinnellys, the Nevilles, the Kellys, the Caseys, who people her stories, there were also the German settlers, the Groharts, the Shimmonds, the Webbers, the Luloffs, as well as the Heinzes. Besides her own people, the Dupuises who came up from Thurso, there were Lepines and Legrees and Gervaises who wandered into the hills of the Opeongo and made farms there. Proba-bly these people were later-comers and certainly some of them were French Canadian rivermen and shantymen who met girls from the area, married and decided to settle there.

When I questioned June Winiarski about the purity of her Irish accent, she explained: "I went to school in Quadville and my first teacher was Izaaih Harrington from Mount St. Patrick and then Claire Salmon from the Salmon Settlement and a Miss Burbidge from Brudenell — all Irish — they all helped out my Irish accent."

Mrs. Winiarski did indeed have a repertoire of Taddy Haggerty stories, but she also re-created for me that March afternoon in her warm and sunny little house, a host of other marvellous char-acters: Uncle Johnny Gallagher, Barney Kelly, Paddy Casey, Sophie O'Hare, Mary Ann Roach, Frank Lavell.

Mrs. Winiarski had some pensive philosophy about the Irish which led into her stories:

"Ah," she said, "they lived from day to day. The Irish are like that. I know my people, they lived from day to day. And everything was at home. The wakes were at home. The births were at home. The weddings were at home. If the house wasn't big enough they built a dancing platform and danced and drank for days and days. They were always playing tricks on each other, too. It seemed to keep them going. They were as poor as church mice and they were as happy as a toad in Hell."

When you get a miserable Irishman, they can be SO miserable. They can put one potato on to boil in the pot. They wouldn't spend a cent to save their lives. Living in little shacks here and there, and they could afford to live better. They have it in the bank. We used to have a German family around here named Luliss. They were like that, too. No wonder they had money! And they'd make such a fuss over nothing, nothing at all. I remember my aunt Jackie Gallagher telling me about one time their neighbour, old Mr. Luliss came over to Grandma Gallagher's. He was just in tears and she thought somebody must be really sick, or his cows had gone through the ice, or the barn burned — some terrible calamity. He couldn't talk he was so teary-eyed. And Grandma Gallagher says, "My! My! Mr. Luliss! What has happened that you're so teary-eyed?"

"Oh, bad luck, ma'am. At my house. Bad luck, ma'am."

"My, my, Mr. Luliss. Do tell me what happened."

So finally old Luliss got the strength up to tell Grandma Gallagher what had happened at his place.

"Oh, Mrs. Gallagher!" he said. "Prince, the big gray, lay on the gander last night."

Things is not what they used to be, you know. There's not a house dance or nothing around here anymore. Every house used to have its dance, yes, after the threshing mill. I'll never forget the old threshing mills and the old boilers coming, and then somebody would make a dance — and somebody would always make a dance for St. Patrick's Day — but you'd have to make that behind the priest's back because it was Lent. And we'd walk miles and miles for Hallowe'en, and knock down fences and over the outhouses and pull key log out of the logs piled on the shores of the Madawaska waiting for the drive, and let them all roll away into the river. Imagine that! Oh, years ago the priest used to be so strict, such a law. Somebody made a dance one time out at Brudenell and didn't the priest find out about it! And he came! And oh Lord! Didn't he clear that place out! And then he went outside with the lantern to find anybody in the dark. And this one lad had been lying in this hole drunk while all this happened inside. And the lad seen the lantern light swinging in the dark and he yells out, "This way with the light! This way with the light!" And over went the priest and found him there, lying in the hole drunk. And he read all their names off the next Sunday at Mass. Oh, if the lad had only kept his mouth shut the priest would never have known he was at the dance, let alone drunk in a hole! But no, "This way with the light!" he has to yell.

Barney Kelly was famous around here. They were always talking about Barney Kelly. They even named dogs and horses after him. The thing about Barney Kelly was that he lived in three centuries. He was born in 1792 and he died in 1908. You

can check through the Old Graveyard at Brudenell and you'll find him there. Mama said he was a tall, skinny old lad, crabby as could be. You couldn't look crooked at him. And she was as broad as she was long, his old lady. She used to be pretending she was sick all the time and nothing the matter with her. She got attention that way. Which reminds me of the cure for Paddy Casey. The Caseys on top of the hill going out by Letterkenny were one of the earlier settlers in the area. Two old Casey bachelors, Paddy and Mick, and their old-maid sister and, oh my God, they were lazy. They were always running out to the road to bum tobacco or sugar or something from anybody that was passing by, eh? And Paddy Casey was another one of these always saying, "I'm sick, and I have a pain here and I'm this, and I'm that." And anything would cure him, you know. My uncle Johnny Gallagher used to mix up a bottle for him, vanilla and water, a little horse medicine, basmayjin, Dr. Bell's Miracle Cure, some vinegar maybe. And old Paddy Casey would take that and it would cure him. There was nothing wrong with him, so anything would cure him, anything at all. One time Paddy was complaining of rheumatiz and Uncle Johnny made up a bottle of pills for Paddy. He had a punch for leather and he took an old shoe tongue and punched out little tiny bits of leather and put them in a bottle for Paddy Casey's rheumatiz. Paddy took them all and said he felt better.

And then old Mick Casey up and died. And didn't Uncle Johnny get an old hollow long steel pipe and run it through the basement of the old log house and, when Paddy was in bed at night on a cold windy November night when the lorigidons were in the swamps, wouldn't Uncle Johnny lie down on his stomach on the ground outside and talk like old Mick into the long steel pipe. And poor old Paddy flew out of the house in only his nightshirt and tore to the neighbours yelling, "Help! Help! Mick is back! He's back in the house again!"

One time Uncle Johnny was talking about old Maguire, a neighbour down the road that had died. And he had got awfully thin before he died. And these two old ladies came and were peering down at him in the coffin and one old lady says to the other, "Ah, deed, he got awfully thin." "Ah, yes," said the other little old lady. "He did. But you should have seen my old man before he died. Why! His legs was just like the sheeps!"[1]

And this is a story about old Mrs. Jack Lepine over here. A long time ago people used to churn their own butter and have it in crocks for the winter.

Towards spring they always got worried if they were going to have enough to last until the cows freshed again, and they'd get very saving on the butter. There was no place to run out and buy some, you know! Well, anyway, some lad from Brudenell was coming to see one of the Lepine girls, eh? And I guess he liked butter and the Lepine girl loaded the butter onto his potatoes and his bread or whatever he ate. And the old lady didn't like that because she was saving the butter. Because they were running out. Anyway, at that time, if a lad was courting a girl, he certainly didn't stay after the folks went to bed. He GOT OUT. The old folks gave him the hint; they went to bed. But Nellie — that was the girl's name — whispered to him, "You slip out and, after they're asleep, I'll let you in again." So he did that. And Nellie quietly later let him in again, and they were in each other's arms. And the old man had the light upstairs so there was no light in the kitchen at all. And the old lady come to the top of the stairs and she yells down, "Has he gone, Nellie?" And Nellie says, "Yah, he's gone, Ma." And Ma yells back downstairs, "And a damned good job, too! Don't have him back again. He's a devil on the butter."

Sophie O'Hare! Oh, my Lord, she'd steal the Lord's Supper, so she would, and go back for the dishes! Oh, Great God! One time she went over and she stole Hartrick's meat out of the barrel. Right out of the barrel! Hartricks were going to have the threshing mill, eh? And they had killed a pig and salted the pork and put it in a barrel. And they went to Killaloe to do some shopping so that Mrs. Hartrick could do some baking for the threshing gang. And they never missed a thing when they came back until Mrs. Hartrick went out to the pork barrel to get some meat to cook for the dinner for the threshers and there wasn't a damn speck left in the barrel. And, all you could see was the big tracks around it of Sophie's bare feet.

She and her daughter, they always went around in their bare feet in the warmer weather. And she and her daughter had peddled every bit of the meat over to her place. And then when Mr. Hartrick went over and accused her of taking it, and her having it on the stove in a pot boiling right in front of his eyes, she said she never touched it. Oh, Lord have mercy on mine, she'd steal! And she was always horse-dealing. We had a horse once that she had. My father didn't buy it from her; he bought it from somebody else that she had traded with. But he met her on the road one day and out she jumps, and grabs the horse by the head, and begins exam-

ining it all over as though he got it some crooked way.

Oh, my God yes! She could do anything a man would do. She could beat up a man if she had to. One time she was looking for whisky, I think it was at Brudenell. There used to be three or four hotels there at the time, and they sold high wines. It's clear — like water. And didn't the old villain Sophie O'Hare fill a jar half with water and she went to this one place where they sold whisky and she said to the guy, "I was over at the other hotel and all they have left there is a half a jar of high wines. Will you fill this up for me?" Well, he filled it up and then she said, "Ach, I can't pay you today." She says, "I'll pay you the next time I'm in town." And he said, "To hell you will! You owe me for a long time and you've never paid me yet." "God — dammit! says Sophie, "If you don't like it, then pour it out and take back what you put in." So the hotelman pours out half of her bottle and away she went with half a jar of mixed liquor.

Oh, a big, husky, raw-boned sort of woman, eh? And rough and rude, too. I remember she came into Aunt Nellie's kitchen at Killaloe one time when I happened to be there. And Aunt Nellie had just made some lunch for me and she had a bunch of fresh bread baked. And in lands old Sophie. She just lived up the road a little ways.

"By God!" she says to Aunt Nellie, "I've had no breakfast yet. And here it is lunchtime!" And she had such a rough way of talking. And nobody asks her to sit down or anything, and she just marches up to the cupboard and gets herself a plate and a cup and saucer, and sits herself down at the table. And, upon my soul, she pretty well cleaned up all the fresh bread, and a big chunk of pork, too.

Sophie had an old farm up Rocheford there. And then there was the Roach lady who had the cure for cancer — if it was on the outside. That was before my time. But I do remember them talking about her. My grand-uncle, Frank Lavell, was married to a Roach, Mary Ann's sister, and after Mary Ann passed away she gave the cure for cancer to him, old Frank Lavell. It was with him for years. Dr. Eggart wanted it, but they wouldn't give it to him.

I know old Uncle Frank put it on different people. He was a kind of foolish old lad, too, and people used to tease him a lot about it, you know. And some Polish woman from up by Wilno came down, and wanted him to try it on her. Well, he put in on her and he wasn't doing it right, I suppose, and the woman quit coming. And down at the hotel they got teasing him about it, you know, and they said, "What about this lady from Wilno, Frank? Did you cure her, Frank?"

"Faith, I did. And she never came back."

"Well, what happened that she didn't come back?"

"Faith, I had a fight with her."

"How come you had a fight with her?"

"Faith, she flew off at me."

"What did she say to you, Frank?"

"Faith, she said I was dirty, and that the stuff was dirty, and that the saucer was dirty, and that I was dirty, too. And where do you suppose she had the cancer?"

"Where, Frank, where?" the lads asked.

"On her tit, of course," Frank replied.

Old Frank Lavell — he was a grand-uncle of mine on the Gallagher side — Frank had this big tomcat. Oh, a great pet of his, eh? And the Finnerty's tomcat came over and they got into fighting. You know how cats fight. They tear their ears and get all chewed up. So Frank's nephew said to him, "I tell you, your old tom's pretty badly beat up now. Finnerty's cat came over and he put it to him!"

"Faith, I saw them, fighting, I did," said old Frank.

"Well," Emmett said, "Your cat was on the bottom and Finnerty's was putting it to him."

"Faith, that's what you think! My cat was on the bottom. But how do you know that he wasn't scratching the Hell out of the other fellow's belly?"

One time up on the farm at Brudenell, old Frank Lavell had sheep. And the sheep in those days used to run — there was no fences — and they'd run from one neighbour's farm to another, and get mixed up in other people's sheep. Well, you have to shear your sheep in the spring, you know, and old Frank Lavell, he left a patch of wool hanging on all his sheep's stomachs. That way he's going to know his sheep from somebody else's sheep.

Well, anyway, one day one of his sheep disappeared. So he said to young Finnerty, "Faith, would you have any idea where my sheep would be?"

"No, I haven't," Finnerty said, "but I'll tell you what to do. Why don't you mention it to the priest on Sunday and he'll mention it at church. Maybe some of the neighbours has your sheep and don't know it."

"Faith, I left a bunch of wool on it," said old Frank. "I'd know it from somebody else's. But you know I'm getting deaf and I can't hear the priest if he mentions it."

"Well, Frank," young Finnerty says, "I'll be sitting with you in church and I'll nudge you if the priest mentions your sheep."

So that was all right. They were at the church side by side, old Frank and young Finnerty, and the priest began reading a marriage announcement.

"This is an announcement of the marriage between Katie Sullivan and Brian Morriarity," he says from the pulpit. "And if there are any objections to the marriage, please speak up . . ."

So young Finnerty nudges old Frank in the ribs and old Frank yells out, "Faith, if she has a tuft of wool under her belly, she's mine!"

Yes, that was old Uncle Frank Lavell with the long, long whiskers that was married to Kate Roach, Mary Ann Roach's sister. And the house was that dirty the ducks were sitting under the stove.

Letterkenny was all Irish people. All Irish and the odd English family. Old Grandpa Gallagher, he used to chew the rag. They hated the English people and there was fights of all kinds. Oh, Glory be to God! They could hold a grudge for a hundred years! And they used to hate the English. They hated the English for driving them out of their country. That's what brought them here in the 1700s. Driven out by the potato famine in Ireland, eh? And then Grandpa Gallagher used to fight with old Luloff. He was a German man that moved in and, of course, they didn't like him and, Glory be to God, my mother said the grandparents fought all of their life and into the next generations. One time old Grandfather Gallagher and old Luloff were fighting up the road and you could hear them all over the country chewing the rag. Finally old Grandfather Gallagher said to old Luloff, "Oh, begone, you old yellow bastard! I was here before you. And I'll still be here when the big blue clocks is hustling in your rump!"[1]

Then one time Grandfather Gallagher and old Luloff were up fighting along the wire fence. Grandpa was fixing the fence on one side, and old Luloff was on the other side of the fence, and Grandpa was blaming old Luloff for poisoning his good dog. They had found him dead up in their field. Lord almighty! They were fighting about that! And finally my grandmother Gallagher sent my aunt Jessie — she told me this story — and her younger sister up to the fence to see what was going on. It was pouring rain. They were standing there fighting in the pouring rain. And just about the time that Aunt Jessie and her sister got up to them, they could see old Grandpa Gallagher hit old Luloff right across the face with a big wet mitt. "And to this day," Aunt Jessie used to say, "to this day I can see the water flying to each side of old Luloff's moustache." Even when she was an old woman of eighty-five she used to say, "And to this day I can see the water flying to each side of Luloff's moustache." And she'd break up laughing.

Billy Turner had a pig in an old building that had no roof on it. And the pig was up to his neck in mud and everything, and he had rickets. A pig gets sick in that, you know. So my uncle Johnny Gallagher was down from Letterkenny visiting the Turners and he looked in on the pig. "You know, Billy," he says, "you'd better get that pig out of there and put him in a dry place or he's going to die on you."

"Oh yes," Billy says, "I will, I will, I will."

Uncle Johnny came back home again and a few weeks later he went down again to visit the Turners. And he says, "Billy, how is that pig?"

"Oh," Billy says, "he died, up and died."

"I told you he was going to die with you leaving him in the dirty place there with no dry bed. I told you he'd die," Uncle Johnny said.

"Well, Johnny, as a matter of fact," Billy said, "that wasn't what killed the pig at all."

"And what then," asks Uncle Johnny, "what killed him then?"

"It was this way," says Billy Turner. "The pig's tail kept curling so tight that it pulled the skin back so far on his back that he couldn't shut his eyes, and he died from lack of sleep!"

The father of this Conway that did the Conway murder, he owned the hotel there in Barry's Bay way back. The Irish and Poles were a terrible mix in some ways. They have imagination. Oh, the Irish were superstitious! And the Polish were just the same. And they like to drink. And fight.

Anyway, one of them Conways, black Irish, was not supposed to get anything more to drink. My father told me this. He told me that the father Conway had locked the bar up tight and the rest went to church on a Sunday morning. Anyway, while they were away at church didn't this Conway lad that wasn't supposed to drink any more, didn't he get into that bar? The bar had bars across it on Sundays, and when it was closed up, the liquor was in behind the bars. And didn't this Conway lad take a buggy whip — they're big at one end and they get real skinny at the other. And Conway tied a knot on the end of that and flipped it in and got the loop over the bottle neck and chucked the liquor out for himself. And got really drunk and went to the church, rearing and tearing, and the whole place was into an almighty fight — they said even the Conway girls was into fighting with the Conway boys, their own brothers.

That's the same Conway that went to the Polish wedding and was killed there. They said he got

what he was looking for because every place where there was anything going on, he was there stirring up a disturbance.

Up in Brudenell, old Mr. Wingle got married for the second time. He got hold of another old lady, and married her, and he was really blowing about the second woman he'd got. Oh, she was a good worker! And she could keep a fire on. And work in the barn. And milk the cows. But mostly he was telling everybody what a good cook she was. Oh, she was a good cook! And one time he was talking to Taddy Haggerty at Brudenell at the church there and he says, "I tell you, Taddy, I got a fine woman this time. She's a great cook. I tell you, she can make a meal out of nothing."

And Taddy says to him, "And by God! She'd often have to do that!"

Then old Mrs. Kelly died. She was a really heavy old lady, well over two hundred and fifty pounds. In those days they had to have a black team of horses to take the corpse to the church. And nobody else had a black team around, so somebody asked old Taddy Haggerty if he would come with his black team.

"Will you come with your black team and take Mrs. Kelly to the graveyard?" they asked him.

And Taddy said, "Good God almighty! I don't know how I'm going to do it — unless I take two boxfuls of her, and make two trips."

One time Taddy gave a goose to somebody. It was a gander. And they're just nicely home with the gander when it dies. So the next time he seen him at church the man says to Taddy, "That gander must have been sick that you gave me because he's dead now."

"Well, now," says Taddy, "the thing is, you know, he's got that new disease."

"What's that?" the old lad asked.

"Well, it's going around among geese," Taddy explained. "It's ganderology."

And then poor old Mrs. Jack O'Brien died and Taddy heard of her death. Somebody said to him, "Did you hear Mrs. Jack O'Brien died?" "Good Lord almighty!" Taddy said. "I guess they'll have to bury her in a daisy churn[1], for I don't think she'll fit into anything else."

My father, Sam Dupuis, was going to Killaloe one time and he got talking to Taddy along the road. Taddy's farm was all rocky and hilly, you know. My father said to Taddy, "Is that all the land you've got, Mr. Haggerty?"

"Oh, God, no!" Taddy says. "I've got a lot more than that. But it's under the rocks."

Taddy had some old horse and the horse got

Allan Davidson, patriarch and protector of the Opeongo, in the kitchen of his home at Davidson's Corners wearing his St. Patrick's Day hat. The Davidsons were first settlers along the settlement road and according to Allan Davidson, "came up before the blaze". Even today the Davidson farm boasts one of the finest complexes of log buildings in the country, including a "first" house where government surveyor Robert Bell is said to have stayed when he came through Opeongo country in the 1840s making preparations for the official survey.

so old that it was a real slow-poke old horse. And he was going down to Killaloe and Mr. Bain used to tease him. Mr. Bain was the miller at the old grist mill at Killaloe and he would see Taddy coming moseying along with the real slow old horse. And Mr. Bain was an Englishman, eh? And so he stuck his head out the door of the mill and he says, "Where did you get that old cripple of a horse, Haggerty?"

And Taddy says, "Faith, I bought him from an Englishman!"

Father Harrington was Brudenell for a long time as the parish priest. He was parish priest for both Cormac and Brudenell. The people of Brudenell bought a new buggy for Father Harrington as a present from them. Well, there was some old lady out at Cormac, living out in some little old house someplace and the two men that owned the place, they were trying to get her out of it. I don't know if she wasn't paying the rent or what. But she wouldn't leave the house and they went in and I don't know whether they threw her out or what they did. But the story got up to Brudenell about these two men throwing the old lady out of the house at Cormac. So anyway, Father Harrington liked to tease Taddy Haggerty and he met him one day on the road when he was driving along in the new buggy and he said, "How do you like my new buggy, Mr. Haggerty?"

"Oh, it's all right," Taddy says.

"Well!" says Father Harrington. "The people up at Cormac are a whole lot smarter than the people here at Brudenell." And he was praising up the people at Cormac for this and that and the other thing like the present of the buggy. And old Haggerty listened for a long time to all this and then he said, "Well, maybe they are smarter at Cormac in lots of ways, and maybe they're richer. People here at Brudenell couldn't afford to buy you a new buggy, or anything like that. But, by God, it doesn't take two Brudenell men to beat up an old woman!"

And I can tell you another story about Cormac. These two old lads were sitting there at Cormac in front of the general store one day not that long ago. They were both really old, eh. They got chatting together and one says to the other, "How old are you now?" And the other one, he said he was in his nineties. And the first old lad said he was in his late eighties. And one old fellow says to the other, "You know, I think the Lord forgot about us down here in Cormac." And the other old fellow says, "Well, I'll tell you one thing. If I go first, I'll remind Him of you."

Paul Madigan used to be a great storyteller here. Paddy Madigan is dead now. And then there is Benny Madigan and Willie Madigan at Palmer's Rapids. Poor old Con Madigan. That was an older generation. He stayed here with me one time and he was telling about one time he was working at Griffith at the farm of some old Irish people, and they were very religious people. No matter how hard a day's work he did on their farm, the Rosary had to be said before you went to bed. And it was a hot day in the summertime and the sheep had been breaking out and getting into the old lady's garden. Oh my, she was raging! Because every time the sheep got into the garden they trampled everything down and cleaned everything up in it. They put the sheep here and they put the sheep there all day long. And they put them to the other place, and first thing they are out again. All day long. So towards dusk the old farmer decided to put them in a cowpen. And the old lad says, "We'll put them in this cowpen for the night and we'll think of something better in the morning. We'll fix a fence someplace and get them in someplace. Meantime, there's no way they can get out of here for the night." So they got in very late. But all the same the Rosary had to be said. And the old farmer got down on his knees with the Rosary in his hand, but keeping watch with one eye. And he began: "Hail Mary full of grace . . . there's them goddamn sheep in the garden again!"

1. The Opeongo Line was one of the early primary settlement roads blazed and surveyed about 1840 to encourage settlers to go inland in the Valley. It was also conceived as a military road in case of attack by the Americans. The line began on the Ottawa River at Farrell's Landing near Renfrew and headed westwards through the Opeongo Hills towards Opeongo Lake in Algonquin Park. The line only progressed as far as Bark Lake. Today, along with the deserted village of Balaclava, the Gillies complex at Herron's Mills, the Opeongo stands as the most exceptional heritage resource in the whole Ottawa Valley, if not Canada. Lined with hundreds of log buildings, houses, barns, shanties, milk-houses, root-houses, schools, churches, stores, built by first settlers from virgin timbers, the Opeongo embodies seventy-five miles and one hundred and fifty years of living history. In importance and richness it compares to the American's famous Outlaw Trail. The actor, Robert Redford, through his writing and his lectures, made the American people aware of the deterioration of the Outlaw Trail and was largely responsible for its restoration as a historical site and a riding and walking trail. Nobody has come forward in Canada to preserve the Opeongo and every day its priceless heritage is being destroyed, sold off, trucked away. Yes, sometimes even to the States!
2. In *Laughing All the Way Home*, Carl Jennings tells the same story. I heard it first in Killaloe but obviously it travelled by word of mouth from one Irish community to another.
3. The meaning of greaads specifically seems to have been lost in time. But obviously they were something fat and soluble.
4. This story in a different version appears also in *Some of the Stories I Told You Were True*.
5. A version of Taddy's image is also recorded by P. J. Ryan in Chapter 5.

Father Tom Hunt of Mount St. Patrick on the Opeongo Line, upon his graduation from Ottawa College. He is standing beside the new car given to him by his father as a graduation present.

2

That makes him related to both of us

FATHER TOM HUNT, MOUNT SAINT PATRICK AND PEMBROKE, ONTARIO

*Father Tom Hunt was born in 1895, third gener-
ation on The Mountain, the eldest son of Margaret Shields and John Hunt. Of eight children, four
took Holy Orders, Father Tom Hunt graduating
from Ottawa College in 1914 and from the Grand
Seminary, Montreal, Quebec, in 1919. He was
ordained in Pembroke on August 15, 1919, and has
since served in parishes at Whitney, Cormac and
Douglas.*

*Over the past two decades he has written and
published a number of local histories:* The History
of the Mountain, The History of the Hunts, The
History of Cormac, The History of Douglas,
The History of the Shields, The History of Sa-
bine, The History of Whitney, *and, in 1982,*
The Memoirs of Father Tom Hunt.

*After his retirement from active service, Father
Hunt continued to be blessed with the good health
that enabled him to actively participate in all diocesan
events, to be present at celebrations in the parishes,
in the local mother-houses, to constantly visit the
ill in the hospitals and the shut-ins at home, to
act as visiting lecturer. His sharp wit and wide
knowledge of the history of the Ottawa Valley and
of Ireland won him considerable popularity as an
after-dinner speaker.*

*The following stories attest to his skill as a
legend-maker and a raconteur.*

You know, I'm an old priest now. Gone through
a lot of days, but wonderful enough. I have
some landmarks along the way. I lived at the time
of the Boer War, and I lived in the First World
War, and in the Second World War and all the wars
they've had, every ten years in some countries, and
I've heard a lot of war stories. I remember the First
World War very well. It was sad. Always difficult
to get the news. They'd wait and wait to get the lists
of who was killed and who was in the hospital and
who was going to be brought home. And I remember
the priest was walking down the street there and
he saw Mrs. Kelly crying and crying. So, he went
over to her and he said, "What's the trouble, my
good woman? Is it about Pat?"

"Yes", she says, "it is about Pat."

"And how is he?"

"Oh, he's dead. He's gone."

"Did you have word from the War Office?"

"No I had word from himself."

"How come you got word from himself and
not the War Office?"

"I have the letter here in my purse and I'll
show it to you, Father. Look here. Read it. 'Dear
mother,' Pat says, 'I'm in the Holy Land'."

An Arnprior businessman was told he had only
a month to live. He called in a lawyer to have his
will drawn up.

"Fix it up," the businessman said to his lawyer,
"so that my overdraft at the bank goes to my wife.
She will be able to understand that and explain it."

"My equity in the car goes to my son. He will
then have to go to work to keep up the payments."

"Give my good will to the supply houses. They
took some awful chances on me in the past and
are entitled to something."

"All my equipment you can give to the junk
dealer. He has had his eye on it for years."

"I would like six of my creditors to be my
pallbearers. They have carried me so long that they
might as well finish the job."

Our home, the ancestral home of the Hunts,
was Limerick in Ireland, and anybody who goes
to Limerick must go out and see the Treaty Stone.
I did when I went back to Limerick to hunt down
the Hunts' family tree. Anyhow, O'Connell's run a
store there — I remember the name well — and
in half of the store there's a fellow, Dinny Cassidy,
has an office there. Over the office door is this
sign, "Livery and Undertaking." Well, I had occasion

to go there for livery (not undertaking yet). And I said to Dinny Cassidy, "I want to go out and see the Treaty Stone." Well, he had one horse and a cart and the passenger's seat had a sliding back. So he used to push it up to a comfortable place on the flat board, and then you got in beside him. Now the sign was there; if you went as a passenger in the taxi, it was fifty cents. Then when he came back, if there was a call, he rolled the seat back and laid it down flat and went over to the under-taking parlour where he'd get a corpse to take somewhere. If you were going as a corpse, you were lying down and then it cost you a dollar. That's why the sign said: "Livery and Undertaking. Sitting

John Hunt, long-time blacksmith of Mount St. Patrick, father of Father Tom Hunt of Pembroke, Ontario. The legendary smitty was photographed in front of the original Hunt house with his unidentified apprentice.

Both the Hunt's blacksmith's shop and the Hunt house remain today in the village. The house has been recently bought by Hunt descendants, who are preserving and restoring the heritage buildings.

up, fifty cents. Lying down, one dollar."

Yes, Red Mick Maloney from Mount St. Patrick. He was way back one time reeve of Brougham Township and he was in here at Pembroke at a council meeting, and the agents for several insurance companies used to be here then on rounds, and one of the smartest of them sold a 1,000-dollar policy to Red Mick Maloney. But when the agent returned to his home base in Ottawa he found there was a mistake in the signing of the policy. At least, his company manager found the mistake and he said to his agent, "Look, you'll have to take that back up to Mount St. Patrick and get it properly signed."

So they gave him the policy and told him to take the train to Renfrew and get a horse from there and go up to The Mountain. The agent landed in at the village of Mount St. Patrick. He saw a man standing in his yard there and he went over to him and said, "Would you know where Mr. Maloney lives?"

"Well, yes, I do," the man replied, "but it would largely depend on which Mr. Maloney you'd like to see."

"Oh," said the agent, "is there more than one?"

"There's more than one" said the man. "But I'll try to help you out. You go up the road here for one mile and a quarter and then turn to the right and that's Black Jim Maloney. Go in there and if that isn't your man, come out and go up a quarter of a mile on the road. There'll be a house on the right-hand side and that's Red Jim Maloney. And if Red Jim Maloney isn't your man, go along that same road and go down the hill and you'll come to Fighting Tom Maloney's place. If Fighting Tom Maloney is not your man, come out the gate and go straight across the road where you'll see another log house. You go into that house. That's Black Paddy Maloney's house and, if it isn't Black Paddy you want, then get yourself back on the main road and then turn left at your first turn and go on ahead in on that road a piece and you'll come to Red Mick Maloney's log place. And if it isn't Red Mick Maloney you want, come out again but don't keep on that road. Turn sharp right and go on down a little piece, about eighty acres and you'll get into Pussy Paddy Maloney's. And if Pussy Paddy Maloney isn't your man, I'd advise you the best thing to do would be come back out to the main road and come on down to Black Jim Maloney's and have your dinner."

My mother, Margaret Shields, came from Brudenell on the Opeongo Line. And she was always boasting to my father, John Hunt, the blacksmith

from Mount St. Patrick, about the beauties and grandeurs of Brudenell, so that he had to take off every year a week in the summer and get a team of horses and a fancy buggy and take her and the children to Brudenell to visit Grandpa.

Grandpa was a great laugh, full of mirth at all times. He gave us all a wonderful holiday. But to get to Brudenell, leaving Mount St. Patrick we drove thirty-five miles along the Opeongo Line. It was a long trip and my father played a game with us to pass the time away. He introduced us to all the places and all the farms and all the people along the way and each succeeding trip he would say, "Now! I told you last time. Who lives?" And we had a means test and then he'd give a little history of where they came from and what they did and who they married. And then we went along another mile and had another means test. And by the time we got to the top of Plaunt's Mountain, where we used to stop at the cousins of my mother's, the Sullivans, for dinner, the means test had given us a good deal of knowledge. After dinner we had a little rest and then proceeded on to Grandpa's at Brudenell. We would arrive there close to supper at half-past five in the evening.

So you see, times have really changed in my lifetime of eighty-some-odd years. What we do in an hour now took us the whole day with horses and a lot of fun. On the road Pa would meet certain ones and he would always stop and talk, whether he knew them or not, and rest the horses — hilly country — and in this way we, as young lads, picked up a good many stories along the way, too.

Everyone in Brudenell parish was known by my mother and friends of hers. We used to go on rounds of visiting while we were on holidays there. I can't remember all the places we visited, but we'd go into Corrigan's. And Grandpa would say, "Pat Corrigan here hasn't done very well and it's the drink."

And Pa would say, "Why don't they get him to take the pledge then?"

"Well," Grandpa says, "he's tried that, too. Yes, Pat Corrigan is always going to mend his ways. But every time he tries to turn over a new leaf, he hurts himself."

And then we'd go along the road a little piece further and visit Katie Costello. And Grandpa or Pa would say to Mrs. Costello, "My, but your little girl is growing up wonderfully!" and Mrs. Costello would say, "Oh, but Tom (or "Oh, but John"), it isn't the times like we used to have. It's so hard to bring them up now."

"How come?" Tom or John would ask Mrs.

Costello.

"Well," said Mrs. Costello, "my little girl went to church for the first time last Sunday and, when her daddy said afterwards, 'How did you like it, Mary?' she stuck her nose up in the air and said, 'Oh, the music was nice but the commercial was too long'."

And then we'd visit the Grogans. And I have this wonderful story to tell about a wonderful pair, Lizzie and Paddy Grogan.

One day Lizzie says to Paddy, "My God, I am not feeling good at all!"

"And what would be the matter with you?"

"I have an awful pain in me stomach."

"Well, it will probably go away."

"No. It won't go away. Get the horses hitched up and take me down to the doctor."

So Paddy took Lizzie down to Eganville and they saw the doctor. Lizzie had an examination. Later, when they got home that evening, Paddy was feeling grouchy and he says, "I'm going over to Costello's Hotel."

"Well," says Lizzie, "I'm staying home."

And there was another fuss. But Paddy went off to Costello's and had a few drinks. When he came home about nine-thirty there was Lizzie upstairs with the lamp burning high. Paddy snuck upstairs and peeked in.

"Lizzie!" he says. "You haven't a stitch on!"

"I know," his wife says.

"And what in the name of God is the matter with you?"

"I know," his wife says.

"Tell me then."

"Well, when I went to the doctor today he examined me everywhere and then he said, 'Mrs. Grogan, you're in wonderful shape altogether.' So now that there was nobody here in the house, I wanted to take a good look at it."

"Well," says Paddy, "did he take a look at your big ass?"

"Oh!" said Lizzie, "he never asked for you at all."

During the summer, of course, relatives visited us at The Mountain. My aunts would come to The Mountain from Almonte where they worked in the Rosamund Mills down there. And my other aunt, Johanna, she was the receptionist for Dr. Lynch — and Aunt Johanna would come home to visit. And like myself she was a terrible talker, always looking into everything. So this one day she went into the little old grocery store at Mount St. Patrick and she says, "Mr. Carter, what do you sell your oranges at?"

There surely must have been some money on the Mountain even in early days, for here is an 1890 wedding photograph of a grand pair, Frank Sheedy and Maggie Kinelly, both belonging to first families settling on the Mountain, taken by no less than the famous Topley of Ottawa. It would have to be surmised that the Sheedys travelled all the way to Ottawa to have this special photograph taken, for it was highly unlikely that Topley travelled to the Mountain.

"Sixty cents a dozen here."

"Oh, my God!" she says. "We can get them in Almonte at five cents apiece."

We had great teachers at Mount St. Patrick and I did well in school. One day in school I remember our teacher said to me, "Tommy, can you spell 'straight' for me?"

And right off the bat, of course, I ripped it through right "straight" through as right as could be.

"S-t-r-a-i-g-h-t," I spelled out for the teacher.

"Very good," says he. "Now tell me, Tommy, what does it mean?"

"It means 'without water,' " I replied.

Whenever we'd go to Brudenell to visit Grandpa

in the summertimes, Pa would try to kid Grandpa along a little bit and they'd tease and chomp at each other, but, in spite of all that was said, they'd end up in the hotel and have a drink or two or more. And then, on the way home, Grandpa'd be saying to John, my father, "Great pair of horses you have, John. Great pair of horses altogether, you know. They go well together. Mary and I had a little bit of a spat the other day and, when I picked her up with the team to go out to eat at Brudenell — the only place you can get a bite to eat out around here — as we went along I said to her, 'Mary, why can't we always be nice and quiet and peaceful like those two horses ahead of us?'

" 'I'll tell you why,' Mary said to me. 'Those horses have only one tongue between the two of them'."

I finished school at Mount St. Patrick and went down from The Mountain to Ottawa College. Aunt Johanna from Almonte, when I was going to Ottawa College faithfully, took me out from time to time and fed me at the restaurants. She worked for the Victorian Order of Nurses and I remember how she was just IT in her little white apron and black cap of those days. And the other nurses who worked with her would be asking me questions about the college and all that. Later on when they had a meeting, they'd say to my aunt, "Johanna, what about that boy Tom? Is he going along all right?"

"Well, yes!" Johanna would exclaim. "My brother, John, that's the oldest boy that he had and he's sending him right through to the cemetery!"

In my schooldays and college days and, I suppose, my seminary days, as I look back now, I think I see one of the greatest curses of the Irish settlers here, and the Irish people in general, is that they were always too fond of the drink. And it dizzied them. And it dizzied their pocketbooks. If you just think for a moment of what the Irishman thinks of the drink. And does with the drink! He gives you some whisky and he says, "Drink it down." And he keeps giving you the whisky and he says, "Drink it down." And after a time, after very much time, you're over at the sink and he says to you, "Throw it up! Throw it up!" And that's a very good illustration of why things aren't very comfortable for the Irishman's pocketbook or his stomach.

I could tell you a good story about when I was in Ottawa College. In my day, you know, we just had to ride streetcars all the time. No way of getting around except we had five cents to get on the electric streetcar. And one day I was going out Wellington Street on the streetcar and an Irishman got on away out at Britannia. And by that time the streetcar was full and he looked around for a seat and there weren't any but only one very fashionable lady sitting with her poodle on the seat beside her. So Pat, nothing daunted, went down and picked up the dog, put him on the floor, and sat down beside the fashionable lady.

"Madam," he asked politely, "what breed of dog would that be?"

The fashionable lady, disgusted with the Irishman, replied, "He's half monkey and half Irish!"

"Oh, begorrah, is that right!" Pat exclaimed. "That makes him related to both of us!"

The priest at Cormac said to Mary Hoolihan, "Surely, Mary, you are not marrying again so soon after the Lord took poor Hoolihan?"

Whereupon Mary replied, "I surely am. As long as the Lord takes them, so will I."

A member of the Pembroke Police Department on traffic duty was scolding the child for running across the street alone.

"Why didn't you hold on to your mother's skirt?" he scolded.

"Please, sir," the child replied, "I couldn't reach it."

I got this story one day while making a parish visit in Douglas. An Irish woman complained to me and exclaimed, "Oh, Father! There's nothing worse than green wood and a tipsy husband!"

"How come?" I asked.

"The minute you take your eye off one, the other goes out."

Up on The Mountain one time Carty phoned Mulvihill to come over for a drink.

"Oh, I can't," Mulvihill replied, "I have a bad case of laryngitis."

"Nonsense. That's a poor excuse," Carty replied. "Bring it along. We will drink anything."

Barney Maloney from Brudenell one time was reading to his wife from the Ottawa *Citizen*. "I just read here," he said, "that an ostrich can see little and digest anything."

"Sure now!" Barney's wife exclaimed. "What an ideal husband!"

One time the priest at Mount St. Patrick preached a thumping sermon on sin. He finished by leaning down over his pulpit and asking, "Now is there any one amongst you who still likes sin?"

There was a long silence. Finally one tiny hand was raised by a very devout lady who was hard of hearing.

"I can't believe this, Mrs. Kinelly!" the father exclaimed. "Are you telling me that after all I have said here today you still like sin?"

"Oh, pardon me, Father," said Mrs. Kinelly,

In pioneer days in the hinterlands of the Opeongo Line a visit from the parish priest was a major event in the lives of the people. In this 1930s photograph Maggie Foley in her ancient log house was blessed with no less than three holy fathers, Father Tom Hunt, then the parish priest at Cormac, on her right, and Fathers Lynch and Tait, on her left.

"I thought you were asking about gin."

Mrs. Mulligan met Mrs. Corrigan on the street in Eganville.

"Oh, Mrs. Corrigan, my dear," said Mrs. Mulligan, "I just got a letter from my son in London. He has got himself a great job entirely."

"And what might that be?" asked Mrs. Corrigan.

"Sure, he's working in a crematorium," boasted Mrs. Mulligan.

"And what's so wonderful about that?" asked Mrs. Corrigan.

"Well, he's burning up Englishmen — and getting paid of it," retorted Mrs. Mulligan.

Everyone says I am like a Texan: I talk too much. Which reminds me of a great story about a Texan in Canada one time. One day while visiting Niagara Falls I overheard a Canadian trying to shut off a boasting Texan. The Canadian pointed in exasperation to the roaring Niagara and said, "Do you have anything like that at home in Texas?"

"Well, no," the Texan replied, "but we have plumbers that would fix a leak like that in a few minutes."

I can round up some old sayings that I like to use when I am giving speeches. I've been lecturing and talking to meetings and groups for so long now that I almost always speak extemporaneously, so it's hard for me to sit down and consciously draw out all the dictums and admonitions that come to me out of my subconscious when I am on my feet in front of a crowd.

You'd better remember that there are more wisecrackers than smart cookies in our world.

Keep smiling; it keeps everyone wondering what on earth you've been up to.

When you throw mud, you are the only one losing ground.

Physically you should always keep yourself in the pink; but financially, keep out of the red.

Our world is one in which some are willing to work and the rest are willing to let them.

A scandal is a breeze stirred up in a couple of old windbags.

I have played considerable golf in my time and I find it's a game much like taxes; you drive hard to get to the green and you wind up in the hole.

3

Going to heaven on dandelion wine

PHOEBE McCORD, SHAWVILLE, QUEBEC

Although now into her seventies, Phoebe McCord of Shawville, Quebec, still wears many of the hats of her energetic and more youthful days. A retired English teacher and indubitably one of great impact, she continues to be wife, house manager, mother, doting grandmother, bird-watcher, writer, friend, lay preacher, popular warmer-upper for political meetings. When Phoebe's dissertation on "The Good Woman" appeared in Some of the Stories I Told You Were True, *one reviewer said her interview "alone was worth the price of the book." And when I began to plan this book I decided that, as one of the great funds of stories in the Valley, she was worth a return visit. I was right. On this second time around I tried to steer her into telling the stories she had used over several decades in her function as warmer-upper at political meetings. She obliged. But, when she got into high gear, in her usual inimitable manner she overflowed into stories about lumbering, Larry Frost, Mountain Jack Thomson, Joseph Montferrand, Charlotte Whitton, and "recreational violence" in the Valley.*

Lady Napoleon Brinkman was very much a leading light in the social hierarchy of early Ottawa in the twenties. I feel sorry for the women who have to try to write the social columns in Ottawa today, for there is nothing to write about. But in the days of Booth and Eddy, the Popes and the Blackburns, the Southams and the Brinckmans,[1] high society was very colourful and nobody needed to dig for a story. Those people were like the Fishes and the Stuyvesants in American society; they belonged to the social class which could say, "If you need to ask the price of a yacht, you can't afford it."

Now I can tell a story about a lady acquaintance of mine who perpetrated a delightful joke on Lady Napoleon Brinckman. Lady Brinckman was a Southam and the Southams were paradoxical because they were both Anglican and Liberal. And this friend of mine was a great Liberal (they later turned Conservative as a dying man is converted on his deathbed). But anyhow, this lady acquaintance of mine was hard put and they tried to burn down their place for the insurance, which was freely given in those days — no questions asked. They weren't too successful because they didn't manage to burn the whole house down, only an addition at the back out of which they had taken an old washing machine before the flames engulfed it. Right after the fire she decided to write a letter to Lady Napoleon Brinckman, who was noted for her generosity. My friend wrote Lady Brinckman that they had had a fire (which was somewhat true), that she was a widow (which she wasn't), that she had thirteen children (which was a considerable exaggeration), and that what she desperately needed was a washing machine, hers having been destroyed in the fire (at the time of writing it was sitting out in the yard). And she sent this letter to Lady Brinckman — she was a Southam and they had such soft hearts — and my friend said to me, "Look what I got back from Lady Brinckman!" It was a cheque for 400 dollars! In those days more like 4,000 dollars.

As I said before, the Southams were paradoxical, being both Anglican and Liberals. In those days things were pretty clean-cut. A Tory was a Loyalist and a Monarchist and very much tended to be Conservative. The Church of Ireland was Anglican, the Church of Scotland Presbyterian, and the Church of the United States of America Episcopalian. (Now, that's a word you can have a lot of fun with as a political warmer-upper.) The Church of England, Anglican, predominated in the Canadian census of 1851. Now, vast numbers of those Church of England people, as they grew older and their knees gave out, changed to different denominations when they found out that some other

The Country Club, Ottawa, Canada

Of course the Brinkmans and the Southams and everyone else who was somebody or who thought they were somebody, belonged to the Country Club on the Aylmer Road. This 1914 postcard was sent to Mrs. John E.

(Carrie) Dennison of Eganville, Ontario, from her sister Mabel. It is August and Mabel regrets in her message that they "will not get up this summer now."

churches didn't require so much genuflection. We are beginning to genuflect again because our rectors want us to be more like Roman Catholics, with whom they are planning to unite — this is an abnegation of all we have fought for. My religion doesn't extend to joining up with people who were responsible for the Spanish Inquisition!

I don't know if it exists today, but for a long time in Quebec it was the law of the Roman Catholic Church that, if it was a case of either saving the mother or the child, the child was always to come first. This applied even to Protestants sometimes. I remember a Protestant — a real good churchman he considered himself — and the doctor came out to him from where his wife was in labour. And the doctor said to the real good churchman, "It's either your wife or your child. Which shall I save?"

And the man said without a moment's hesitation, "Oh my goodness! Save the child!"

Oh, I do so remember the gypsies — remember how Maggie Tulliver ran off to join the gypsies in *The Mill on the Floss?* — but perhaps even more wonderful were the Syrian peddlers.[2] Very wonderful people — I know now that they were mostly Jewish. Many of the great fortunes began that way; the Caplans of Ottawa began that way. I remember one in particular, Sam Lacoven. He'd come up on our verandah in the summer and throw that sack down. It was like a "box of wonders."

"Ladies' earrings, brooches and bloomers," he would chant. As children we would say that over and over again. It was a chant that haunted our sleep and our play, and haunts me yet.

They always stayed at our place — my mother was the soul of hospitality. We just loved one Syrian peddler in particular because in the spring, dying for green vegetables — we lived almost like pioneers in those days, you know, during the winter surviving on carrots, turnips, potatoes — and he would come from Ottawa with his little sleigh in early

The amazing but short-lived Cage Ferry, which crossed the Ottawa River during the 1920s at a narrow point at Deux Rivieres. It was devised by a lumber baron to get his men, animals and supplies quickly into his camps. It was run across the river on cables above the water. Carl Jennings of Sheenboro, Quebec, aged eighty-four, remembers this contraption and says that terrified animals roared and neighed and stamped all the way across. It is also likely that brave men shook! Jennings also remembers the intrepid Syrian peddlers crossing with their wares on the Cage Ferry, looking for new markets on the Quebec side of the Valley.

March and out from under his old horse blanket he would take **Fresh Green Onions**. What a treat! We thought of him as a most wonderful man and, as children, we would get up on his knee and sing with him "Abdul Abubhul Amir."

On a hot day my mother would treat the Syrian peddlers to her dandelion wine. My mother always believed that wine that was made in the home was therefore nonspirituous. So she used to always give it to the clergymen who came to our house. Of course, the clergymen enjoyed it all to pieces because it kicked like a mule. There was never a shortage of visiting clergymen at our place, and my mother never seemed to realize that we were all going to heaven on dandelion wine.

I got stinko on my mother's dandelion wine when I was about fifteen. We got home from school and my father immediately put us to work digging those early Rose potatoes for the Ottawa market. It was very hot. And I came into the house and said, "I am dying of the heat."

So my mother sits me down and says, "Well, have a glass of dandelion wine."

So, as the Irish say, I takes a glass. I went down into the basement and filled up a glass with this lovely yellow tart stuff — golden — and brought it up, sat down on the sofa near the window, and drank it. And I said to my mother, "Mother, this is really good."

And my mother said, "Well, it won't hurt you. It's homemade. And it's last year's."

When I had finished the glass, I said, "I must get back to the fields. Father will be looking for me." But I was unable to get up. Indeed, I was unable to lift a hand or a foot! I was stinko on vintage dandelion wine. They decided I was suffering from the heat and, I believe, put me to bed.

I think the French and English language mix is just beautiful. We had a lot of French in Navan and they came to our school. They loved the train. Now Navan was only ten miles from Ottawa and we went in from Navan often. It was a great thing. You stopped for Blackburn and then you were in Ottawa. We went in and out on weekends, back and forth to the Navan station and then walk down the tracks to home.

One time there was a big crowd collected at the Navan station waiting for the first train that came through there. It had taken a group into Ottawa that morning and was coming back in the evening. The group included a Mrs. Poirier, and her little boy was waiting for her on the platform. The train always blew a big blast at Blackburn — it was only five or six miles away — you could always hear it fairly well. And then it would start to blow for Navan. And the little Poirier fellow starts jumping up and down in excitement. And the people on the platform said, "There she's blowing now! She's coming now!"

And the little Poirier lad, jumping up and down, yelled out, "Listen to dat! My mudder! My mudder! She blow for Navan!"

My brother, Bill Rothwell, went to school one day in Navan all rigged up — or so he thought.

Bill had asthma until he was nineteen. He did Dr. Jackson's diet in the Ottawa *Journal* and he cured himself and he never had it again. He's an older man now down in Trinidad or Tobago playing golf most of the time. But anyhow, he went to school all rigged up and his friend Alec Robinson (his mother was French, so he had a French accent) was waiting for him at the school gate. And Alec saw Bill all dressed up and he started to chant;

> "Oh, he's all dress up
> For see de girlies
> He's Pass on de school."[3]

An old shantyman of few words was working for Gillies up near Petawawa on the ice road. An ice road — it's a place where when they were taking out these huge timber loads they had to have the roads iced and horses sharply shod to ease the loads safely onwards. Well, anyhow, timber baron John Gillies[4] was out with my father-in-law, Big Jim McCord, examining the ice roads. And this shantyman came along. He was a chickadee. A chickadee is the man who takes the horse manure off the ice roads. He's called that because there's nothing chickadees like better than fresh horse manure. But it had to be taken off the ice roads because it might slow down the load and get it stuck. This shantyman of few words was also highly contemptuous of any authority and he was chewing tobacco — they all did it — so he spit a great big rotten spit on the ice road and, of course, it splattered and splashed. And John Gillies said, "That's horrible! I'd just as soon chew horseshit."

And the old shantyman chewed a few chews more and drawled out: "Well, just whatever a man's used to."

In those early days, men measured distances by horse-hours. I remember one time a long time ago a young girl asked my husband, Henry McCord — he worked in the shanties like his father and his grandfather before him — she asked him, "How many miles from Shawville to Danford Lake?"

"Well, my girl," said Henry, "I don't know how many miles it is. But I can tell you it's a good forenoon's trip with the horses. When you get to the Danford Lake Hotel, you're ready for your dinner."

This is one of my favourite political warmer-upper stories. It can be adapted to all places and all situations.

One day this man with a constipated tomcat met the vet on the street in Fort Coulonge. The man asked the vet to prescribe for his constipated tom-

cat. And the vet said, "Go to my office and get such-and-such a thing." And the man did.

A couple of days passed and the man met the vet (and I would say as an aside, "Now doesn't this remind you of what our opponents are doing in government?" The French-Canadians loved this and would already be laughing) again on the street in Fort Coulonge. So the vet asked the man, "How is your tomcat? Did he get better of his constipation?" (And, of course, by this time they'd all be in stitches anyway.)

"Yes, he certainly did," the man said. "And furthermore he has five cats working for him now." (And I'd say as an aside, "Doesn't that remind you of the fat cats in the government who are getting the money for doing this, doing nothing?")

And the vet said to the man, "Why would your constipated tomcat have five cats working for him?"

"Well," said the man, "there's two digging, two covering, and two looking for fresh territory!" ("And," I would say as an aside to the audience, "that's exactly what our opponents — the Liberals — are doing!")

This is a Twelfth of July story. You can turn this story and tell this story with all kinds of political parallels in all kinds of situations.

This particular family lived quite a distance up the railway tracks above Shawville. The lady of the house was very elegant. She thought she was quite a dresser and all that. And it was the Twelfth of July celebrations. And unfortunately she had sent her favourite dress down to the dressmaker's in Shawville to be altered. She had to have that dress, she told her husband. So they decided to send her husband's brother down to Shawville to fetch the dress. Now, her husband's brother had not any more brains than the Lord had endowed him with. In fact, some of them had worn away through the erosion of time over the years. And he was quite simple-minded.

Anyhow, they sent him down on the morning train, early about seven. He was to walk back home, a distance of five miles. They figured he would be back around nine o'clock, plenty of time to allow the lady of the house to ready herself in her finery for the big celebrations in Shawville.

Well, nine o'clock, ten o'clock came, and he wasn't back home. And eleven o'clock came and he wasn't back. Lunchtime came and he wasn't back. The lady of the house was beside herself. They had missed the big Orangeman's parade and were in danger of missing the picnic. The heat increased both inside the house and outside the house as the

While legendary figures like Mountain Jack Thomson, Big Jim McCord and the Gillies Brothers were involved in the white pine business in the Valley up "at the front", a man named Delano Dexter Calvin (1798-1884) was engaged in making a like fortune in the square timber hardwood trade along the shores of the Great Lakes. The centre of his operation was Garden Island, just off the Kingston shoreline. In this photograph square timber hardwood, having been collected from forests along Lake Ontario, is being unloaded for rafting to Montreal and Quebec. Since Calvin's hardwood did not have to go through timber slides, rafts could be any size at all.

long wait went on. Finally at sunset the messenger arrived back in the yard with the dress. The husband pounced on him. "My wife has been waiting all day for that dress and we have missed everything! What the hell kept you so long?"

The man just sat down on the stoop and quietly lit his pipe. "Begad, Bob," he said slowly, "I wasn't going to kill myself in the hait."

I didn't always need jokes. When I walked into a classroom or a political meeting, they all knew it was going to be, at the very least, entertaining. As a political warmer-upper I was supposed to limit myself to seven to eight minutes. But I never could. Because it was going too good. I would have the crowd in a receptive mood by the time the VIPs arrived on the platform. If I knew we were slated for a poor speaker, I would have to work harder to warm up the crowd. Sometimes I would look down at the crowd and say, "I can see staunch Conservatives here. But I can see a few Liberals hiding there, too. That's a funny thing. And you know what the Liberal said," — and I'd fill in with a pithy one. "Well, maybe these Liberals can't be turned. Now, what do you people think? Do you think we can do anything with them? Or should we just let them go on outside?" And then I'd go on to tell a favourite:

You all know, of course, about the Liberal who got very very animated about his Liberalism and his party policy. And he was up on the platform telling everybody why he voted Liberal.

"Yes, yes," he shouted, "my father voted Liberal. My grandfather voted Liberal. My great-grandfather voted Liberal. We've always been Liberal. And I vote Liberal." Boos and cries from the audience.

"Furthermore," he shouted out, "my father was a Catholic. My grandfather was a Catholic. My great-grandfather was a Catholic. My great-great-grandfather was a Catholic. And I'm a Catholic. **And I'm Going to be a Catholic to the End of my Days!**" (Use Protestant here in a Catholic area.) Boos and cries from the audience.

"Yes, yes, my friends," he went on. "I do what my forefathers did — right down to the last letter. I'm a bachelor — my father was a bachelor. My grandfather was a bachelor. My great-grandfather was a —— " He is drowned out in boos and cries.

Yes, there he was — hoist on his own petard. By the time I got through that story, everyone in the audience knew that to be a Liberal was a very bad thing. And I used to work very hard to appeal to the women in the audiences. I had one piece called "Yes, I vote the way John votes." I'd tell them something like this:

"Remember, girls, I don't care how old you are — I was young then myself — I don't care what age you are. It doesn't matter. You are still girls, aren't you? You are *not* boys. Are you?" This would appeal to the men always and make them laugh. "There's 51 percent voters in Canada who are women." And I said, "Most of these women — **But Not You** — are under subjection to their husbands. And a great many of them — **But Not You** — say, "Well, I vote the way John votes." And I would fold my hands piously. And I said, "Of course, I don't have any trouble with that at all. I vote the way my husband votes. But then he votes the right way. He always knew how to vote the right way — Conservative.

"A lot of women when they get in that polling booth (tomorrow or next Friday) will do whatever their husbands tell them to do — well, not **You**; but unwise women will. They are the kind of women who do what their husbands tell them to do — always. If he says, 'Go to this church,' they go. If he says, 'You can go to Shawville to shop on such-and-such a day,' that's the day they go. If he says, 'This is how much money you can have,' that's what they take. Yes, these women do what their husbands tell them. When they go behind the curtain on election day they are the ones who take the pencil up and say to themselves, 'This is how John

would want me to vote.' And they vote that way. But not **You**. Remember, when you go behind the curtain on voting day you have 51 percent of the voting power in this country. And when you get in behind that curtain, forget that you were ever married. Forget you were ever married if your husband told you to vote Liberal. And put your X in the right place. **He'll Never Know. He'll Never Know.**"

I believe French Canadians have more capacity to laugh at themselves than do the Anglo Saxons. The French Canadians loved me. They laughed at my crazy stories and my crazy accent and my racism, my anti-bilingualism and all that. Irish Catholics have less sense of humour. I don't know why. But the French Canadian can have fun laughing at himself. I can tell you a couple of stories which illustrate this capacity:

Up in Big Jim McCord's lumber camp, a great horned owl had been stealing and killing the cats. Now, this was a very bad thing, for the cats kept down the vermin — not the lice or the bedbugs — but the rats and mice. So the men in the camp killed the owl. Being very short of any change of diet in the lumber camp, they cooked and ate the

As Gillies foreman, Big Jim McCord of Shawville always used to say, "The Frenchmen were quick, agile, good river-drivers." Here they are in an early action shot *"running on the loose" over a mass of logs in a quick dash to shore and out of danger.*

great horned owl. The next morning one of the shantymen — a Frenchman named Pierre — came in to see Big Jim McCord in his office. The Frenchman was holding his stomach.

"What's wrong with you, Pierre?" McCord asked.

"Oh, sick in de stomach," Pierre replied.

"What made you sick?" McCord asked.

Pierre began laughing to himself.

"Oh, Jeez," he said, "I think I ate too much of de chick with de big hye!"

When the French and Irish mixed and married, they had a wonderful sense of humour and they got along well together. If I was warming up an audience which had a goodly number of French in it, I would often say to them, "I have a relative who lives up in Resolute Bay and he says Resolute Bay is the ideal place to live; there are no mosquitoes, no humidity — and no Frenchmen." Well, everybody would hoot. But so would the Frenchmen. Can you imagine if I changed it around and said "no Englishmen"?

I had a cultured uncle in Ottawa named Marshall Rothwell who used to run for Parliament but never got in. He was like Charlotte Whitton — "pretty near there." He was too honest and he had a very sharp tongue. Only a silly tongue can get you elected. One time my uncle Rothwell was running on the Conservative ticket — what else? — and was addressing a meeting at Navan. As I said before, Navan had a large French population and one of my uncle's dearest friends and staunchest supporters was a Frenchman named Ernest Lariviere. At this particular meeting, Lariviere was to introduce Uncle Rothwell to the audience. Lariviere didn't speak English very well at all and, once he got up to face the audience, he got stage-struck and tongue-tied. He fumbled around for words and finally blurted out, "I guess de first ting on de programme, I take off my coat."

It brought down the house and I use it yet. To certain audiences I will say, "I guess de first ting on de programme, I take off my dress." Usually they yell, "Take it off! Take it off!" And I yell back at them, "Don't say that because I might!" And we're off.

I value Charlotte Whitton because she kicked Paul Tardiff in the shins for something sexist he said. They hated Charlotte Whitton — the men — because she was honest, always honourable, and swept the dirty men out of the corners. They couldn't stand her for that. I don't think she was a feminist, but she wanted to be acknowledged the equal of men. I can tell you a delightful Charlotte Whitton story:

Charlotte Whitton always got her hats in Ogilvy's.[5] Besides having the smallest feet in Ottawa — size four — she had a very large head, like mine. When I went in to stores in Ottawa I was often called Dr. Whitton. She was a small woman and she always got her hats in Ogilvy's. She would go into the hat department — they don't have them anymore, you know — and try on hats and hats and, of course, they wouldn't fit her. She'd put one on and look at it in the mirror and then say to the salesgirl, "Take that damn thing away!" And she'd throw it on the floor. And then she'd take up another one, try it on, look in the mirror and then yell once again, "Take that damn thing away!" She'd try dozens on, take them off and throw them on the floor. Imagine that! The Ogilvy hats! Until she got one that fitted her. They suffered her gladly. They knew she'd be back for an Ogilvy hat.

The Kilreas of Ottawa were relations of ours. The first Kilrea, Jack, was an Irishman, pure Irish, over from Northern Ireland. He got work in a lumber camp with my uncle, John Armstrong, a big, handsome man. And John Armstrong brought Jack Kilrea home with him because Jack had no place to go. And then with his bride, Sara Armstrong, Kilrea moved to Ottawa and got work with J. R. Booth — oh, he was poorly paid — and he bought a little house on Laurier Avenue West. It's still there — just off Bank Street — and they had a little back yard. And Kilrea was having this large family. Fourteen they had, you know. Anyway, he was an Irishman and he was an Orangeman. And he rose on the Twelfth of July before sunrise. At the first gleam of the sun he would be out there in the back yard in his "couth."[6] And he had a revolver and he'd be firing shots into the air and yelling, "Hurray for King Billy! Hurray for King Billy!" At the top of his voice and already drunk! Yes, he would already have had two or three good shots of good whiskey. He collected whiskey for the Twelfth, the Glorious Twelfth; he wasn't drinking beer that day!

And the police would come. In those days they were all Irish Catholics — not now though — and they would come and say, "Now, Mr. Kilrea, you mustn't make such a noise."

And Jack would yell, "Get out of here or I'll drill you full! Hurray for King Billy! Out of my back yard, you damn Dogans!"

And the police would say, "Kilrea, you are causing a disturbance ——— "

And he would shout, "Are you a Dogan?"

"No," the policemen would say, "we're Catholics."

And he would say, "To hell with that! You're all damn black Dogans, every last man jack of you! Out of here or I'll drill every one of you!"

And the policemen would go — partly because he was armed and partly because he was a fiercesome-looking man. He wasn't a big man but he was full of presence and he had yellow curls and a great yellow whisker. Another reason the policemen would go was because Jack Kilrea was the father of the later-famous Hec Kilrea of the Ottawa Senators.

Every Twelfth of July, Jack Kilrea petrified his neighbours. But the police stopped coming to his place on the Glorious Twelfth. "Oh, it's just Jack Kilrea" they would say when the complaints came in. "He doesn't shoot at anything. He just shoots up into the sky!"

Jack Kilrea was an Orangeman first, last and always. For years the Kilreas lived from hand to mouth on Laurier Avenue. But then some of the girls got work and got married, and Hec was making all that money with the Ottawa Senators during the twenties and early thirties. And one Kilrea married a Jewish lady and when the first child was born her Jewish grandfather gave her a white mink hat and coat. It was the talk of the town.

The Rush End at old Day's Arena in Ottawa was a section at both ends of the rink where you stood up. You'd get a ticket for five cents and you stood up all night. But that didn't matter. You were watching the Montreal Maroons play the Ottawa Senators and Aurel Joliat was playing. Oh my, that little wee Frenchman! Just absolutely gorgeous! And my uncle Jack Kilrea was there, of course, in the Rush End, telling everybody around him that that was his son down there, big, blonde Hec Kilrea. Jack would be having a few, maybe even had managed to save up some whiskey for the game, and he'd get bragging in a very loud voice: "That's my boy down there." And somebody would answer him with a vile insult, or slanderous French, and they would be into it. And more and more people would be into it, taking sides until the whole Rush End would be a melee — everyone fighting and hitting and cursing and swearing, in both French and English! Oh, it was audience participation in the truest sense of the word!

I can tell you some slapstick fight stories, full of fun and so typical of the Ottawa Valley. My brothers used to come up from Navan and Ottawa on Saturday nights for the sheer pleasure of being there for the Saturday night fights. In Shawville they used to hire a couple of Saturday night policemen. One night this young man — he was an Irishman, of course — resisted arrest. Oh, how he resisted arrest! The two policemen dragged him out of the bar of the old Pontiac House and the crowd began to gather until you could walk across their heads. They got up on the cars, on the trunks, on the hoods, and you could yell, "Get off my car!", 'til you were blue in the face. And the crowd began to get into the melee because a policeman is always an enemy. And everybody got into it and the policemen barely escaped. Of course, they never arrested the Irishman.

I'll tell you about the best fight I ever saw. An absolute beauty in Charteris. There was then a long-standing vendetta between two families from Thorne. And on this particular Saturday night the feud erupted between two members of the families in the Clarendon Inn bar. They rolled out of the side door into the hotel yard, fighting on the ground. And the rest of the two families began to collect and join in. You know, in the old Celtic battles, the leader used to cry out, "To me! To me!" or in French, "A moi! A moi!" Well, the battle cry was sounded and they came from every nook and cranny. Word sped through town, and more and more came in to join the fray until eventually men, women, children, grandparents, were involved. They fought the whole length of the main street, fought with everything they had: fists, sticks, belts. They took off their boots and shoes and hurled them; they used their handbags. It was the best fight I ever did see. And my relatives were all there to see it.

Well, after the fight broke up and we were all heading home, the trailer hitch came unhooked from the car and the trailer went into the ditch. It took us hours to get it out. When we got home exhausted and all ready for bed, a bat got loose in the upstairs hall and we had to get rid of that, chasing and batting around with the brooms and the mops for a considerable length of time. And my poor sister-in-law finally fell into bed at dawn absolutely tired out. She was used to a quiet life in Montreal, "And to think I came to the country for peace and rest!" she proclaimed.

And I can tell you another fight story with a really funny ending. One time the Charteris Orange Lodge was notorious for its dances and its battles — you know people came out from Shawville to the country to have a great time at the dances. Oh, the little wee floor, but oh, the dances we had there! There wasn't room to turn but we did the grapevine and we swung and we sweated — we didn't perspire, we sweated. And we had one glorious time. The men went outside and drank, and we women stayed inside and danced with the men who were still standing up. And I never missed a dance — maybe two weeks over the birth of a baby or maybe six months pregnant — and dance until morning. We didn't stop at twelve or one in those days, you know! Anyhow, this was a cold November night, very moonlit, and the ground was frozen. There was a couple of Fighting Hawkins boys present and there was also present one of the Onslow boys who was a Roman Catholic but a very gallant gentleman. Now, in those days, you know, there were the drinkers and the fighters. And the Onslow lad was a fighter and a drinker. One night I saw him drinking outside a dance in the back country. There were buggies parked outside the hall and Onslow was sitting in a buggy seat having a drink. The buggies nearly all had a step on the side where you lowered yourself onto the ground. But he stood up in the buggy, took one giant step forward, missed the buggy step, and stepped forward into thin air — and of course, fell flat on his face.

And these two — the Fighting Hawkins lad and the Onslow fellow — got into a row. The Protestant engendered the fight by making some derogatory remarks about what the hell was a Roman Catholic doing in an Orange Hall and this Onslow fellow said, "Now, now, let's not fight in here before the ladies." I said he was gallant. So they went outside, followed by everybody in the hall. The set broke up; the musicians stopped; we all went outside.

Now the church was right beside the Orange Hall and the church steps, at that time, came down to what is now the highway. But, anyway, they got down these steps. And everybody was beautifully excited, *joie de vivre* and all that. Half-past three in the morning. And they got down and the Protestant Hawkins was underneath and the Roman Catholic lad was sitting on top of him banging his head on the frozen ground. So the Protestant fellow's wife took her shoe and began to pound the Roman Catholic fellow on top of his head with her shoe heel. And he turned around and said to her, "Oh lady! That's not fair!"

And in the meantime as well, the sister-in-law

A lone sorter works with Calvin's square timbers. In the timber trade, the hewer was always one of the heroic experts. Can you imagine the strength, stamina and expertise required to square hardwood like oak, ash, maple, walnut, butternut! Calvin also built sailing vessels on Calvin Island and used them to take his timber to Great Britain. In 1881, Calvin launched his first lake steamer, the D. D. Calvin.

of Fighting Hawkins, seeing that he was getting the worst of it, she was sitting on the church steps keening, "Oh, remember your heart! Oh, remember you heart!" — he had evidently just had a heart attack a short time before the fight. And she sat down on the church step, keening away. And then she fainted. And this fellow who was a real joker caught her in time and upheld her with his strong right arm. And she came out of her faint and leaped to her feet, yelling out, "Oh, they're going to kill him! Oh, they're going to kill him!" And the fellow who was such a joker yelled out, "Get back down here! You're supposed to be fainting in my arms!"

Meanwhile, back at the fight, the Protestant underneath, in all this commotion, withdrew himself from his position on the bottom, went over to the store across the street — a hen's race away — and he came back — Fighting Hawkins was a dirty fighter — and he came back with an axe, swinging it around his head. And we ladies withdrew back to the sanctuary of the rectory lawn.

Fighting Hawkins came back swinging that axe and somebody — a fellow who came up to Otter Lake to summer and was there for the weekend, a Roman Catholic — said, "What are we going to do now? He is going to kill; he is one of the fighting ones; he can't win for himself, so he is going to win this way." And this summer visitor decided to do something to stop what was beginning to look like a disaster. Before anyone could stop him, he ran under Fighting Hawkins's arm and caught the axe.

Loyal Orange Lodge number 65, Charteris, Quebec. So peaceful it looks here, it is difficult to believe it was once the scene of some of the Valley's most memorable recreational violence!

That ended it all. But it was the most terrible and horrifying and enjoyable fight I ever saw. It was a dandy, and after it was all over, the Roman Catholic fellow said, "I am sorry if I caused a disturbance. Now shall we get back into the hall and continue the dancing?" Which we did. I said in the beginning he was gallant.

Children were a wonderful thing but they sometimes could spoil a good sale. One time Henry was selling a cow of ours to a cattle buyer, a Jewish Mr. Myer. And if you wanted to "Jew him down," as the saying goes, like a horse-trader, you didn't tell him too many of the deficiencies of the beast, but rather emphasized the good points. So Henry was saying, "Yes, she's a very good milker, quiet, good" — not telling any lies — "yes, she feeds up well and comes out well in the spring," and so on. And the young lad pipes up to my husband, "Oh, Daddy are you selling the one with the three teats?" And there went the sale.

Whiskey cured a lot of things in this country. In the year of the flu — 1919 — this was a cure. Our dear Dr. Powell — a Christian gentleman who happened to be a doctor and we remembered him as such — he was immaculate, he was a picture to see, just the way a doctor should look. Anyway, when Big Jim McCord was taking the flu, Dr. Powell went around to our place early one November morning in 1919. Henry, my husband, his sister and his mother were down with a mild form of flu — they didn't die of it — a great many people around here died of it. Anyway, Dr. Powell came and it was a farm kitchen and poor Grandpa, Big Jim McCord, had cooked the sick members of his family a big pot of turnips. That was his cure. Imagine! And Grandpa said, "How are the Hazards up in Thorne?" And Dr. Powell said, "They'll both be dead by morning." They left a big family of children. And he said, "How are you?" to Grandpa. Grandpa at that time was a man about fifty. And Grandpa said, "I'm taking it. And I'm taking it damn bad, too!" Dr. Powell took his temperature; it was high. "Yes," the doctor said, "you are taking it. James, do you want to die?" And Grandpa said, "No, not yet." And the doctor said, "What are you going to do then?" And Big Jim McCord said, "I'm going to hitch Belle to the buggy and I'm going out to Campbell's Bay and I'm going to get a bottle of castor oil and a bottle of high wines and I'll come home and I'll drink the two of them before I sleep tonight." And Dr. Powell said, "If it were anybody else, I would say it would kill them. But you are six-foot-four; you weight 240. You have an exceedingly strong constitution. You do that." With that

Dr. Powell went on his way. And Big Jim McCord drove Belle to Campbell's Bay, got himself home again, drank the two bottles and went to bed. And he went instantly to sleep and when he got up in the morning he was a little shaky on the legs, but otherwise he was fine.

The famous riverman, Mountain Jack Thomson of Portage-du-Fort, one cold misty early spring morning was once standing on the banks of the Black River surrounded by a bunch of French Canadian river rats. The river rats were standing there beside Mountain Jack wondering whether or not they should tackle the terrible white waters of the Black River. And finally Mountain Jack, angered by their indecision and anxious to get on with the work and meet his deadlines, yelled at them, "Jump in, boys! It's boiling but it won't scald you!"

One time Big Jim McCord went in to visit this Gillies camp, to inspect it I guess, since he was foreman. There was one toad-strangler of a rainstorm raging outside. The roof of the sleep camp was made of cedar shakes — you know, just one shake laid roughly over another to give some sort of protection. The rain was coming down in buckets and there was just silence in the sleeping camp; the men were lying in their bunks just suffering it through. And he said all of a sudden he heard this voice — it was Jim Ebert from Campbell's Bay and he was a jolly fellow — he was the one who put the sock in the stew — and all of a sudden came Ebert's voice from the top bunk: "Easy, Lord! You know damn well I can't swim!"

They were always playing tricks on one another, you know. I guess it was a way of easing the boredom and having a laugh. And one time in the camp they had this wonderful stew. They all had partaken of it heartily and at the very last, someone cleaning out the pot put the ladle in and brought up this dirty sock. Of course, it didn't hurt the flavour and no one really minded.

Which puts me in mind of another trick. In the camp one time this fellow thought he would play a trick on the other lads. Of course, they had to go outside to the facilities, the convenience, the john, the head, whatever. He caught a big bear in a trap and at night put it on the convenience seat — I love that word "convenience" — it was so damned inconvenient! And, of course the men had to go out at night. And it would be dark and they would feel their way out and in and back into this great furry creature sitting on the john — and come howling back into the camp. Very funny.

It was the same lad who one time thought things were pretty slow — it was Little Alec Hodgins, by

the way — and he thought he would make a brew for all the lads who were suffering from the cold. So his brew was cherry bark. Cherry bark, when it is brewed, will make exceedingly strong cough syrup; when it ferments, it is something wicked. He said it was good for chest cures. And it was, of course, because there was so much liquor in it. When it ferments a little, it is pretty near pure alcohol. So he was making this medicinal brew. And this other lad in camp thought he would have a little fun, got up in the night, and put a pound of Epsom Salts into the cherry-bark brew stewing on the stove. The next night he almost died laughing in his bunk. That camp door never quit banging all night long. Bang. Bang. Bang. And the fellows cursing in the dark.

There are so many amusing incidents to relate about the bushman, the ingenue, coming into civilization. Like the shantyman who went to this big spread in an Orange Hall one time and looked at the potato salad and said, "One hell of a thing to give visitors — cold potatoes." And Grandpa McCord used to tell of one time he went into a store in North Bay with the famous strongman Larry Frost (and Larry was "full" at the time, of course) and he bumped into one of the store manequins and said in all seriousness, "I beg your pardon, lady."

Granpa McCord was lumbering in the 1870s and 1880s and from him comes a story — an amusing one, too — of the time that Mountain Jack Thomson from Portage-du-Fort beat Big Joe Montferrand on the dock at Fort William, Quebec.

One time Joe Montferrand — the bully from Montreal, that's what they called him — and Mountain Jack one Sunday morning were sitting on the wharf at the Fort. And Big Joe Montferrand said, "I can beat anyone from Montreal."

No answer from Mountain Jack.

"I can beat anybody in Fort William," said Montferrand.

No answer.

"I can beat anybody back at that camp," said Montferrand.

No answer. But Mountain Jack edged a little closer to Montferrand on the wharf.

Montferrand stood up and roared out, "I can beat any man around here in the whole Pontiac."

That was it for Mountain Jack. They had a knock-down, drag-out fight on the dock at Fort William. And after Mountain Jack had finished beating up Montferrand, he said to him, "Do you not think, Big Joe, that you made a mistake?"

"*Oui,*" said Montferrand, "I tink me take in too much territory."

After Calvin's sailing vessels were superseded by his steamships, he used old sailing vessels as scows to ship *timbers to Quebec and Montreal. In this photograph, they appear to be loaded and ready for departure.*

My father-in-law, Big Jim McCord, always said that in the bush work for top loaders[7] you always took the Bretzlaffs from Ladysmith. The little Frenchmen were quick, agile, good river drivers, but they got lonesome in the bush for home. Big Jim said one time he went into a camp back of Jim's Lake and there was a little French lad on the top bunk suffering from homesickness — he was probably only fourteen or so — in those days they took youngsters and tried to make them into men in the camps. And anyhow, he was crying and Big Jim said to him, "What the hell's wrong with you?" — the foreman was supposed to be big and rough and gruff — and he was — and the little French lad said, "Oh, I never was away from my house before, away from my mudder."

And Big Jim said, "Hell! You're not very far away. You just come from Masham."

"Oh, I miss my home," the little French lad repeated.

"Have none of you ever been away from home?" Big Jim asked.

"*Oui.* Oh ya, my brudder he been away as far as Maniwaki," the lad replied.[8]

1. The Brinckmans, the Popes, the Blackburns, the Booths and the Eddys were all families of power and influence in Ottawa and the Valley in the first half of this century. The Southams founded the Southam chain of newspapers across Canada. J. R. Booth and E. B. Eddy established lumbering dynasties.
2. With a pack of the rare and exotic on their backs, these peddlers travelled the countryside in good weather. The more remote the homestead, the greater the excitement and curiosity with which their arrival was heralded. The designations "Assyrian" and "Syrian" seem to have been used interchangeably throughout the Valley.
3. Phoebe's translation of this is "all dressed up to watch the girls go by."
4. John Gillies was one of the second generation of the Gillies lumbering empire established at Braeside, Ontario.
5. Along with Bryson-Graham's and Caplan's, Ogilvy's was one of the big department stores of Ottawa.
6. "In his couth" would be mostly undressed, perhaps naked.
7. A top loader was a man whose expertise was in being able to load and balance the top timbers on the haul sleigh.
8. From Masham to Maniwaki is only about sixty miles, but a long distance in those days when most people walked wherever they went.

4

My God! And so small for its age

ED AND TED, AND WALTER FAIRCLOUGH, ARNPRIOR, ONTARIO

These three storytellers, Ed and Ted, and Walter Fairclough, are grouped together here because they combine to give a composite picture of "growing up in Arnprior." Ed is an Arnprior businessman whom I taped at his home. While I was interviewing him his old friend and neighbour dropped in to chat, as was his daily wont. Ed decided he wished to be recorded here anonymously and when he expressed these wishes Ted, an old shantyman, decided to follow suit.

Ed: My mother came from Quyon, an O'Donnell from there. My uncle, Garrett O'Donnell, was the purser on the old *J.B. Green*, and the night it burned at the Quyon dock, he decided he'd sleep at home that night instead of on the boat. And another old uncle of mine went down to meet him and they were walking home and they were hardly at the door when the call went out through the town: "The *J.B. Green* is on fire!" She was tied to the dock at the time and the sad part about it was that one man was killed. But the funny part was that the cook's husband escaped in the altogether off the boat. He was so busy helping his wife to escape off the burning boat that he forgot he was in the altogether until there he was in the altogether on the dock at Quyon in front of everybody. Well, after all, they had to get off real quick, no matter what was going on! Some man went home and got him a pair of pants.

Ted: There was a lot of Gahans at Glasgow Station and in Braeside. They were real Irish right out from Ireland. Pat Gahan, "Grandpa" Gahan to me when I was a young lad and he was an old man, he used to love to tell us young lads stories. He loved to laugh and joke. Years and years ago he used to have an old horse and he used to draw junk and draw water around Braeside. Cartage, you know. With his old horse and wagon he used to draw water up the Braeside Hill. He had a barrel on two wheels on the wagon and you paid a quarter a barrel, that's a wooden barrel, for fifty gallons of water. We had a barrel of water in our house, too, in the wintertimes, Well, Pat Gahan had this old horse doing all this hard work pulling and Jesus! didn't the horse keel over one day dead, dead from a heart attack. Everybody knew about old Pat Gahan's horse falling over dead. And the old grocer in Braeside said to him, "That's too bad about your horse, Mr. Gahan." And Pat Gahan said, "Yes, and you know, he never did that before!"

Ed: During Prohibition, Chief Roberts, Timmy O'Toole, Tippling Tom Mulvihill and Dr. Sanders were rumrunning out of Arnprior. You see, they used to bring lumber down to the CNR here, and what these guys were doing was putting the booze inside the railway car, in the centre, and then they were packing the lumber all around it, and I guess they put a little on top, just enough to cover it. And then they were getting it across the border to the States that way. Oh, they were making money at it! My father was a town councillor and somebody tipped him off about what was happening down at the railroad tracks at the Arnprior station. So he went down and watched for a while and caught them in the act. But, my God, when he saw who was involved in the rumrunning, he couldn't believe it! It was Who's Who in Arnprior. So he didn't blow the whistle on them. He just said, "OK, lads, you do that once more and I'll call the RCMP on you." There weren't any more loads of *that* kind of lumber run out of Arnprior, I tell you.

When you think of drinking and cops trying to catch illegal drinkers and boozers and all that stuff, I think the best one I ever heard in my life was this one. In some of the older General Motors cars there was a windshield-washer and there was a hose which led up to the windshield, and it squirted up on the windshield when you pressed a button inside the car. And these fellows up at Forester's Falls were playing around with illegal booze and the cops

Granny Bean's stopping-place at Quyon as it still stands today. The legend goes that when Edward VII was Prince of Wales and making his grand tour of Canada in 1860, he decided to make an unscheduled stop at

Granny Bean's. She is said to have scurried about town to borrow china, silver, and linen from the Egans, the Bronsons and the Mohrs.

were trying to catch them all the time for drinking and driving. There was no open bars up there then, and you couldn't go in and get a drink, and it was illegal to carry it in a car. So what these lads used to do was put the goddam stuff in the windshield-washer and pipe it through the fire wall and into the car. All you did was hit the button on the floor and put the hose in your mouth and you got a mouthful of the pure stuff. This was in Forester's Falls when I was playing for dances up there. And the cops were up there all the time trying to find out where in hell they were getting the booze. They knew they were drinking and they knew the booze was there. But they could never find it. These country bumpkins, my foot! They buffaloed the cops for years.

Ted: Yes, Mr. Sawsay — this was back during the Depression times — and he was cutting up his wood for the winter and carefully piling it up. But

when he got up the next morning he was always missing some. So he got some dynamite caps. He took the knots out of his wood and put the dynamite caps in and then put the knots back. He waited until the next morning and, sure enough, there was the darndest explosion up the street a few houses, and he knew right away who was stealing his wood.

Years ago in Arnprior there used to be the Slaters and the Whites. They were bakers; they ran Slater and White Bake Shop. Scott White was a wee short fellow with red hair and he was one hell-driver. One time he was taking a big load of bread from Arnprior over to Norway Bay for all the tourists and cottagers over there. In those days you could cross on the ferry with Captain Gamble.[1] So Scott slams over the railroad track hump at Sand Point and down onto the ferryboat wharf lickety-split. And when he puts on the brakes, they fail on his truck and he goes right over the wharf and into the

Ottawa River. When he comes up, he is surrounded by hundreds of loaves of floating white bread.

"By gar," he says to the crowd gathered on the dock, "that's good white bread. It floats."

Ed: There was a councillor here in Arnprior one time who was being chased by the police for drunken driving. He was weaving and bobbing all over town. So, when they chased him, in order to make his getaway, he took up off the railroad tracks in his car. The railway gauge matched the width of his car. So he escaped and they didn't catch him.

Oh, I could tell you lots of stories about the elite of this town. Like most people around here still remember the big dance up at the airport during the last war when one lady of high society here had a little too much to drink and she did the Dance of the Seven Veils — right down to the seventh!

And, of course, the McLachlins and the Gillieses were the hoi-poloi of Arnprior. There used to be Jimmy and Arthur and Norah Ward and Tommy Wood and myself and my sister, and once a year we would be invited to the Gillies place for a party. And it would be a swim and then there would be brown sugar sandwiches and milk, and then Norah Wood, who was the one who took us down there to the Gillies place, brought us home. It was always such a big disappointment because we were all going to the Big House in Town and we thought we were going to get something really special, and all we got was brown sugar sandwiches — and we got the same at home.

Ted: There were a couple of old-timers in Arnprior and they hadn't met for years. To celebrate the reunion one lad said to the other, "I'm going to give you a good drink of Irish whiskey. You've never had the like of it in your life." So jeez, he brought out a little wee nip — not big enough to put in your eye — and gave it to his friend in a little wee bitch of a glass, you know. And as he was handing it to him, he warned him, "Don't you drink that like an Irishman. Just sip it."

So the other old-timer took a couple of sips of the Irish whiskey and it was so damn strong he pretty near coughed to death.

"Jesus!" he said. "That's really good! It burns all the way down!"

And the other old-timer said, "Do you know how old that whiskey is?"

"No. How old is it?"

"It's one hundred and five years old," said the first old-timer.

"My God!" said the second old-timer. "And so small for its age!"

Ed: Arnprior used to be great for amateur "theatah."

Cock-eye George McNee, one of the most famous of the early shantymen from Arnprior. This family portrait was believed to have been taken in Thessalon when McNee moved north to follow the timber trail.

In those days there was another section of the Arnprior Town Hall. It looks like a hunk of junk now, but then there was an auditorium and that's where all the shows and plays were held. In this particular play that I remember so well, an actor was supposed to run out on stage and shout, "If anybody moves, I'll shoot!" But he got all excited and mixed up and ran out on stage and shouted, "If anybody shits, I'll move." The whole cast broke up and the audience was in stitches and the whole play fell apart. They couldn't go on.

Another time, Fred Dodds used to play in the band, with an old friend of mine, Johnny Hudson. Fred got into the booze at a very early age and Jack Dodds and my father were friends. They were both farmers near Glasgow Station. And it was graduation night at Glasgow Station. You can imagine with the size of Glasgow Station that everybody knew everybody else. And that night Fred got behind the stage and got half-snapped. And he was the one who was supposed to go out and thank all the people for coming to the event. So at the end they pushed him out onto the stage. "Fred, you go out now," they said to him, "and thank all the people." So Fred staggered out to front stage and said, "Ladies and gentlemen, you can all kiss my ass."

Ted: Speaking of Glasgow Station, I heard a story somewhere one time about the Scotsmen at White Lake. Way back in the 1800s they used to come from White Lake to Arnprior for a beer. And those old Scots fellows, when they got half-corned, when they were coming back from Arnprior, they'd walk to White Lake but they wouldn't follow the road — they'd cut through the fields. And this old Scots fellow, he had this tam-o'-shanter on and he was crossing to home cutting through the fields where there were a lot of cattle pastured. And jeez! he jumped over the fence and he lost his tam-o'-shanter. And there he was feeling around in the dark and there were meadow muffins all around him. And he's feeling around 'til he got one and it's kind of dried out, you know. And he puts it on and goes home.

Ed: There was a Doc Myers here in town whose political career was very brief. There used to be some Cleghorns here in Arnprior who ran a department store; they had mostly dry goods and flooring and that sort of thing. You could buy food or clothes there as well. Or anything. You remember back to the time when women used to have "a fit of the vapours"? Well, Mrs. Cleghorn of Cleghorn's Department Store used to have this strange illness and Doc Myers was the only one who could cure her, it seems. Then one day Mr. Cleghorn walked in and Doc Myers was giving Mrs. Cleghorn "the cure," and he shot him. They took Doc Myers to Smiths Falls and they got the bullet out of him and he recuperated and some time later he went into politics. Now the Cleghorn – Myers shooting was all hushed up and nobody in town was supposed to know about it. So anyhow, Doc Myers was up in the Burnstown Hall giving a big political speech. And my dad was there. And he said Doc Myers was shouting out, "You show me Such-and-Such, and I'll show you such-and-such —— " And somebody at the back of the hall yelled, "What about showing us where Cleghorn shot you?" Oh, oh, end of meeting. End of politics for Myers.

Ted: I remember Lloyd Duncan up at Braeside years ago. I always thought Lloyd was a wee bit off, odd; but now I know that maybe it was me. We used to go to the movies together, all the shows, Walt Disney, Mickey Mouse and all those science-fiction men-from-Mars movies. Lloyd thought the Buck Rogers movies were the greatest. "It's all going to happen," he used to say. Now I know he was away ahead of me there. But anyhow, Lloyd was talking to me one time going to the movies.

"Know what happened to me the other day, Teddy?"

"No. What?"

"Well, I was cutting the bread for Mother. Baker's bread, it was. I was cutting away and all of a sudden I saw a black speck, and I kept on cutting and do you know what happened?"

"No. What happened?"

"I cut the rear end right off a mouse."

And I can remember when Scott White played goal for a hockey team in Arnprior called the River Rats. I was just a young lad in Braeside and he was in goal and they were shooting hard on him. They were all crowded around him, eh? And I don't know whether Scott was half-cut or not, but all of a sudden he yells out, "Don't crowd! The puck's for everybody!"

But the old ladies in the crowd didn't think that was what he said at all. And they reported his foul language to the head coach and Scott was reprimanded for using language unfit for the ears of elderly ladies.

Ed: White Lake for whiskey
And the Bellamy Road for fun!

Yes, there was another version they used to say, too:

White Lake for fishing,
Pakenham for blueberries
And the Bellamy Road for fun!

Well, back of White Lake up in the hills there they used to have some fun, too. When I was a young lad growing up around Arnprior there were only a couple of OPP to service the whole area. At that time I think the OPP was Johnston. Well, Johnston and this other policeman, they spotted this still in a shack back of White Lake. They left their car at the bottom of the hill, climbed up, and dismantled and carted away half the still. While the policemen were portaging half the still down the hill, the White Lakers went into the still shack and dismantled and carried off the other half of the still. When the policemen went back up the hill to dismantle and carry down the other half of the still, it was gone. When they went back down the hill to their car to check on the other half of the still, *it* was gone. So they had no evidence at all, and the White Lakers put the two halves of their still back together in the shack and business went on as usual.

Which reminds me of a story of not too long ago when the police found a stolen-car ring near

The entire Dionne family, including the Quintuplets (white outfits), in earlier, younger and perhaps happier days.

Carleton Place. They found a whole barn full of stolen cars. And they raced back to Ottawa to report the great find. But they didn't put a guard on it. And when they returned the next day with more policemen, there wasn't a goddammed car left in the place. Cleaned out completely by the ring.

We lived across from the police station when we moved to Arnprior, so I can tell you more police stories. This place used to be policed by the OPP and there was a policeman who decided he was going to quit the police force — it's no easy job, you know. So he locked himself in down at the police station and he took his service revolver and got stoned on a bottle and shot the ceiling full of holes. That was his farewell to the force!

I remember another time a policeman who became — and still may be, for all I know, in some other town — a very prominent member of the OPP who celebrated Christmas Day in a rather peculiar way. From our house across the street we saw him get out of his car — the whiskey bottle hanging out of his pocket — weave, and stagger his way into the police station where he locked himself in for the whole day. We never saw him come out

again. And that lad really went up in the ranks!

Ted: I heard a good one here the other day. The McComb boys used to peddle ice. Back years ago in the twenties and thirties they all had good cars and money because back then you could make money out of ice. Anyway, Gerard McComb, one of these McComb lads, a big stout man who lived up on the Third Line, he was an awful one for the booze when he was younger. Anyhow, he was up at the shopping centre one day and he went into the washroom and fell down right across in front of the door of the men's washroom. He weighed about 300 pounds and when he passed out there nobody could open the door. So they called the police and they sent down their smallest cop and he managed to crawl through an opening and into the men's john. "You must have had a heart attack," he said to Gerard. "No, no," Gerard said, "this is a pure rum attack."

My father was in politics and naturally he knew Charlotte Whitton. One time she ran on the Liberal ticket and she didn't make it. So a while later my father met her on the train going to Ottawa and she was running this time on the Conservative ticket. So my father asked her why she was switching around like that and she said, "I'm going to make it, by God, one way or another!"

Dionne, father of the famous quintuplets, attended a formal dinner shortly after the birth of the five babies. Charlotte Whitton was mayor of Ottawa at the time and Dionne struck up a conversation with her at the affair. He didn't recognize her at all, so he said, "And who are you?" And Charlotte said, "Oh, don't you know me? I'm Charlotte Whitton, Mayor of Ottawa."

And he said, "I guess you don't know me either. I'm Dionne, Cock of the North."

I first met Walter Fairclough in 1982 when I was giving a reading to a senior citizen's group at the Kanata Public Library. Right on the spot he created for me a marvellous group of characters he had known as a child growing up in "The Prior," amongst them Johnny Look-Up Slater, "Professor Jones," John T. Waite. I resolved there and then that I would get to Walter Fairclough to tape his stories. When I finally did visit Mr. Fairclough in his home in Kanata, a year later, the circumstances and mood were different and the second time around had less of the spontaneity and more of the cautious circumspection that is sometimes a frustrating problem for the oral historian. However, some loss of Johnny Look-up Slater and John T. Waite stories was counterbalanced by new stories Mr. Fairclough told of his times at the McLachlin Lumber Mills in Arnprior, Ontario, and the McLaren Lumber Mills at Buckingham, Quebec.

Mr. Fairclough's ancestry was English, but his step-father was an Irishman from Arnprior who must have passed on to Mr. Fairclough his "turn" for telling stories. Mr. Fairclough's wife is the former Laura O'Donnell, daughter of John O'Donnell, who owned one of the five hotels in Calabogie, the one now run as the Whippletree Shanty. Mr. O'Donnell's mother's maiden name was McConnell; she was one of the McConnell lumbering family from Aylmer, Quebec.

My father was killed in the Battle of Lwos in 1916 when he was twenty-six years old. Mother worked for three years and then she married an Irish Canadian who had enlisted in the 21st Battalion

in the First World War and went overseas and stayed in England until 1920 when he met my mother. They were married in England and that's how we came to Canada. I was young, about eleven years old. I kept my father's name. My new father was a gentleman, just like a father to me, and he brought me up. His name was James McCabe. He was an Irish Canadian born in Manchester, England — to his sorrow. When he went for his old age pension, they couldn't trace him in Dublin and they went to Manchester and found that his mother had left Ireland to visit her sister just two weeks prior to his birth. So here's that poor Irishman born in Manchester, oh, to his sorrow!

The Madawaska River! We had a Boy's Bay and a Girl's Bay and never the twain shall meet. The Boy's Bay was over what we called Number Two Pier and that was on the opposite side of the river at the bridge. One time there was an old lady complained that we were skinny-dipping — boys being boys. She complained to the policeman. We only had one and his name was John Rogers. He came to her house and she laid her complaint about us boys swimming with no suits on. John Rogers looked at her and he looked out her window and he said to her, "I see. The boys are swimming over there. Well, that's a long, long way away to be able to see if they're swimming skinny." And she says to him, "Here, take my spyglass. You can see them quite clearly."

When I was a boy the big pine was ending. I can remember as a boy of twelve or thirteen there was a lighthouse out in the river halfway across Shaw (Chats) Lake and I can remember almost getting out to the lighthouse on logs, running those McLachlin logs with our bare feet.

When I was about twelve I was water boy at McLachlin's Number Four Mill at Arnprior. Up at the Gillies mill at Braeside two and a half dollars was a day's pay for a hard-working man. I don't know what I did for it. I galloped around here and there and I enjoyed myself. But one thing I didn't do: I don't remember ever giving anybody a drink of water!

They always used to tell stories about this Frenchman named Baptiste and I remember one of them. McLachlin's had this Colonel Johnston, whom we only called the Colonel, and he was the superintendent and a graduate engineer. Anyway, it was a very, very cold day and they had these long sheds and, if they got too much snow on them in wintertime, they'd cave in. So they used to hire Baptiste to do the job. He was a very solid-working man and he'd have a big wide shovel and he'd go

Until the 1940s, there was still a lumbering operation and boom house on one of the islands offshore from Sand Bay, Quebec. In this photograph, the men are at *leisure on Cheneaux Boom standing with their cook and the cook's helper.*

up on the roofs and cut it out like cheesecake and throw it off. They only put one man on to do this job, and it was very cold up there in the wind, and the Colonel was going by and he yells up to him, "How are you doing up there, Baptiste?" And Baptiste yells back to him, "I'm all right, but it's too damned cold up here for one man."

The McLachlins were a very tender-hearted company and when Mr. Lapierre was dying they hired him as a superintendent for piling the slabs and he got paid by the cord. He had a contract for it, too. Well, he couldn't do it because he was dying, so he hired boys from the town, and he'd pay them two and a half dollars a day to pile the wood for him. What he did was he would go and feel the wood and make a little mark on his tally board to keep track. But the boys would sit there and make noises — bang-bang-bang — pretending they were working and they thought it was all really very funny. But I couldn't stand that, so I put a stop to it.

The drive used to come down the Madawaska

and, as boys, we'd go down to the cookhouse for the food. They fed us beans and pie and gobs of butter, but you had to help the cook round up some bread in town, maybe wash some dishes. They always got a little work out of you and if you didn't do anything, you weren't invited back. Sometimes they'd have pieces of wood from the river shore and we'd have to saw that into stove lengths for the cook.

Sometimes some of the rivermen would be there with the cook, and they would tell us young lads that we had to play games or tricks to earn our pie. We often had to play "Black Hat." It was a favourite. Somebody had an old felt fedora — you know, the kind with the big bands inside them — and the inside bands of the hat would be all filled up with soot from the fires and the stove. And then you would catch the New Boy — this was always played on the New Boy — and you'd sit him down and tell him he had to put his head in this hat and then guess who ran past and thumped him

41

on the back. If he guessed right, then the thumper was to take his place underneath the hat. "Get your head down there," they'd say to the New Boy. "You can see. You're peeking." And, of course, it wasn't true at all; he couldn't see a blessed thing. The rivermen or the cook would take turns pressing the soot-filled hat down on his head further, and the soot would fall out of the bands and turn his face coal-black — but of course, he didn't know that either! Except that everybody would be starting to laugh and he'd be beginning to suspect something fishy.

And people would run past and thump him on the back and say, "Who am I? Who am I?" And the boy in the black hat would say, "Is it Joe Mulligan?" "No, no! It isn't Joe Mulligan." "Is it Gid Adams?" "No, no! It isn't Gid Adams." And the cook or the rivermen would push the hat down further and the soot would fall into his eyes, and he would begin to suspect. But even if he wised up, he had to play the game until someone else took his place. And everyone is rolling around now, holding their sides looking at this black face and these soot-filled eyes. And the New Boy in the black hat finally calls out when he's thumped on the back, "Is it Billy Barber?" And all of a sudden the cook or the rivermen jump up and grab Billy Barber and yell out, "Yes, yes! It's Billy Barber!" And into the black hat would go Billy Barber and the game would go on — and on — until everyone was tired of laughing.

They often played "Jump the White Horse." The biggest lad would bend over with his arms and head on the bench, and then the next biggest boy would jump on his back, and then the next biggest on his, and then the next biggest. They played it in teams and the highest team got the pie. It was the drivers coming down the river. We were playing it for the men. Just pick out your team. You could be on that team one night and that team the next night. But, no matter if you won or lost, you got the pie anyway. Those men were good men. With my knowledge of today's life, I'd be afraid to send my boy to a place like that. But they were all good men when I was a boy.

When I was a boy, John Rogers was the policeman. He was an Englishman and he ran a pig farm there where the hospital is now, and the wafting breezes from the pig farm — well — they got rid of that and made Rogers into a policeman, and a very good policeman he was. Now I grew up in the era when each town had its "Best Man." Ned Culver was the Best Man in Arnprior and Jim Dempsey was the Best Man in Renfrew. When the big, blustering trouble-makers came into town, of

course it was Rogers's duty to get rid of them. Well, one day Jim Montgomery came into town from Renfrew. He wasn't the Best Man in Renfrew — Jim Dempsey was, there was no question of that — but Jim Montgomery was one of the best. Anyhow, he was brawling for trouble down at the Newborne Hotel and they sent for Rogers to settle things down. And Rogers appeared and Montgomery saw him and bolted. He started to run down towards the Madawaska and he started to cross on the CN trestles and Rogers couldn't follow him. Let's face it, Montgomery was a riverman and he could run trestles blindfolded, and Rogers couldn't do that. And the Englishman didn't like that, so he stood on this side of the river and he yelled at Montgomery, "You get back to Renfrew and don't come here again!" And Montgomery yelled back, "Why don't you come over here and tell me that?" And, of course, Rogers couldn't do that, but he was so mad he took out his revolver. We young lads were all standing there watching and thinking, "There's going to be a murder here! We're going to see a shooting!" But Rogers fired a shot up in the air — and went home.

As a young man I worked for Jim Dempsey up on the Baskatong Reservoir. That's a long time ago and it's all been taken over by Bourassa. Dempsey was a lumber contractor there and I worked for him and I didn't like it and I came home. I felt he didn't pay me enough. Some years later I met Dempsey in Arnprior — he was a contractor for the Sanitare Soft Drink factory. The building is there yet. They used to get their water way up the Madawaska River from a spring. And it's there yet. The spring water used to be brought down and they bottled it as Sanitare's Mineral Drink. Dempsey had contracted for the delivery of this. I remember him and Mr. Charbonneau and they had an old truck and my step-father, Jim McCabe, was also in on that, and they'd deliver this around the countryside. And I had always resented that he didn't pay me enough up on the Baskatong. So I said, "Yeah, Dempsey, I worked for you up on the Baskatong and you cheated me." It was the wrong thing for a slight young man of eighteen to say to the Best Man in Renfrew. Even at his age, he could have lifted my head off. So he says to me, "So you worked for me on the Baskatong, and you say I cheated you." I backed off. "No," I said, "I guess I was wrong about that." And I managed to come out of it alive.

There was another old character who used to turn up in Arnprior when I was a boy. His name was Enright and he came from Renfrew. He was a con man. I can remember him coming into town in an old fur coat, and he had a pick over his shoulder, and he was carrying a great big bag of rock samples. And he used to go around from door to door and hotel to hotel. And they tell me he'd get five or ten dollars here and there from people as a grubstake for him to go back and work some vein he told them about in the north. He'd show these samples and he'd tell them these stories about going back to milk this great vein of ore — gold or silver, I suppose; fool's gold and fool's silver, perhaps. I saw him come through three or four times. Every year. Maybe it was the same samples of rock every year. I don't know.

And once a year Johnny Bolton from Torbolton in full regalia would come through town playing the bagpipes. Only once a year. Some said he was a little slow mentally but I don't know about that. He was a fine-looking man and the spats were — well, I got into the 42nd Highlanders and I know the regalia, and he had one beautiful costume. Real legitimate 100 percent Highlander costume. Spats and beautiful brogues. And a more handsome-looking man you never seen! I can remember him coming down along side the station and going down John Street. And of course we young fellows were beneath looking at that corny thing. But I often think of it now and wonder why did he do that. It was in the summertime. I'm not sure now if his name was Tommy or Johnny. My wife always said that he came from Braeside and that he walked from Braeside all the way in to John Street.

Everyone knew Professor Jones. He was called "the Professor." The "Professor" was about four-foot, four inches. I guess he didn't have a full deck, but harmless. He could talk all right but in a parrotlike way. If you recited a poem to him, he could recite it right back to you. They used to tell me some awful stories about him. This is the one I remember the most. It's about the time the boys were swimming in the Boy's Bay — I wasn't with them at the time — but they were swimming across Shaw Lake at Braeside and it's about three miles across there. And the "Professor" swam halfway across with them and then he thought he couldn't make it, so he swam back. I've heard that story so many times I accept it for the truth.

And then there was Mr. Havey. Mr. Havey couldn't tell the time but he had a gold watch. He was a big pompous-looking man. Big, big coat and this big, big gold chain. Of course, everything looked big to the eyes of the small one I was then. Anyhow, he was a retired farmer and we'd know he'd be coming down the street and we'd make sure to meet him. Me, Big Mouth again, I'd say, "Hello,

Mr. Havey. Have you the time, Mr. Havey?" And he'd pull out his great big gold watch and he'd look at it and say, "I don't know what time it is, my lads. I've left my glasses at home today." So we'd tell him the time and laugh and snicker. That was his house on top of Havey's Hill. It was a log house that had been bricked. And you know what? We lived in that house one time and it had a walk-in furnace. You could walk right into it with four-foot-long sticks and lay your fire down. We never had to cut our wood!

I remember a wonderful story about the time that John T. Waite walked on water. That was hearsay. But they say it was true. John T. Waite was a natural, like a homeopathic. I can imagine that he was probably one of the forerunners of natural foods and things like that. I understand he was

As a young boy, James McLaren was sent off to be schooled in Scotland. He proved to be such a cut-up and so unmanageable that he was shipped back home to Canada. He did stay long enough to have this angelic photograph taken at Tunny's Art Photographic Galleries in Edinburgh, Scotland.

a very religious man, a very good-living man and a good man. No one ever said a word against his character. But this story is about how for many months he said that he was prepared to show that man, by faith, could walk on water. His relatives kept at him to the point where he had to face up to his claim. So this Sunday morning was appointed and a great crowd was gathered to watch man, by faith, walk on water. It was down in front of where the Oblate Fathers are now,[2] down where the cement wharf is now. But it was an old wooden wharf then. And John T. Waite went down this Sunday morning and he walked off the end of the wharf into the Ottawa River and of course . . . But he wasn't nonplussed at all. John T. Waite simply waded back to the end of the wharf and said to the crowd of his supporters and the onlookers, "My faith wasn't strong enough, as you can see."

I grew up in Arnprior and went to school in Arnprior and got married in Arnprior. Then I left Ontario and went to Quebec to work in the paper mills of John McLaren at Buckingham, Quebec. By that time the McLaren family was pretty well run out. There was the two girls, Jessie and her sister, and they married two Kennys, R.M. Kenny and T.F. Kenny. I knew R.M. Kenny very well. He almost adopted me. I was then only a small little fellow working around the mill, but I got on very well with him. I had had a lot of experience in church and house decorating, and I remember going up to the big McLaren house in Buckingham to do some work there. There was Jessie McLaren, old Mrs. McLaren and R.M. R.M. raised and showed Wyandotte hens and he had prize ribbons all over the place. The Silver Wyandotte is a show hen, great big silver feathers and so on, and they don't lay when they are on show, or going to be. I know that now, but I didn't know it then. Anyhow, this day I wanted to impress R.M. that I knew something about hens, too. He was coming out and he used to give me some eggs. If he liked you, he'd give you half a dozen eggs from his prize hens, big, brown, warm eggs. So this day when I saw him, I thought I'd get some of those big eggs and I said to him, "Are they from your Silver Wyandotte, sir?" And he glared at me and he said, "Any person that doesn't know a Silver Wyandotte hen from a laying hen doesn't deserve any eggs." And I never got another egg from R.M. Kenny.

I can well remember one time there was a tie vote in the council election in Arnprior. I can see yet the results of the vote in O'Toole's drugstore window:

711 for Stafford R. Rudd.
711 for Con Mulvihill (the lawyer)

Stafford R. Rudd was a Masonic member in good standing, a Protestant. Con Mulvihill was his exact opposite, Roman Catholic, Knights of Columbus. The poor town clerk had to cast the vote to undo the tie. And Mr. Rudd said to the town clerk, "If you vote for Mulvihill, I'll take you to court for discrimination." That upset the town clerk and he said, "I'll show you, Mr. Rudd; I'm voting for Mr. Mulvihill." And he turned to Mr. Mulvihill and said, "I hope you have a very successful office." And he shook hands with him.

Funny, isn't it, the sometimes strange, sometimes foolish, sometimes funny things you remember as a child? Like I remember that tie vote so well, and it seemed so funny to me at the time. Con Mulvihill and Stafford Rudd were on the opposite sides in everything. And yet I remember so well as a boy those wonderful Decoration Day parades down the main street of Arnprior when the Knights of Columbus and the Masons and the Oddfellows all marched to the same band music — all together in the same parade.

Peter McLaren, who founded the McLaren lumber empire on the Clyde, later became a senator in Ottawa. This photograph of his wife was taken at J. Dynes, No. 17 St. John Street, Quebec. Mrs. McLaren obviously accompanied her husband on business trips to the great timber markets of the world.

As with almost every other river in the Ottawa Valley, big or small, the Quyon River was used to move timber down to the Ottawa. Quyon in its early days was a most colourful and busy river-town, settled by both French and English. It was the site of many lumbering and mining activities. One of the narrowest stretches of the Ottawa River is at Quyon; it was logical, therefore, that it should become the site of a ferry crossing. This photograph is of the first Quyon ferry, a horse-powered cadge-ferry. The animals circled on a wooden platform above a steel cable attached to an anchor. The man at the back is steering.

1. For the story of Captain Dudley Gamble see *Some of the Stories I Told You Were True* by Joan Finnigan.
2. The Oblate Fathers bought the McLachlin estate in Arnprior on the Ottawa.

A 1906 postcard view of the Main Bridge on the Main Street of Renfrew. It is also the perspective of Wyman Townes from his vantage point on the spire of the *Eganville Roman Catholic Church that day when he said he saw Noble Dean talking to a salesman in Renfrew.*

5

The good roads gang

VI DOOLING, DOUGLAS, ONTARIO

For the past sixteen years Viola "Vi" Dooling has been writing homey reminiscences of life in Grattan Township for the Renfrew Mercury, *a Valley weekly. Her columns tend to be charming, folksy pot-pourris, and random rememberings. But in a face-to-face encounter, Vi Dooling turned out to be a gutsy, lusty seventy-eight-year-old, outspoken and honest. She reminded me a little of Phoebe McCord of Shawville, Quebec, in that, although she had lived for many years in the insularity of a small town and some of her perspectives had been severely narrowed by that view, still and all, on many occasions she could step outside her small-town, rural community and look at it objectively, philosophically and with considerable awareness of its manners and mores. These she could both laugh with and laugh at. She had a writer's feeling for the characters she had known in her tough, long lifetime. She was very often able to view with highly contagious humour the vicissitudes of her life both as the wife of a charming bounder and as a provincial widow. As she says herself, "You have to have had to face tragedy before you can enjoy a good joke."*

My father's name was Peter Gilmour and he came from Shepherd's Bush, England. He was Irish-English, six-foot-two, very handsome, talented. He sang with Beatrice Lillie in Toronto. He and I could play duets on the piano. I went to the Toronto Conservatory of Music when I was young and they threw me out because the teacher would say, "Vi, this is the way the piece is going to sound when you're through," and I would have it all "up here" in my head. But I couldn't read a bloody note. I can still play you any piece you want on the piano.

My mother's name was Cronin, Helen (Ella) Cronin. My grandmother, Annie (Burns) Cronin was born in County Kerry, Ireland; my grandfather, Richard Cronin in County Mayo, Ireland. So I go back Irish four generations. There was the Cronins, the Penders, the Burnses, the Gallaghers. My parents came out and got married in Toronto and I grew up in Cabbagetown. I never knew my paternal grandfather, Peter Gilmour, and I'll tell you why. Peter Gilmour and Martin Denny, both Irishmen, were bringing people out from England and Ireland to Halifax and Kingston and they were given so much per head as they did this. They made three or four trips out and they came back to Canada and they brought their wives and they brought out Grandma, Harriet Gilmour, with four children. They brought Martin Denny's wife out with eight children and they stationed them in Kingston. And the women said, "Now, you're going to stay with us." But the men said, "Just one more trip and we'll be back and we'll settle down." They went back to get more immigrants and they were never heard from again. They say they shipped out on the *Winnipeg* and disappeared. Never heard from again! Peter Gilmour was a big man with red hair and his daughter, Lil, was the same. But they were never heard from again. They either got into a fight in a pub or were thrown overboard, or whatever. So my grandmother Gilmour in Kingston had to take in washing to support four children, and Mrs. Denny had to go to the government for help because she couldn't work with eight children at home. But they both ended up in Toronto.

I still remember Mrs. Denny. She was stoutish and a loveable lady and she and my grandmother Gilmour were the best of friends. My grandmother was typically English. She always carried a snuff box about with her, she wore a black velvet band at her throat with a diamond brooch there, and she wore black lace silk over purple and she insisted on her four-o'clock tea. We had to bring her down to our house for four-o'clock tea, which would be strawberry jam, tea biscuits, and tea.

I was not supposed to be born until May 7 or 8. My father was working at the Redways Saloon at the corner of Sherbourne and Queen streets in Cabbagetown, Toronto, and my mother decided to wash out a few things that night. And when she was throwing the water out into the yard, she looked up at the sky and saw the tail of Halley's Comet. And she ran down to the store that Kathleen Sinclair — she was Gordon Sinclair's aunt — ran on the corner of Queen and Parliament. And my mother cried out, "Oh, glory be to God, Kathleen, I just saw the worst thing in the sky and I can't describe it to you!" And with that, she went into labour. So she didn't blame my birth on my father; she blamed it on Halley's Comet. (That might explain a lot of things about me. Halley's Comet is coming around again and I wonder about me . . .)

I grew up with an exposure to many of my mother's old sayings. She always used to say when in despair about my father: "There are two kinds of Irishmen. There's the one who says, when trouble comes along, 'I'm going to fight this.' And then there's the other kind who says nothing and buries his head in the sand, hoping it will all go away."

One time when I came home from school with lice — there was always lice or itch or impetigo in the schoolroom — my mother said to me, "Don't worry, Viola. Everybody has to get lice once in their lifetime because, if they don't, the lice will come out when they're in their coffin."

She was always giving us warnings about and signposts about judging men: Never trust a man with tight eyes. Never trust a man with ears close to his head. Never trust a man with pouches under his eyes. Never trust a man with pockmarks. And so on.

Of course, when I was growing up the word "sex" wasn't invented and the word "pregnant" wasn't invented. If a woman was pregnant she was "up the creek without a paddle" or she was "in the family way" or, worse still, she was "*that* way." When I was thirteen and beginning to fill out, I went to my mother and said, "Mother, the girls in school are talking about training bras. I wonder would you get me one?" She said, "Just a minute." She went to the medicine cabinet and she brought me two strips of adhesive tape and she said, "Put one over each nipple. That's all you need."

Like a great number of Canadian families during the Depression, we made the trek to Detroit, where there was work. I got a job as a telephone operator when I was sixteen. I met Joe when I was seventeen in a bootlegger's joint.

Actually, I worked for a bootlegger when I was sixteen, putting a thimbleful of sugar into each bottle of home brew. You'd give it a tip and then the guy'd cap it. I was given a penny for each bottle and I gave the money to my mother. Anyhow, it was the last day of May, which is a big day in the States. It's Decoration Day. And I had come home from work. I was on a split shift, ten to one and six to ten, so I got home about eleven o'clock. There were bootleggers on both sides of us where we lived. There was the McHales on one side of us and the Mulligans on the other. And I could hear all the Decoration Day whoopee going on. You see, they were selling bathtub gin and bootleg beer, so I said to my mother, "Can I go over to Mulligan's and play the piano over there?" And she said, "Well, you know you can't drink at your age." (I never had a drink until I was twenty-five.) And I said, "Mother, you know I don't drink or smoke." And she said, "Well, you can go over for an hour."

So I went over and these guys were sitting around playing poker and I stood around watching them and somebody said, "Hey, kid, do you know how to play poker?" Well, that was like asking is the present Pope Polish! I had watched all those poker games in my mother's boardinghouse and sure, I knew how to play poker. So I said, "Well, I could try, but I didn't bring any money with me." It was Joe Dooling — this freshly scrubbed face, this black curly-headed fellow with the wide grin — who said, "I'll stake you, kid. Sit in." So he gave me two dollars and I sat in. When I made nine dollars, I went out the back door through the loose boards at the fence and buried seven dollars and brought two dollars back to get back into the game. I made nineteen dollars that night and that's how I met Joe. My mother liked him, too, and when Mother asked him what nationality he was, he said, "Irish."

"And would you be Catholic, too?"

"Oh yes, I'm Catholic."

"Oh, you are, eh? Do you know how to say the Rosary?"

"Yes."

"And the Stations of the Cross?"

"Oh, yes."

"Well then, come on in," she said.

In 1927, Vi Gilmour at the age of seventeen was married in Detroit, Michigan, to Joe Dooling of Douglas, Ontario, aged twenty. Their first two children, Mary and Pat, were born in Detroit. The Doolings were forced to leave the United States during the Depression. In Arnprior for two years they lived with the Doolings and Laderoutes: seventeen people in one house. They then moved to Barnet's Subdivision, a poor section of Renfrew. Finally, Mother-in-law Dooling gave them ninety-nine acres of land at Douglas where Joe built the log bungalow in which they lived for forty-nine years. Joe died in 1972.

When I first came to Douglas I would see these two men on the street and they looked so alike I thought they were brothers. But they were in no way related at all. Now at that time we had about six head of cattle. This day Larry Forest came to our door and he said, "Vi, I have about seven or eight head of cattle in there and I have a red cow due to calve any day, and she always has troubles. Now if you see her amongst the cows, get word to me as soon as possible. She'll probably be in the bush somewhere and she'll need help."

I said, "All right, Larry. I'll keep an eye out for her."

And I did. And the next day I was at Jim Purdy's store and Larry Forest came in. And I said to him right off, "Remember what we talked about yesterday?"

And he looked at me very strangely, but he said, "Yeah."

"Well," I said, "I think it's happened."

And he looked at me in a very funny way and said, "Oh!"

And I said, "You'd better come on down because Joe's in Sarnia and I'm all alone there."

But I thought to myself, "By God, Larry Forest, you're stupid! You're not catching on at all."

So he went out the door and I said to Jim Purdy, "What's wrong with Larry Forest today?"

And Jim Purdy said, "Hell! That wasn't Larry Forest. That was Harold McQuittie!"

They looked so much alike it was scarey and I hadn't been able to tell them apart. But ever after that, Jim Purdy used to tease me unmercifully: "You'd better come on down now because Joe's away in Sarnia and I'm all alone."

Oh, my God, the false modesty and prudery and downright ignorance of those days! Why, I can show you wedding pictures by the score where neither the bride nor the groom is smiling. I have passed these photos around amongst schoolchildren of today and they are always asking, "Why aren't they smiling?" Well, it just wasn't done. It was immodest. So, poor Honora Burke was going to marry a widower of Douglas. In those days once you reached the age of thirty or thirty-five you'd had it. You

were an Old Maid. So here was Honora — at the age of thirty-eight — about to take the plunge. And they, the neighbour women, were all making sandwiches for the event the night before — they didn't have the big fancy spreads we have these days — and one of them said to Honora, "Just think, Honora, this time tomorrow night you'll be in bed with a man!" And Honora said, "Faith, I knows it and I dreads it!"

Hannah O'Leary was marrying another widower of Douglas. Before the wedding Hannah confided to her friends about how nervous she was, how she didn't know what to do, how she didn't know anything about anything. Well, anyway, they got married and went off on their honeymoon. In those days nobody ever went any further than the Newborne Hotel in Arnprior. Why waste the money? So they went down to the Newborne overnight and when they came back Hannah's friends asked her, "How did you get along?"

"Well," she said, "when he was in the bathroom putting on his nightgown, I flung on my flannelette nightgown and I jumped into bed and pulled up the covers. And I made the Sign of the Cross and I said, 'Well, here goes nuthin'.'"

Joe's aunt, Sarah Manion, was a midwife. In those days almost all the women helped each other in the time of having a baby. They went out as midwives, or, as Johnny Quinn would say, "They were midways on eternity cases." He never got anything straight. Anyhow, this lady in Douglas was expecting a baby and she started having labour pains so she said to her husband, "Johnny, run up the tracks and get Sarah Manion." And Johnny said, "What like's the matter?" That was the way they talked. And she said, "Never you mind, man, what like's the matter. Just go and get Sarah Manion."

When she told me about this, all I said to her was: "Well, for heaven's sakes! Hadn't you already told him you were expecting a baby?" And she said to me, "Why should I tell him? Let him find out for himself." And I said, "My God! He *is* your husband!" And she said, "Well, that didn't ever matter. When the time came and I showed, then he'd know something was up."

Yes, in this country after you were married, they quit looking at your face and started looking at your stomach.

Which reminds me of a wonderful story. This nun went into the maternity ward in the Catholic hospital in Pembroke and she went up to one of the patients and she said, "And how many is this for you, my child?"

"My fourth, Sister."

"Well, God bless you. You're Catholic, of course?"

"Yes, Sister."

The nun moved on to the next one and she said, "And what one is this for you my child?"

"This is my sixth child, Sister."

"God bless you both. You're Catholic, of course?"

"Yes, Sister."

She went to another patient and said, "How many is this for you?"

"Seven."

"And you're Catholic?"

And the patient said, "No, Sister, I'm a Protestant."

So the nun went out of the room and she turned to this other nun and said, "That's a horny old bitch, that one, isn't she?"

My journey to visit Vi Dooling in Renfrew was instigated by Mr. W.T. James in Carleton Place who told me a number of Wyman Townes stories and then said, "But you must go to see Vi Dooling. She has many, many more." This was a slight exaggeration. Mrs. Dooling, unlike Mr. James, had not known Wyman Townes personally, but had absorbed stories which were part of his legend. These she passed on to me.

No, I never knew the man actually, but I know a lot of stories about him. One day Wyman Townes went into John McKean's store in Douglas. Wyman had a wife and a large family. Yet he frequently went out working for widow women who had lost their men, and he helped a lot of them with the farming they couldn't do. So one time Wyman went into John McKean's store. It was at night — the stores stayed open at night in those days — when nobody was around, so John McKean took the opportunity to say to Wyman: "Wyman, you know I admire you, you work so hard and everything and even though you've got a big family yourself, you help out a lot of other people, too. I see here that you bought a wood range from me and there's forty dollars owing on it. Now, to show you I'm a gentleman, Wyman, I'm going to knock off half of it — twenty dollars." And Wyman thought for a while about it and then he said, "Well, I thank you kindly, sir. And to show that I'm just as much a gentleman as you are, I'm going to knock off the other half."

Sometimes, though, Wyman worked for farm women who were mean and stingy in the food department. At this particular place back at McDougal, he would get an egg on his plate one morning for breakfast and then the next morning, he'd get the bacon. But never the two together. So finally one morning he said to this woman, "You know, Mrs. Cameron, you're a very neat and tidy woman. The last woman I worked for was real sloppy because sometimes she'd put an egg and bacon on the same plate."

He worked for another widow woman who made him get up at five o'clock in the winter in the dark to milk her cows. Finally, one evening he said to her, "I wonder, Ma'am, if you'd give me a lantern for the milking tomorrow morning?"

"Why should I do that?" she snapped. "Sure it's break of day when you get to the barn and you can see then."

"Oh, it's not that," said Wyman. "I don't want the cows to have a heart attack when I go in to feed them in the dark."

Wyman Townes said this helper went up to Eganville to fix the spire of the Eganville Roman Catholic church. It was tremendously high. Wyman said, "I'll go up, I'll go up. I'm not afraid of heights." So Wyman went up while the helper held the ropes on the ground. And he said to Wyman when he got to the top of the spire, "Can you see anything, Wyman?"

And Wyman yelled down, "Oh yes, faith and I can!"

"What can you see, Wyman?" yelled the lad down below.

And Wyman yelled back, "I can see the main street in Renfrew and I can see Noble Dean[1] talking to a salesman on the main street."

There was this lady that lived on a farm near Douglas and her husband had died and she had a pig that needed to be bred. It had to be put in a little box and placed on a wagon and taken to the boar. The fee was five dollars. So the widow lady called in Wyman Townes to do that job. She said to him, "Wyman, you know what to do with that pig?" And he said, "Of course I do." So he took the pig away and had it bred. But the widow lady didn't know who she owed the five dollars to. So the next time she saw Wyman she said to him, "Wyman, you took the pig and had her serviced, eh?" And Wyman said, "Yes, indeed, I did, Ma'am."

"And where did you have her serviced?" the widow lady asked.

"Fair in the arse, Mrs. Burns, fair in the arse," Wyman replied.

Stoney McShane was also one of the great wits and great characters of Douglas. He fenced his farm with hand-picked stones all the way around it. And when they put the Good Roads through in 1922 through Douglas, he got eight dollars a cord for the stones. Oh, he was a dry wit! And one time he was down at Frank Neville's blacksmith's shop, which was across from the Neville Hotel and two strange women — they weren't Douglas women at all — they were crossing just in front of Mick Neville's hotel. And Frank said, "Stoney, Stoney, come here quick. Sure, there's two strange ladies out there. Do you know them?" So Stoney peered long and hard at them, "Wal," he says, "I don't know the one on the outside at all." And Frank said, "Who's the one on the inside then?" And Stoney said, "Sure, I don't know her either."

My husband, Joe, had a wonderful aunt, Ellen, a superstitious, ripe-tongued, pseudo-religious lady who always began everything she said with "Oh Cross of Christ!" When I knew her she was a widow woman, but her husband had been the butcher, Jack Neville. She used to keep Jack's pants hanging on the back of the kitchen door on a hook there, and every once in a while she'd cast a look at them and say, "Sure, there's Jack's pants and no Jack in them."

Aunt Ellen was always afraid to cross the bridge at Douglas, afraid of meeting a car on it, would you believe? So this one time she asked me to go out with her to Aunt Maggie Gallagher's for a visit. I had to walk from my farmhouse over the bridge and meet her on the other side and get her across. Then we went on out to Gallagher's. A great big beautiful brown collie dog came out to meet us there, barking and jumping up all over us. And Aunt Ellen said, "Oh, Cross of Christ! Look at that beast! Maggie! Maggie! Call your beast home!" She was afraid of dogs, too. So Aunt Maggie called the dog home. The dog went in the front door — and on out the back. Aunt Ellen says, "I'm not going in the front door." And she went around to the back and there was a great big brown beautiful collie coming out the back door. And Aunt Ellen says, "Cross of Christ, Maggie! You have two of them!"

Aunt Ellen Neville of Douglas had eight hens and two roosters. This is a very bad ratio — you should have about ten hens to one rooster — but Aunt Ellen didn't know any better. So one day she was out in the henyard in her black alpaca apron,

Dated "Autumn, 1915", this photograph captures the feeling of sweat, muscle and hard work so characteristic of a threshing gang of the era. The steam thresher is working on the farm of Ernie Humphries, 8th Line of Horton Township. George Humphries is at the engine, "Granpa feeding" the inscription says, and "Lorn and Ernie Stack, two neighbours on the bags."

which she always wore to feed the hens, going, "Chick, chick, here chick, chick," to the hens. And the two roosters were busy topping off these eight hens as they bent over to eat the henfeed. Aunt Ellen kept trying to chase off the damn roosters, but finally she came into the house and said to me, "Vi, I give up. I just left them to it. I just left them to it."

I was really sick in bed one time and Joe wanted to go out and play poker. So he got Aunt Ellen to come and sit with me. She had me trapped; I was the captive audience, so she decided to give me some religious thoughts. "You know, Vi," she said, "when you die, you go to purgatory. And the fire starts to eat in between your fingers, eating, eating away at your flesh." I'm sick and I'm in bed listening to this. "It starts at your fingers and then it moves on, eating away at you. And even your best friend can't give you a drop of water." Having to listen to Aunt Ellen, by the time Joe got home from his poker game, I was much worse.

Aunt Ellen's son, Tommy Neville, owned a

grocery store next door to her house. And Duncan Stewart owned the general store, up across from the gas station. But Duncan Stewart gave a cent more for eggs. So Aunt Ellen would pull her hat down over her eyes so Tommy, her son, wouldn't see her. And she'd go up to Duncan Stewart's store with her two dozen eggs to make two more cents.

There were Nevilles all over Douglas. Undertaker Tom Neville kept the old-fashioned hearse in those days with the tassels and the cross on the top and the curtains at the windows, and all. They had no car then. So his wife Eva used to see Tom getting a little tipsy now and again and she wondered where he was getting and keeping the liquor. So one day she watched him going into the hearse and she found out this was where he was keeping the spirits. So when he went up the street, she crawled into the hearse and waited. When he came back for another little nip and reached back for his bottle, she grabbed his hand. They heard him yelling all over Douglas and they saw him running down Main Street as though the devil were on his tail.

Mick Neville owned the hotel and when the men would come out of the shanties they'd give Mick Neville a bunch of money and they'd say to him, "When I have spent this for booze and meals and lodging, you tell me and I'll go on home." Well, when a man had used up his money and there was nothing left, punctual as the sunrise, Mick Neville would knock on his door and he'd say, "Good morning John. Your stake's all gone. Your knapsack's in the hall. That's all."

John Pierunik, lisp and all, drove the milk around the village. He would let his beard grow until they had to take it off with clippers. So he saw an ad in the Douglas paper where they wanted a milk inspector in Pembroke. And he decided to upgrade himself. So he went up to Pembroke, long beard, old rubber boots, patched clothes, and all. And he went in and he said, "I thee in the peper tar yer lucking fur a milk inthpector."

"Yes," said the girl, "we are. But do you realize, sir, that you have to have a university degree in order to apply?"

And he said, "And wot makth you think I ain't got one?"

The O'Brien family of Douglas was noted for great wit. And especially Tim O'Brien. One day he and Father Quilty were walking up the main street of Douglas in the fall and there was a banner strung across the street. It said, "Quit working and come to the Cobden Fair!" And Tim O'Brien turned and said to Father Quilty, "Well, Father, I guess you and I can go any time."

Tim was drinking heavily, so he went up and took the pledge for a year. But he was having a hard time cutting down cold turkey. So he said to Father Quilty, "Do you think it would be all right if I just took a thimbleful in the mornings?" And Father Quilty said he could see no harm in just a thimbleful of liquor each morning. "Yes, I think that will be all right, Tim," he said. So later on that day Tim O'Brien was in Neville's hotel sitting with the lads at a table there. And he said, "What I forgot to tell Father Quilty, you know, was that I was using a tailor's thimble."[2]

Word got around that there were bootleggers in Douglas — as, of course, there were! So the police came to check out the story and they stationed their car right in front of the O'Brien house. It's the oldest house in Douglas and it is there yet. And the OPP were parked there a long time and the O'Briens were looking out through their Irish lace curtains for a long time, too. So, finally the police started up to pull out and Mary O'Brien stuck her head out the window and yelled at them, "Next time you come, be sure to bring your knitting!"

Tim O'Brien got sick and he had to go down to the Ottawa Hospital. And Mary wanted to go down and see him. But the O'Briens, you know, were poverty-poor. So the women all got together and gave Mary O'Brien enough clothes to get dressed up and go down to see Tim. But he died anyhow. So when Mary O'Brien came back she called in Seriphican Enright — that's another great name after an Irish saint — and she said to Seriphican Enright, "You know, Seriph, those doctors in Ottawa, they're a bunch of damned ijits. They don't know nothing at all. They told me Tim died from having two bladders. Sure, Lord God! Everybody knows he wasn't big enough to have one!"

Now, I'll tell you one about Paddy Enright. There were about fifteen or so of them so I'm not giving anything away. Anyway, Paddy Enright used to sit all the time on the steps of the bank in Douglas. He had a gamey eye, and he smoked a pipe, and he'd always say to everybody going in to the bank, "Are you going to be putting in or taking out?" Well, nobody paid much attention to him because he was just Paddy Enright, or because they were so used to him sitting there and asking his question.

Well, one day a new section man of the CPR came to town and he came to the Douglas Creamery where I worked then and he bought eggs, bacon, cheese, and so on. And he said to me, "I want a bill for this, please."

"What is your name?" I asked him to write on the bill.

"Ami Huneout" (pronounced "You know"), he said to me.

Well, after that, Ami Huneout (pronounced "You know") went to cash his cheque at the bank. And, of course as usual, Paddy Enright was keeping vigil on the bank steps. "Ha," he said to himself, "here's a strange lad coming in now!" And he said to the Frenchman, "Hey, lad, what's your name?"

And Ami said, "Huneout" (pronounced "You know"), and went on into the bank.

So Paddy thinks to himself, "Ha! This is a smart-ass fellow, this is." So when Ami came out Paddy said to him, "Hey, me lad, I asked you a question there when you went into the bank. I asked you what your name was."

And Ami said, "Huneout."

And Paddy yelled out, "Cripes, man, if I knew, why would I be asking?"

Billy Laplaunt and his wife, Hannah, were another wondrously funny Douglas pair I remember so well. They were always down on their knees, it seemed to me, saying their prayers or their Rosaries. But anyhow, Hannah got very, very thin and she had to go and see the doctor in Renfrew. And afterwards I went in to see how she had made out, and she had these electric blue tights on — real violent blue. And I said to her, "Well, Hannah, how did you make out? Did you ever go down and see the doctor in Renfrew?"

"Yes," she says, "Billy took me down and the doctor looked me over."

"Yes," I said, "but did he examine you?"

And she said, "Yes, he got the full of his eye of me."

There was this man in Arnprior who was held in very high esteem. And there was this lady of very questionable virtue who charged him with rape. Everyone said that a man who was held in such high esteem certainly must be innocent. But anyhow, they went to the trial in droves. And the man was called upon the stand and the judge said to him, "Sir, did you touch this woman or try to rape her in any way?"

And the man replied, "Your Honour, I have not serviced a woman in over ten years."

There was this girl in Douglas and, if she was the only girl in town, she would not be called beautiful, that's how homely she was. But she was going with a man for quite a long time, such a long time, indeed, that the parish priest decided they would have to get married. So he more or less pressured them into getting married. You could not call it a love match, eh? But they got married and, in due time, had a baby. Then the man went up north to work and he was away a lot. But one weekend I knew he was in town visiting his wife and when I came out of the post office she was sitting in his half-ton truck. And I said to her, "Hi, Theresa! I see Frank is home for a little while."

And she said, "That's right, Mrs. Dooling."

And I said, "How long is he home for?"

And she said, "Oh, God! For eleven pricely days!"

These settlers came out from Scotland and settled in the Scotch Bush. W.T. James of Carleton Place, his family was one of them. Now in Douglas in the early days there was a wonderful man named Canon Quartermain. He looked after the Children's Aid and neglected children, and poor widows and misguided and pregnant girls and all that sort of thing. So when they put the Good Roads through Douglas in 1922, he got word that one of the Douglas girls was expecting a baby and she was not married. So Canon Quartermain went to visit her.

"Tell me, my child, who is the father of this baby you will be having soon?"

"I can't say, Rev," she replied.

"I am going to see that he does right by you, and marries you."

"I really can't say," the girl answered.

"You must know his name," the Canon said testily. "I have to have a name to put down here if I am going to help you."

"Well," said the girl from Douglas, "to be honest with you now, I guess you can just put down 'The Good Roads Gang.' "

---

1. Noble Dean was a tall and outstanding citizen of Renfrew at the time.
2. A tailor's thimble has no bottom in it.

6

Yes, but he has a rich father

W. T. (BILLY) JAMES, CARLETON PLACE, ONTARIO

In the spring of 1983 when I first went to tape W.T. James at his home in Carleton Place, he was then eighty-seven years of age, twice a widower, and, except for a partial blindness, remarkably fit and sharp for his age. His house was strewn with signposts of activity: newspapers, CNIB books-on-tape, taped music, letters from fans and friends, bits of his own writing. He was then working on his memoirs, which have since appeared under the title, W.T. James, Reminiscences of My Life, *published and distributed by the Almonte Gazette.*

The second son of John Webster James and his wife, the former Maggie Jane Byers, Billy James was raised on the family farm at Eganville. The Byerses' ancestors came from County Antrim, the Jameses' from County Wicklow, Ireland. When Billy James was nine he raised a pig until it was big enough to market. It was then sold and his parents kept the money since they needed it. The next year he raised a calf and again it was sold when ready for market, the money going again to his parents. These very early ventures in livestock production were true indicators of the young boy's future; for the past sixty years the name of Billy James has been synonymous in Canada with prize-winning cattle and Registered Herefords. Time and again, Billy James, "Appleton's dirt farmer," put his stock against those of millionaires like M.J. O'Brien of Renfrew, and time and time again beat them out for best herd, best breeder's herd and best exhibitors.

In 1920 Mr. James married Florence Belford, the eldest daughter of George Belford and his wife, the former Elizabeth Lotan, all of Pakenham, Ontario. Billy James was most anxious to get away from the stony ground of the Scotch Bush and in 1924 sold that farm and moved to much better land at Appleton. As the marriage partnership flour-

ished over the years, Spring Valley Farm became a showplace and a social centre for the cattle people from far and wide. In 1957 and 1965 Florence and Billy ("Jessie James and Billie the Kid") hosted the Ontario Hereford Picnics and in 1964 the International Ploughing Matches.

When he was young, Billy James had had many wonderful adventures threshing in the West during the First World War, horse-trading and surviving during the Great Depression, working the cattle drives for the Foster Brothers of the Scotch Bush, George Sparks of Vars, Ontario (son of Nicholas Sparks, founder of Ottawa), Gillies of Braeside.

However, Billy James seems to be more proud of one outstanding achievement he made while working for the Crop Seeds and Weeds Branch for Lanark County than of all his ribbons, cups and accolades won as a Hereford cattle-breeder. His alertness made a real contribution to cereal grain crops in Ontario.

The barberry bush, a European shrub, had the highest concentration in the Appleton–Carleton Place–Merrickville area. This rather pretty-looking bush was the host for the spores of the black-stemmed rust that was ruining thousands of acres of cereal crops, including wheat across the country. Mr. James began the fight for the elimination and control of the barberry, and eventually a million-dollar federal grant resulted in the almost total elimination of barberry in Ontario.

It was, however, not cattle or barberry but my search for stories of Dinny O'Brien of the Burnt Lands of Huntley that led me to Billy James. In 1983 I wrote a letter to the editor of the Almonte Gazette explaining that I would like to get in touch with anyone who had stories of Dinny. Mr. James's step-daughter, Jean Lyons, wrote me that not only had her step-father some Dinny O'Brien stories to tell, but he had actually known Dinny when he was alive and walking the Burnt Lands of Huntley forty years ago.

Mr. James's stories of Dinny O'Brien are included in Laughing all the Way Home. *But Mr. James could contribute many other stories of other legendary characters he had known: Frank O'Brien and Maloney of Carleton Place, George Comba the undertaker, and the Towneses of Douglas.*

In the 1920s Billy James married, sold his farm in Renfrew County and moved to richer lands in Appleton. He left behind him the stoney hillsides of Ryan's Mountain back of Renfrew, where long ago two lads named Martin Ryan (left) and Pat Bruce, posed before pitching in to some back-breaking and probably heart-breaking work.

Oh the Towneses! The Towneses of Douglas! They all stuttered a little and they all seemed to like to talk in rhyme; there was Stephen and Heman and Wyman and Erin and Calvin. And Wyman, who was perhaps the wittiest of them all, seemed to have a lisp as well. Well, anyway, he always used to say "Flord!" for "Lord!"

One time my cousin, Thomas John James of Douglas, met up with old Mr. Heman Townes. Tom hadn't seen Heman for quite a while and he commenced by asking him what he was doing. "Oh," Heman said, "I'm still hunting and trapping and fishing. But right now I'm trapping."

And Tom says, "Is there anything in it, Heman?"

"No, Tom," Heman says to him. "When you count the going and coming, the sitting and catching and fetching, the skinning and stretching, no, there isn't a hell of a lot in it."

In his time Wyman Townes worked at a lot of different jobs, like most of us in those days. One time he started to work for some people called Knight and McCrae, shanty owners. And Wyman said, "It wasn't long before I was working there night and day."

Another time, Wyman was cooking on a boat for a bunch of wealthy people from New York. They asked him if he would cook eggs for breakfast. And one of the party said to him, "Do you like eggs yourself, Mr. Townes?"

And Wyman said, "Flord! Sure there's nothing that I like better that a hen lays!"

Another time Wyman was cooking for this wealthy bunch. He asked them if they would like him to cook some tongue. And one of the ladies said, "Ha! I wouldn't eat anything that comes out of an animal's mouth!" And Wyman said, "Flord! What about an egg?"

One spring on the farm at Douglas, Wyman was getting low in laying mash. So he mixed the balance with sawdust and fed it to his hens. When somebody asked him how the hens did on that mix he said, "Oh, they laid fine. I even set some of the eggs."

"And what happened when you set the hens?" somebody asked him.

"Well," said Wyman, "when the chickens came out, some of them had wooden beaks and some of them had wooden legs. And one was even a woodpecker!"

Another time when Wyman was out hunting he seen this deer away up the side of this great big hill near his place. And he kept raising his sights and raising his sights and missing the deer. Finally, he raised them as high as they'd go and he told everyone afterwards, "I got the deer, but I bent the barrel."

One time Wyman was hired by this man, old Mike Murtagh from Admaston, and Murtagh wanted to have some fun with Wyman. Before Wyman come, he was out cutting some hay and come on this wasp's nest. So he put it in a little bundle where Wyman would run over it with the hay rake. And, sure enough, Wyman did. And the wasps came out of the nest and started to sting Wyman. Wyman just dove over the back of the hay rake and let the horse run away. Murtagh called out to Wyman, "Oh, catch that horse! Catch that horse! It's running away!"

And Wyman said, "Flord! Catch me! I'm running away, too!"

And there is the one about Wyman and old man Bob Bowes in Douglas. Bowes one day came along to where Wyman was digging this well and Wyman was down in the bottom of the well and old man Bob Bowes stood and turned his waterworks down on Wyman in the well. And Wyman was so mad! But he waited until hunting season and he got old Bob Bowes at the hunt camp lying in bed this day, dead drunk. And Wyman got this big tomcat and he raised old Bob Bowes's shirttail and pushed the cat up onto his shoulders and drew him right down his back. That's a true story and it got things evened up a bit, and it sobered up old man Bob Bowes.

There was some Towneses that lived over at Madawaska, too, and one of them, Danny Townes, was a great yarner. He told this story about how one winter it was so cold up there that he had his thermometer hanging outside the door on the nail, and this one night the temperature went down so far that it bent the nail. Danny Townes went on to tell how one night he heard a wolf howling underneath his bedroom window. But he had no weapon there. So he up-ended the chamberpot over the wolf and, on the way down, the contents turned into a block of ice, struck and killed the wolf, and he got his bounty. They still say that, if in that country in the deep of winter you see Danny Townes out with a long pole jabbing it down here and there, don't ask any questions because he's still out looking for his horse stable.

Wyman Townes and Mrs. Myrtle McMaster were always great friends playing tricks on one another, joking, teasing and trying to outdo one another. Apparently, this one time Myrtle had got ahead of Wyman and he didn't like to be outdone.

So he comes up to her house the next day and he bangs the door open and he says to Mrs. McMaster, "Flord! Myrtle, do you know what's afoot this morning?"

And Myrtle turned around quick — she thought it was something awful — and she says, "No, my God! What, Wyman?"

And he says, "Twelve inches."

Mr. James had many stories of other people and other events he remembered from that early period of his life spent in the Douglas–Eganville–Dacre area.

The Richardses were very wealthy in Balaclava when I was young. And of course, they couldn't get along without old Geordie Morrison, a jack-of-all-trades, a crusty, snappy old Scot. One day, finally, anyway, old Bill Richards was away and Mrs. Richards had old Geordie down to do something at the house or mill there, and whatever happened that he did, she had one hell of a row with him. And, of course, old Geordie got mad and told Mrs. Richards to kiss his ass and walked up home. So old Bill came home that night and he was awful mad about it and he went down to Geordie and said, "Come on now, Geordie, you've got to come down and make an apology to Mrs. Richards. You can't get away with the likes of that." So old Geordie came down and he says, "My Lord, Mrs. Richards! I told you yesterday you could kiss my ass, but you don't need to today unless you like."

Richards got into a big lawsuit up there over the Bowman Grattan Telephone Company. The Foster Brothers undertook to get a new line out for the farmers because we had no service at all with this other one. Every time the lines on the Bowman Grattan Telephone lines came to even a waterhole they'd cross the road with the lines and it would zigzag here and there all over — and of course, weaken the lines. Anyhow, there was then thirty ratepayers on the wires and Foster was very strong on one side of it and a lot of people went with Foster. Then the owners of the Bowman Grattan Telephone Company — Richards and oh, I've forgotten who else was mixed up in that one — they went after a bunch of weaklings and split it all up so that some stayed with Bowman Grattan and we built our own line with Foster Brothers, instead of everybody going over to Foster and running Richards out and making one really strong telephone service. So anyway, Joe Foster and Richards hadn't

Along with the Opeongo Line and Herrons Mills, the deserted village of Balaclava remains one of the great heritage resources of the Valley. Like them, it shares the ignominious fate of being allowed to fall into ruin. With its log buildings, its old houses and early squatters cabins, its great old store and storage-shed, its lovely water site on Constan Creek, its old mill — the last water powered lumber mill in North America — Balaclava could and should become something better than Upper Canada Village, for all the heritage buildings are still on site.

spoken to each other for months over this telephone business. I was only a young lad and Foster appointed me as secretary for his line that they were going to build. It was going to be the "Foster Bros. Telephone Co." Anyway, there was a big lawsuit came up and the court case couldn't be held anywhere else but in the school at Hyndford because a telephone expert from Toronto was coming up to settle this thing. Richards served the summons himself to Foster to save money. And Foster said to him, "By God, Richards, it's too bad you didn't get the sheriff's job because they'd never have been stuck for a hangman!" Both companies stayed in business until Bell took over.

In 1911 when there was that big fire in Eganville there was this cousin of mine, Johnny Sharp —

he was real Irish, too — and he had this friend, Matt Egan. They were always jibing at each other although they were great friends. Matt comes out this morning after the big fire in Eganville — it had burnt nearly everything down, including the Roman Catholic convent. And Matt comes up to Johnny and says, "By God, Johnny, it's too bad that Father Dowdall didn't have time to get the holy water to work to save the convent." "Yes," said Johnny, "But wasn't it damned lucky he got it to work in time to save the Orange Hall."

When I was in my early twenties and from then on, I was chosen to be the one to be trusted to handle money and to handle cattle. I drove big droves of cattle, fall after fall, from the area of Douglas and Eganville and around there, even to

Killaloe, to the lumber woods. This was for Gillies. I mostly went to Rowlington on the Dumoine River where the Gillieses had a Depot Farm and they used to take those big herds of cattle in there and hold them there at the slaughtering house and they'd slaughter one or two, according to their different needs for the different camps. We always used to try to arrive at the camps at dinnertime in order to get a big feed. Sometimes we'd see the Frenchmen hauling a moose or two. We'd always arrive there on a Sunday and they'd haul in a moose or two very often. Twice — more than that, I guess — I drove cattle from around Cahill Station and from the little village of Hyndford up to Pem-

broke and drove them up the main streets of Pembroke and put them on a boat and took them up to the Mattawa River that goes into the Ottawa River, and came down the next day on the boat to Pembroke and took a train home. There would be thirty or forty cattle on a drive. The boat was the *Oiseau*.

I worked for Gillies but I remember stories about timber baron J.R. Booth, who was the greatest of them all, I guess. The first one is about J.R. Booth and the Young Upstart.

This young fellow had got through college from up the line, probably somewhere at Pembroke or Renfrew, and after he graduated, he seen that there

A group of Quyon residents gather in 1911 for picture-taking on a crib of the last raft of square timber to go down the Ottawa River. The owner was J. R. Booth.

C. B. Mohr of Quyon, himself a timber operator, took this photograph just after the crib had passed through the slide at Chat's Falls.

was an opening advertised for a clerk at J.R. Booth's mills. So he got on the train this Monday morning and he went down to Ottawa. Everything was very quiet around Union Station. As a matter of fact, when he got off the train at the station there was only this one old man around there at all. So the young fellow sat down for a while and waited. But still no one appeared. Finally he went over to the old lad and he says to him, "What would you take to carry my grips over to J.R. Booth's office?"

And the old lad said, "Oh, anything at all you'd like to give me."

So the old lad carried the young fellow's grips over to J.R. Booth's office. The young fellow threw the old lad fifty cents for his trouble. Then he noticed that the old lad was still hanging around so he said to him, "Say, you couldn't tell me where J.R. Booth is, could you?"

And the old lad pointed at himself. "Yes, right here," he said.

One time at the Chateau Laurier, J.R. Booth gave the waiter a quarter tip. And the fellow says to Booth, "Your son always gives me a dollar tip."

"Yes," says J.R., "but he has a rich father."

The following stories emanate from Mr. James's middle and later years in the Appleton–Carleton Place–Almonte area.

I've known some great characters in my time and quite a few of them around Carleton Place. Frank O'Brien was one of them. One day Frank was going down the highway between Carleton Place and Almonte with an old hay-press, which was nearly half an acre long. And didn't this OPP officer come along in this car and was passing Frank. But then he pulled off to the side of the road and went back to Frank.

"What kind of a thing is that you've got there?" he asked O'Brien.

And Frank sighed and said to the OPP, "It's a German gun."

One time this fellow sold a horse to Frank. He palmed off this old "kicker" on Frank. And, of course, Frank had an awful job to get the horse harnessed. It took him nearly half a day to get the horse harnessed. How he did it was he finally moved some of the boards off the loft and he leaned down and got the collar on him. And then he removed some more of the boards and dropped the harness down over him. Then Frank got down and buckled the harness on the creature. Frank left the harness on the horse all spring. He never took it off all spring. And then the fellow that sold Frank the horse got curious, and he was back that way, and he went in to see Frank and asked him how he was getting along with the horse he had sold him.

"Oh, fine, fine," Frank said.

Finally the fellow got around to the point. "Did you ever have any trouble harnessing him?" he asked.

And Frank said, "Yes. Once!"

Another great character around Carleton Place was Maloney. Maloney had a terribly big nose. One day he was walking down Main Street and two ladies were coming to meet him on the sidewalk. And one said to the other in an underbreath, "Oh my goodness! Look at that man's nose!"

And Maloney puts his two hands up to his nose and he pulls it over sideways and he says to them, "Can you get by now, ladies?"

And there's another story about the infamous Maloney nose. One day Maloney was walking down Main Street with two ladies walking in the opposite direction towards him on the sidewalk. Just as they got near him he put his finger up to one side of his nose and gave it one awful blow. And one lady said to another in an underbreath, "Oh my! Look at that! Isn't that just awful!"

And Maloney right away put his finger up to the other side of his nose and said, "Watch out, ladies! The other barrel's loaded, too!"

Maloney used to work for a long time for Holly Acres and Holly Acres was an MP for Carleton County for years and years. Holly always wanted Maloney to get up on Sundays and go to church with him. "No," Maloney would say, "I'll just sit here in the shade. You go." So one Sunday Holly came home from church and he says to Maloney, "What religion are you anyway, Maloney?"

And Maloney says, "I have no religion and I live up to it."

One Sunday while Maloney was working for Holly Acres, the minister came out to visit. He was fresh out from England and he had a very broad accent. Holly gave Maloney an introduction to the minister and the minister says, "I take it for granted by your name that you're an Irishman."

"Yes," says Maloney, "I'm Irish. But I'm not imported."

George Comba, the Almonte undertaker, was a great after-dinner speaker. He would always finish up a speech by telling of all the sterling qualities of the people of Almonte. He said that in Almonte people got along so well together that there was once this Orangeman and this priest who lived side by side, and they got along so well that the priest always took his water from the Orangeman's well. "But," said George Comba, "what always puzzled me about that was how he could ever make holy water out of it."

This fellow from Carleton Place was a big bettor on the horses at the track in Ottawa. And he always noticed that, before the race, the priest would go out and touch the winning horse. He was losing a lot of money, so he thought he would try this horse that the priest touched this time. So when it came time for the race to start, his horse dropped dead at the starting gate. So he went up to the priest and he said, "How come that the only time I bet on the horse that you laid hands on, he dropped dead at the beginning of the race?"

And the priest says, "Well, now, it may be just that you don't understand the difference between a winner and the last rites."

This old gentleman named Jedediah Hunt lived in the village of Pakenham. He and his daughter, Sarah Ann, lived together and she had raised this big steer up as a pet and for their own meat, too. And this elder of the church had a ranch up on the Pakenham Mountains and he drove the big steer up and put it in with his own cattle. When this news got to old Hunt's ears, he went after the elder of the church for having stolen his steer. So they congregated at the ranch to identify the steer. And Jedediah said to his daughter, "Sarah Ann, call your steer now."

So she started to call, "Jim-eye, Jim-eye, Jim-eye," and Jim-eye came right up to her with his tail over his back.

And Jedediah started to curse and swear because he had been robbed. And the elder of the church who had stolen his steer turned to him and said, "Tut, tut, man. There's ladies around here, you know."

"Yes," said Jedediah Hunt, "pray and steal, goddam you."

Old Tom Johnston from Douglas was a great supporter of the church. He was also a terribly dirty old bachelor. And, of course, he was always inviting the minister in for dinner. And the minister was usually able to find some excuse for not going, but this time he had to go. In the kitchen old Tom starts throwing one egg after another into the frying pan. And the minister says to him, "My, Tom! Sure, we wouldn't be able to eat half of those."

"Acht," says old Tom, "that's nothing. Sure, half of them may be rotten."

These two maiden ladies lived out in the countryside near Hopetown. And they had the minister coming in to see them, but they happened to be out of meat. They had this old pet rooster, poor old Joe, that had been around their place for years and years and years. Of course, rather than see the minister go without meat, they killed poor old Joe and put him in the pot. After the minister had eaten and gone, the two maiden ladies from Hopetown were sitting rocking and mourning about poor old Joe.

"Oh dear," said one of them, "we won't have poor old Joe around for company anymore and to waken us in the morning with his grand crowing."

And the other maiden lady from Hopetown thought about it for a while. And then she said, "Well, maybe it's not so bad after all that poor old Joe has entered into the ministry for he was one hell of a poor layman."

It can be fairly well documented that farmers tend to like earthy, salty, raunchy stories that have to do with basic bodily functions and pretty fundamental sex. Farmers have their good points, as no doubt their wives and children can testify, but they do not tend to be a romantic group of people. Hard work, long hours, closeness to the earth, obeisance to the seasons, moulds their characters generally into that of the practical down-to-earth, pragmatic individuals who have had to watch the pennies, been able to improvise, invent, innovate with what they have on hand — a piece of old haywire or binder twine — in order to keep the farm and its machinery and animals going. The farmer looks like a simple man on the outside, but very often inside he is a paradoxical complexity combining ruthlessness and gentleness, reclusiveness and gregariousness, pragmatism and love of beauty, ignorance and philosophy. In Mr. James's earlier years on the farm in the first half of this century, religion was an integral part of life, whether one was a fundamentalist or a Roman Catholic; therefore many of the original stories he has to tell involve his religion — Presbyterian — and the deep-rooted animosity between Protestants and Catholics of his time. This sometimes murderous conflict was often diluted socially through humorous stories about the Orangemen and the Catholics.

This man who was very constipated finally went into a Renfrew doctor. The doctor gave him some medicine and told him to come back the next day for a check-up. So the man came back the next day and as soon as he arrived in the office, the doctor said to him, "Well, my good man, what did you pass?" And the man said, "Well, I passed Stephen Henry on a stick of square timber, and an old sow, and a litter of pigs."

This one is about Padre Young, who eventually became padre at Ontario Agricultural College in Guelph. He gave his first sermon this Sunday morning and he was awfully badly worried about it all that afternoon. Was it good? Was it bad? He didn't know how the congregation felt. And the next morning he went out looking around the place and he thought to himself, "Well, if I can't preach, I can at least keep this home looking a lot better than it was before I came here." So he goes along and he sees this farmer next door to him out in the field pulling in a load of manure. And Young went over to him and he says, "Would you sell me a load of that manure?"

"Sure," said the farmer.

"When could you bring it to me?" the preacher asked.

And the farmer says, "I could bring you the next load."

So the farmer brought Young the next load and when they got it off, the preacher pulled out his purse to pay him. "Oh no," said the farmer, "I'm not going to charge you anything for it."

"I'm not going to be a bum around here," says Young. "I intend to pay my way."

"No! No!" exclaimed the farmer. "That sermon of yours yesterday was worth two loads of manure."

This minister was talking to this old lady and he said to her, "Well, my dear lady, you know we should always be thankful for anything we have." And the old lady said that she was, that she had only two teeth and she always thanked the Lord that they "mashed."

Pat went to church but he slept there. So this time at church in Almonte the people, as usual, were all sitting at the back, and the minister said, "Everyone that wants to go to heaven, take the front seats." So they all moved up, but Pat was in a great slumber and he never heard anything. And the minister started to lash out at the congregation again. But he looks up and he sees Pat still in the back seat and still asleep, and he yells out, "Everybody that is going to hell, stand up quick!" And Pat just heard the words "going" and "stand up." So he jumps up and he looks around and then he says to the minister, "Well, I don't know where you and I are going, but we seem to be in the minority."

This Anglican and this Presbyterian were always arguing about their religions. This day the Anglican was getting away ahead of the Presbyterian and the Presbyterian got so mad he said, "Oh, it doesn't matter a damn! You Anglicans are all going to hell anyway!" "Well," says the Anglican, "I'd rather be an Anglican and know I was going to hell than be a Presbyterian and not know where the hell I was going!"

This Presbyterian missionary went away up into the Far North Country, as far as Moosonee, looking for Presbyterians. And he went into this place in Moosonee and he asked the young boy there if his parents were at home. And the missionary said, "I just came around to see if there were any Presbyterians around here that might need me." "Well," says the young boy, "I don't know. My father is a trapper and he has a lot of hides out in the back shed and if you look amongst them you might find a Presbyterian."

These two lads were at a Holy Roller immersion baptism up the Pontiac in the Ottawa River. They were pretty impressed by the way the new members who were going "to be saved" were submerged in the waters of the river. So, when they got home — they had a batch of new kittens and the old cat — they decided they were going to practise it on this batch of kittens and the old cat. They got the tub of water out and they dipped all the kittens in and they got along fine with them, but the old cat scratched the devil out of them when they tried it on her. "Ouch!" said one of the young lads. "Let's just sprinkle her and let her go to hell!"

This one Sunday morning the preacher at Almonte was lashing out at his congregation. He took for his subject "Enemies." Yes, he was lashing out at them about having enemies and finally he asked if there was anyone in the church that had no enemies. Eventually, this very old gentleman in the front seat put up his hand. And the preacher said, "Good for you, my dear man. Would you mind getting up on your feet and turning around and telling this congregation how it is you have no enemies?" So the old lad started to get up. And the preacher said, "Take your time, take your time, my man. I want everyone to hear this." Finally, the old lad was on his feet and the minister said, "Now, would you mind turning around and telling the whole congregation how it is that you have no enemies." And the old lad turned around and faced the congregation and said, "I outlived the buggers!"

And a time for everything. Including a time for courting on the Opeongo Line. Here are Harry Kinnelly and
Maggie Lynch of Kinnelly's Mountain in their Sunday courting best.

The farmer, from the moment he was aware as a child, was exposed to sex and mating on the farm amongst the animals he observed. This constant visual presentation of the facts of life gave him a forthrightness about sex that was probably manifested in his private life and most certainly in the jokes he found humorous — and which were far too often too raunchy for repetition here in print. The jokes that cattlemen tell each other in the barn are probably best kept a private affair. On the other hand, whether the farmer was Bible-thumping evangelical or Roman Catholic, the repressive hand of religion, the Cyclopean eye of prudery, eventually overlaid his spontaneous naturalness. The feelings and attitudes about sex and mating that these influences push down into the subconscious even-
tually, through time, re-emerge wearing the many masks of humour.

This fellow from Carleton Place was walking down the road one day and it was a hot, hot day and he seen this pool and he thought he'd pull off his clothes and jump in and have a swim. But, anyway, there was this bunch of young lads hiding around in the bushes and they stole all his clothes. All but his hat. And when this fellow got out of the water and found his clothes all gone, he run down the road chasing those young lads. And he was using his hat to cover his nakedness and this lady met him on the road and she started to laugh to beat the dickens. And he says to her, "You're not much of a lady or you wouldn't laugh at me."

And she says to him, "You're not much of a

gentleman or you'd lift your hat to a lady."

This fellow was in Almonte one day. It was in the horse-and-buggy days and he had to ford the Indian River to get to town. He discovered when he was in town that it was his twenty-fifth wedding anniversary and he had had no new clothes or anything since the time he was married. So he thought he'd buy everything from the hide out and put them on and go home and surprise his wife Nelly. So he got the big parcel in the back of the buggy and he thought he'd change at the place where he had forded the river. He pulled off all his old clothes and threw them in the river to float away. Then he reached around to pull the parcel of new clothes out of the back of his buggy, but he discovered that the young lads in town had stolen his parcel. He stood up and scratched his head for a while and then he said to his horse, "Well, giddy-up. We'll go home and surprise Nelly anyway."

The doctor in Pakenham was busy explaining one time to this old lady that, if you were blind in one eye, you were always sure to get stronger in the other. And if you were deaf in one ear, you were always sure to get stronger in the other. And the old lady listened to him and then she said, "Sure, by God, I often noticed, too, that if a man was short on one leg, he was always sure to be longer on the other!"

This couple, they weren't too well off, and their boy was up to the age when he could go to university. So they scraped up enough money and they thought they would put him through college, and they sent him up to Queen's. Anyhow, when he got up there to Kingston, he got stepping out, and the money ran down, and he knew that his parents had this old dog, Rover, that they thought so much about. And he put up this plea to them. He told them that, at Queen's University, they could teach dogs to do all kinds of tricks and, if they would just send Rover and 100 dollars, he would get him learned all those tricks. They sent the money and the dog. But, after a while, all the money got done and he wrote them and told them that Rover had learned to do all kinds of tricks, but that at Queen's University they could even learn dogs to talk. And wouldn't it be grand and nice now that Rover could do all kinds of tricks, if he could learn to talk? So they sent down another 100 dollars. So, finally, it was time for the young lad to go home in the spring to Carleton Place, and when he came home in the spring he went up to his mother and they greeted each other. And he says, "Where's Father?" "Oh," says his mother, "he's down at the town hall at a meeting." So the lad goes down there;

he meets up with the father and they greet each other and the father says, "Where's Rover?" And the young lad says, "Oh, Father, we've got to talk that over privately." And the father says, "There's an office here. Let's step in here." "Well," begins the young lad when they get inside the office, "Rover learned to do all kinds of tricks and he learned to talk and everything. But the night before I left Queen's to come home, he couldn't talk about anything except how you and the hired girl were running around together. And I had him shot because that would never do." "Good for you, son," the father says. "Are you sure that damned dog is dead?"

Traditionally, farmers in the Ottawa Valley and, for the most part, elsewhere, have always been Tory, Conservative, right-wing, hard to change. Next to the weather and the crops, politics has been the butt of most of their jokes in the past, although things are changing now and Liberals have actually gained and held seats in the rural Valley. At eighty-nine, Mr. James can claim to be one of the oldest supporters of the Conservative Party in the Ottawa Valley and has voted for them for the past sixty-eight years. He probably has in his repertoire a hundred political jokes, but I have only recorded here a few of them.

This one is about John Diefenbaker and I heard it long before he died. John D. had died and gone straight up to heaven. But he got awful tired on his way up and he was sitting down by the road when who should come along who had just died, too, but Trudeau himself. And Trudeau said, "You look tired, John." And John said, "Yes, I'm afraid I'm not going to be able to make it into heaven." So Trudeau says, "Get on my back. I'm in good shape and I'll take you on up." So John Diefenbaker got on Trudeau's back and when they got up to the Pearly Gates St. Peter came out and he said to Dief, "You're late, John, but it's all right. Just tie your ass to that fence over there and come on in."

This Toronto Hogtown mayor — he was such a blow — and he came to Ottawa to visit and, of course, the officials of Ottawa tried to entertain him all day. Finally, when the day was all over they took him to one of the finest hotels in the capital to get him a bed for the night. They told the proprietor of the hotel how the mayor of Hogtown was such a blow and a windbag. So he decided to play a trick on him. He slipped a big mud turtle under the covers on the bed before the mayor of Hogtown got in. And it wasn't very long after he got in that the old mud turtle got hold of him by the toe and the mayor came to the top of the stairs shouting for the proprietor, and with the turtle still hanging onto his toe, and yelling and shouting, "What's that! What's that!" And the proprietor came running up the stairs and he says, "Sure, that's one of our Ottawa bedbugs! Now don't try to tell us you have ones ten times as big in Toronto!"

This Manitoba fellow and this Ontario fellow from around the lake country back of Kingston were always blowing about each other's provinces and bragging about how much one was better than the other. The fellow from Manitoba would brag about all the great untouched lakes of his province and the fellow from Ontario would boast about the Great Lakes that border Ontario and the lakes that run up to the northern seas. But finally, anyway, the lad from Manitoba was getting ahead somewhat of the lad from Ontario. So the lad from Ontario finished it off by saying, "Look, some fine night you just lay a pipe up to those lakes up north and, if you can suck as hard as you can blow, you'll soon have all

the lakes of northern Ontario down in southern Manitoba!"

Canada was never and probably never will be the melting pot that was the United States. The Irish, the Scottish and the English were the principal migratory races into the Ottawa Valley and they had to live together and join forces for survival here. But the old hatreds didn't disappear magically; they went underground and surfaced in a socially acceptable way through racial jokes.

This Scotsman had his two fingers taken off in an accident in Almonte. The Almonte doctor told him to take them home and bury them in consecrated ground. If he didn't do that, the missing fingers would pain him all the rest of his life. So the Scotsman went home, but he didn't want to be bothered with burying his fingers in consecrated ground, so he just went out into the barnyard and threw them into the manure pile. Well, it wasn't too long before the fingers started to ache something terrible and, unable to bear the pain, the

A midsummer view of Carleton Place with the ruins of a Gillies mill to the left and the town hall tower to the right. In his youth Mr. James worked for both Gillies and Booth lumber companies.

Scotsman went back to the manure pile to try and find his two missing fingers. But he could not find them. Then he heard about this great Jewish doctor in Carleton Place and he went to him and told him the story and the Jewish doctor said to him, "What nationality are you?" "I'm Scots," he replied. "Well then, my good man," the Jewish doctor said to him, "you just go home and put fifty cents into that manure pile and, if those fingers are in there, you'll soon see them start to work."

The Scotsman, the Irishman, and the Englishman were discussing what they'd be if they weren't what they were. And the Scotsman said to the Englishman, "If you weren't an Englishman, what would you be?" The Englishman says, "I'd be a Scotsman." And the Englishman says to the Scotsman, "What would you be if you weren't Scots?" And the Scotsman said, "I'd be an Englishman." So then they both turned to the Irishman and said, "What would you be if you weren't Irish?" And the Irishman says right off, "I'd be damned well ashamed of myself!"

There are whole repertoires of humorous stories — some true and some old chestnuts — about the ingenue going to the Big City. Very often the ingenue is the simple farmer taking his first trip away from the farm. Mr. James had a number of these in his collection of stories.

This old farmer from Killaloe had never been out anywhere more than ten miles from his farm. And one time between seasons he decided to spend a few pennies and take a trip to Toronto. He went to the Royal York and the first time in he was standing watching the elevator go up and down. Of course, he had never seen such a contraption before, and he seen this old lady get on and go up and he stood there gawking at it till it came down again. Of course, he expected the same old lady to get off. But, instead, this grand young big blonde got off. And he said to himself, "Boy, I'm sorry I didn't bring my old lady here and have her run through that machine!"

This young man from Rockingham had never got out anywhere to see the rest of the world, and he was always plaguing his father for money to go on a trip. So, finally, his father gave him a lot of money and he went down to the station and he spent a lot of it on a return ticket. And he got on the train and he started passing through all the towns and cities and he started cursing and swearing about how he had missed so much all his life. And there was this minister sitting near him,

listening to his profanities. And finally, the minister stepped up to the young man from Rockingham and said to him, "Say, young man, do you know where you're going?" And the young lad said, "No," and the minister said, "Well, you're going straight to hell." "Well," says the young man, "I don't give a damn. I have a return ticket."

The farmer tends to have an ability to laugh at himself. His pragmatism and his closeness to the earth seem to obstruct any tendency to take himself too seriously, a fault more prevalent amongst people who work in the more abstracted levels of society. Mr. James told some wonderful stories that demonstrate the farmer's capacity to take himself lightly.

One time back there when the livestock got so plentiful in the States that they sent the government fellows out to the farms to shoot off the surplus stock, this government fellow who knew nothing at all about farming went out to shoot off the surplus livestock. He had to take a book along with him because he didn't know one animal from another. So he went out to this farmer's place and he says to this farmer, "I've come to shoot your surplus livestock. How many cattle have you got?" So the farmer told him and he says, "Well, I have to shoot so many of them." So they drove out and they shot so many cattle. The same with the pigs. The same with the horses. The same with the sheep. And then the government man says, "I guess my work is all done here." And the government man was beginning to drive away, but just then an old billy goat stuck his head around the corner of a building and let out a bleat. The government man took out his book and looked it over but he couldn't see a picture of any animal like that in it. So he says to himself, "I guess I'll have to call up Washington." So he calls them up and he says, "I have a species here and I have no picture of it in the book and I don't know what it is." So the government man in Washington says to him, "Well, describe it." So the government man in the field says, "It's got a long face and a tear in its eye and a goatee." And the government man in Washington yelled out on the phone, "For God's sakes, don't shoot that! That's the farmer."

This farmer from along the Opeongo Line got fed up with trying to farm unfarmable land. So he sold out and moved to a farm down near London. He made a deal with a farmer there who told him what good land it was, how it would grow anything. He could even grow nuts on it, the farmer said. So the lad from the Opeongo moved down to his new farm near London and he tried it for a couple of years. And then he phoned up the farmer who had sold him his new farm and gave him hell. "Goddam you," he said, "you told me I could grow nuts on it." "Oh no," said the other farmer, "I said you could *go* nuts on it."

This income-tax inspector from Ottawa was checking up on this farmer one time. And he says to him, "How many hired help have you got?"

And the farmer says, "I have one hired man."

"And how much does he get?"

"He gets a hundred dollars a month and his board and room."

"Have you any more hired men?"

"I have another hired man. He gets seventy-five dollars a month and his room and board."

"Is that all your hired help?"

"No, my wife has a girl to help around here."

"What does she get?"

"She gets a hundred dollars a month and room and board."

"Is that the extent of your hired help?"

"Well no, there's a half-wit around here."

"And what does he get?"

"He gets his tobacco and some old clothes now and again."

The income-tax inspector pulled off his glasses and rose to his feet and he said, "This is a rather interesting case. I'd like to see this man. Where is he?"

And the old farmer says, "You're looking at him right now."

1. In *Laughing all the Way Home* Jack Jewel of Fort Coulonge tells stories of Josh Billings and the Balmoral Hotel in Barry's Bay.
2. The Tom Murray referred to here is the late Tom Murray of Barry's Bay. See *Some of the Stories I Told You Were True.*
3. Graham's Lake is in the Griffith area, off Highway 41.
4. This story was also told of Wyman Townes.
5. This story was also told by Ed Hubert.
6. A decking line was a chain run through block and tackle; the hook on the end of it was snagged into a log so that a horse could haul it to the top of a skidway pile or a sleigh load. A gin pole was a primitive hoisting gear for loading logs.

The Roman Catholic Church at Latchford bridge on the Madawaska River, where "the drive" began.

7

The man in the coffin, Sir

WILLIE MADIGAN AND P.J. RYAN, PALMER'S RAPIDS, ONTARIO

In the Palmer's Rapids–Quadville–Latchford Bridge area the Madigans have long been renowned as fiddlers, singers, and storytellers. Six years ago I arrived too late at the Barry's Bay hospital to tape Dan Madigan, who had long been on my list of old-timers to be interviewed; Dan died just two days prior to my arrival. Another name on my line-up had been that of P. J. Ryan of Palmer's Rapids. Several years ago when I first went to visit him I discovered he had no electricity and ran his television off his tractor battery. I had not had the foresight to take batteries for my tape recorder and so had to depart that country once again frustrated.

Then in early March, 1983, on an off-chance, I drove from Renfrew to Palmer's Rapids, hoping to catch either Willie Madigan or Ryan. Before I left Renfrew, following an intuition that proved well grounded indeed, I stopped and bought a wee tot of rye whiskey at the local groggery. Widower Willie Madigan was at home and was also, as I have so often found, most glad of visitors in that dreadful in-between kind of weather. And I hadn't been long there either before he suggested that we drive up Wingle's Hill and get his long-time friend, bachelor P.J. Ryan.

Willie Madigan's and P.J. Ryan's families had been early Irish settlers in the area around Palmer's Rapids, famous as the place "where the drive began" on the Madawaska River. But as the French rivermen of yore met and married the local Irish girls, the area began to be also characterized by a good sprinkling of Franco-Irish. Madigan and Ryan were a case in point; although they were both obviously of Irish origin, their mothers had been Canadians of French descent. Dan Madigan had married Zelpha Beaudry and Paddy Ryan was wed to Louise Parisienne (now pronounced Pershall)

of Bell's Rapids, today a deserted settlement above Lake Kiminski on the Madawaska.

Madigan had worked in the bush for the Bronsons and the McCreas and, back in the Dirty Thirties, for the railway. He moved on to the Department of Highways and stayed with them for twenty-nine years until his recent retirement. Ryan all his life has farmed the Ryan place.

As the afternoon wore on and the bottle went down, Ryan and Madigan peopled the Palmer's Rapids world with Proudfoots, Mahons, Sullivans, Mantibles, McCarthys, Pilgrims, Hickses, Cowleses, Hares, Watsons, Byerses, Muddigans, Goleens, Pennicks, and Jessopses, as well as with a large German settlement of "good neighbours."

Neither Madigan nor Ryan, probably because of their French infusion on the maternal side, had outstanding Valley-Irish accents. And physically Madigan revealed a good mix of both races. But P.J. Ryan was all-of-a-piece Irish and, furthermore, the breed that comes out as ascetic genteel Irish, very serious of mien and very specific in historical detail. He was the only old-timer I have taped who chewed snuff and lifted the stove lid and spat it out — quietly and discreetly, of course. But when he laughed! It was as though his whole face peeled off — and became another — while his entire body shook.

It was an unforgettable afternoon of storytelling and singing. But, as it turned out later, most of the stories in this chapter were told by Ryan. Madigan was the dominant singer.

Willie: Right off I'll tell you a funny story, funny-sad. In the Dirty Thirties I was building a highway from Barry's Bay to Pembroke with wheelbarrows. There was eighty or ninety men there, but that was in the winter and you couldn't do nothing. We had no machinery and what could you do with everything froze up? There was five out of each township, Raglan, Radcliff, Brudenell. That's all they could take. But that five could only stay for two weeks and then they'd have to come home and let somebody else take a turn so they'd make some money, too. And there I was on the pick and shovel trying to move this whole great big hill with a wheelbarrow. Well, you know how far we got! We got noplace. We never moved that hill away from there.

P.J.: That's not all. This is just as crazy. I forget the name of the company, but I remember when they used to cut ice up at Hudson Bay and bring it all the way down to sell it in Ottawa.

Willie: I can tell you another funny story you wouldn't believe. Down the road here there's a lady who's one hundred and one and her son she's living with is eighty. When she and her husband were ninety-five, they decided to separate, and they lived two or three miles apart for three more years when he died at the age of ninety-eight. Fancy that!

P.J.: One time my old dad took out telegraph poles for the Hydro in 1916. He cut them and barked them and piled them on the banks of the Madawaska and he got a part payment on them through the winter. But then he heard no more, so he got connected with a couple of lawyers in Pembroke — White and Williams — because he was not going to roll them in until he got paid the rest. And a lot of people said to him, "Oh, you're going to end up in jail, Paddy Ryan." And he said, "I might as well be in jail as slave away my life working for them bastards." And he refused to roll them in. But they didn't rot there. Some of them Hydro poles were fills for that barn of Coyne's up there where Malcolm Muddigan lives, and some of them went into that big barn that Goleen has there.

In those days they sold alcohol over the bar. It was three dollars a gallon. They called it high wine, eh? I think it was old John Windle and old man Pennick — he was a friend of Windle and the Moores that lived up on the hill there — and they were down in the Windle yard having a talk. And they had a bottle of high wine and they didn't want the women to know it. They were in a bad way because they'd have to go up to the house to get the water to mix with the high wines. When they seen Paddy Ryan coming down the hill with the team and buggy coming home from The Palmer, they thought maybe he'd have a bit of water in the buggy for the horses or something. They told him their troubles. And he said, "Nope, I've nothing

here. No water pail or anything. But I can certainly make room for water in it, if that's what you want." And Paddy Ryan reached for the bottle and began to put it to his mouth. But old man Pennick was too quick for him and grabbled it from him, yelling out: "Oh no! There ain't no man alive can drink high wines pure! Sure it would kill you, Paddy Ryan."

This Josh Billings[1] from the Balmoral Hotel in Barry's Bay, he was an awful card. His son, Jack, was the game warden that got burnt. Anyway, Josh was a-walking this time along the boardway in Barry's Bay and he met a girl who was leading a little dog, and the dog's tail was curled right up like a **9**, you know. And Billings stopped and he asked her, "How old is that dog?" And she says, "It's 90 years." "Oh, now," says Billings, "how could it be 90 years old?" "Well," the girls says, "you see that curl and the dot under its tail. That says 90." And Billings says, "It's too bad it isn't a bitch. Then it would be 900."

Cooey Costello was reeve one time. He ran against Tom Murray[2] at one point. Costello owned that hotel at Brudenell and there was a racetrack at Brudenell in the early days. Them old-time Billingses, they were great horsemen, you know. This old Josh Billings, he travelled a stallion up around Carson Lake. They didn't travel in no damned truck the way they do today. They drove them on the road. Old Josh started out on his schedule run, but he got sick with the flu or something and he had to send his son, Johnny, out with the horse. Once he started, he had to hold up to that schedule, you know. Well, anyhow, this Johnny fellow was up around Carson Lake — that's about ten or fifteen miles from Barry's Bay — and he ran into a bunch of good-looking girls around there, and he decided to stay there for three or four days. To hell with the stallion! And old Josh found out about it and he sent him this note:

> Dear John;
> You eternal bastard! Bring back my horse and cart.
> From your loving father,
> Josh Billings.

Josh and his son Jack were having a few drinks one time at the Balmoral. And they got into some kind of a real row and Jack threw a glass and hit the old fellow in the face. A glass half full of whiskey and it broke and cut up his face. A day or two after that, some lad came in to the hotel and he says to Josh,

"What happened to you, Josh?"

"Son stroke!" Josh says, "son stroke."

In the days before the hydro came on the river, there used to be ice on the river. And that big Kiminski Lake — that used to be just like Main Street in Barry's Bay for all those Polish people to go to the Bay. They went straight up that lake. You can't do it today. Hydro doesn't want ice on the river. Well, anyhow, he had a great team of French Canadians (horses), and he was out to the Bay and on his way back to Bell's Rapids across the lake and one of his horses got sick with the colic. You know, when they got sick with that colic it damned well killed them within half an hour, if they got it bad enough. They'd lie down and roll and get their feet under the pole. Well, my grandfather met old Josh Billings coming across the lake from someplace or other. And Billings said, "Don't worry, I've got a cure for that. I've got some Dr.

Bell's Miracle Cure." And Billings pulled out half a gallon of whiskey and poured it into the horse. And it wasn't too long before it was on its feet and away.

This farm that Howard Jessop has up there now, that was what they called the Old McLachlin Farm. They raised hay and potatoes and pigs, pork for their camps. Instead of drawing it up from Arnprior. They had another one up above Bark Lake and these fellows that live around here now, the old-timers, they bought their land from the McLachlins after they got the pine off it. But McLachlin didn't buy a hundred acres. They'd buy a couple of thousand acres. Well, anyhow the time my grandfather Paddy Ryan died — it was long before my time, but I heard the story. It was when there was only one church and one graveyard at Brudenell. I think this is about Bill Hartney. Hartneys were relations of the Ryans. And, of course, they had to take the

Cooey Costello's stopping-place along the Opeongo Line, at Brudenell. Once one of the grandest places in the country, it is now uncared for and falling in. Legend has it that the grand piano from its days of former splendor still sits in the dark gloom of the parlour.

corpse down and across the river in a log canoe, and Hartney met them with a team and wagon and took the body from there out to Brudenell. Hartney was pretty short on the grain. He wouldn't tell you to go right to hell, but he'd give you a pretty short answer if you started asking him any questions. But they met this lad on the road near Brudenell, Hartney drawing the corpse and a few more wagons of relations behind him. And the lad says, "Who's dead now, Mr. Hartney? Who's dead now?" And Hartney snapped, "The man in the coffin, sir. The man in the coffin."

In the old times they never had no undertakers or anything like that. You had to dig the grave and make the coffin and do the waking. In those days the corpse was never left alone until it was under the sod. Well, it was hard times, you know, and Bill Hartney and his uncle used to go to all the wakes, away out to Brudenell to a wake. But it was in order to get the smokes. The tobacco. They'd pass round the clay pipes and the tobacco. But it didn't suit Bill well enough — the tobacco wasn't coming around often enough to suit him. So finally he says to all around, "At the death of he or she, tobacco should be passed around at least every twenty-five minutes."

You know where Graham's Lake is?[3] They say there was an old fellow lived one time near where Larry O'Brien lives now. His name was Graham and that's how it came to be known as Graham's Lake. And there was the old Addington Road; it joined the Opeongo Line out near Brudenell and came out near Tweed. Across the river below the Snake Rapids — the log bridge burnt in a bush fire and that was the end of it — there was an old fellow by the name of Graham lived there and he was a cobbler. He worked in leather and fixed shoes. He died sitting down at his cobbler's bench, all hunched over, and it was some days before he was found, and he was stiff and cold and bent. The body wouldn't fit into the coffin and they had to find some way to straighten him out. So they put some stones on his legs and knees and down and around, you know, and they tied a rope to his neck and bored a hole in the coffin and tied the other end of the rope to a board behind the coffin. In those days it would be lit by coal oil and not too bright — and old Curley Jim Ryan, my uncle, and Crombie and somebody else, they bent over and cut the rope on the corpse and the old cobbler tightened up into his hunched-over position right in the coffin. Well! What a scatteration that was!

In this country out here toward Quadville long

ago there was a great big powerful man named Big Jim O'Brien. He wasn't fat neither. And, if he got a dollar ahead of you, you'd have some fun getting it out of him. And Jim Johnston up here, he had a store here and Big Jim O'Brien run a little bill there. I don't know how much he owed, but the laws them days was that if a man moves away from a town where he had run up a bill, you couldn't follow him up and collect it from him. Big Jim was moving down toward Eganville with his niece. He had a team of horses and a few cows and a few hens and a couple of pigs. Johnston was in his store one day when Big Jim came in. Johnston knew he wasn't going to get paid. So when Big Jim O'Brien said to him, "What's the best way to move them hens down to Eganville?"

Johnston said, "Drive them with the cattle, Jim. Drive them with the cattle."

Back in 1931 when I was only seventeen I was working at this place where there was this old man named Jack Sullivan. He used to tell some awful hunting stories. And Paddy O'Brien came over one day and this Sullivan said to him, "Paddy, what was the largest flock of partridge you ever saw in your life?"

"Oh," Paddy says, "I guess about twelve or fifteen."

"By dang," Sullivan says, "I once saw ninety-nine."

And Paddy says, "Come on now, Jack, you may as well make it one hundred."

And Sullivan, he says, "Do you think I'd tell a lie over one damn partridge!"[4]

Years ago, down in the lower country, it was good farming country and there was a family lived there one time. They had a team of horses and a bunch of cows, and one thing and another. And they had a damned good dog. In the evening the dog would go to the pasture and bring the cows in all by himself. This one night there was to be a dance some distance away and the young people would have to drive there with the teams to get to the dance, and they wanted to do up the chores real early. So earlier than most times they told the dog to go out and get the cows and bring them in for milking. They waited for some time and went on with their other chores. But still the cows weren't home. The cows weren't that far away that they couldn't see them or hear them. They wondered what was the matter with their good dog that he didn't round up the cows. So they went out looking for the dog. And there he was, around the corner of the barn with his paw up over his eyes, looking at the sun. He knew it wasn't time to bring in the cows.

There was a townie traveller one time out in the country west of Bancroft where you fall off the world. He was travelling around taking his orders from these country stores. And he came to this town there and hardly anybody could say "Goodday" to him. It was ducks, ducks, duck-hunting season, hunting ducks. He never hunted ducks before. He was a townie and he thought he'd try his hand at this, so he bought himself a shotgun and got himself a nice big overcoat and he hired this guide, an old mountaineer, an old fellow dressed in rags. The townie had got himself a new shotgun, but this old mountaineer, he used to hunt with a rifle. And they went out this afternoon and rigged up what they call a duck blind out in the slough someplace to watch for these ducks.

The old fellow says to the townie, "Meet me up here tomorrow morning at daybreak or before. And I don't mean morning. No damned ten o'clock."

So the townie had his overcoat on and Thermos bottle of hot coffee in his overcoat pocket. And the old mountaineer, he had a bottle of good rye whiskey. The townie wouldn't touch the whiskey and the old fellow wouldn't touch the coffee. So they sat out there in the blind. And they're waiting and waiting and waiting. It was about nine o'clock when at last there was one lousy duck comes flying over. So the townie is up with his shotgun and he fires two or three shots at the one lousy duck. But he misses. So the old fellow, he's up with his rifle and brings it down.

"Holy Moses!" said the townie. "That's a good shot! Can you do that every time?"

"Oh yeah," the old fellow says. "When you shoot into a bunch like that, you're bound to get some of them."[5]

There used to be a Charlie Mahon, an uncle of Harry Mahon at Brudenell. I don't know if he was a great man to hunt or not. But he used to tell some awful tall tales. He said one time he was out hunting in the wintertime on snowshoes, and he shot at a deer and wounded it, and he followed it up on his snowshoes for so long that he finally came out to a field where old John MacDonald was cutting his oats down by the creek.

Now this Paddy Gainey lad, he wouldn't come to church. And we had a mission down there then. Father Kehoe was a missionary priest and, at that time, they used to tell you it was a lot harder to get into heaven than what they tell you now, you know. Now, Paddy Rafferty and Johnny Sullivan,

they used to try to get Paddy Gainey over to the church. And they got him this time. It just happened that this night the missionary priest was preaching about hell and describing how terrible hell was. Then after the Mass and the sermon was over, they all went outside. And Paddy Rafferty asked this Paddy Gainey lad, "Well, what did you think of the sermon, Paddy?"

"By damn!" he says. "If hell is like that, it must be quite a smudge!"

One time the wolves were very bad and, if you shot a deer and didn't hang it up and couldn't get it out that night, the wolves would eat it all overnight, and you wouldn't have it. So John Sullivan was watching on this side of the hill and over across the valley, and he saw this tremendous big buck. He said it had these great wide horns on. He said he'd have liked to have got that big buck, but he knew it was so big he couldn't carry it out by himself before night. It was getting near dark and he would have lost it to the wolves. But there was a doe running ahead of the buck — that's the way the deer goes — the buck will always let the doe go ahead. So the doe came running ahead and there was a tree about eight or ten feet up the side of the hill with a great big crotch in it. And Johnny Sullivan watched there and he seen the doe run up and jump through the crotch of this big tree. And he says to himself, "Here's my chance!" And the buck came and followed the doe through the crotch of the tree. And Johnny Sullivan shot it right there. And it was all nice and safely hung up for him in the crotch of the big tree on the side of the hill.

Kerr his name was. He lived down in the snakepit country. And he married — I don't know what her name was — but she was a Catholic and he was a Protestant. And he wouldn't come to church. They had a terrible long piece to go to church from there anyway. Anyway, she didn't go either. Whether Protestant or Catholic, they couldn't get there. So the priest came in there one time and tackled them.

"Don't you know that Jesus Christ, the Son of God, died on the cross for your sins?"

"Really?" says Kerr. "It was the young fellow that died on the cross? I thought it was the old man himself."

Willie Madigan, aged seventy-three, has memorized literally hundreds of Canadian and Irish songs, collected into his repertoire over the past fifty years. He explained it this way:

I used to like that back in the twenties and thirties. From four or five o'clock in the morning there was good cabaret songs and everything like that and I used to listen to them on the radio until I went to work at nine. Then in the evening it was "Summertime Frolics" from Chicago. I got tunes and airs and parts of songs from that programme. I didn't have no tape recorder back then, but now I have a 900-dollar one, and a lot of music books. Back in the forties and early fifties there was a weekly that came from Montreal called the *Family Herald* and every Saturday there used to be one whole page in there of songs. There'd be requests from all over the breadth of Canada for the names of songs and the words of songs. And maybe if someone in New Brunswick requested it, somebody in Alberta would know it, and they'd send it in.

Willie went to a room off the kitchen and brought back the back issues of all the old Family Heralds *he had saved so carefully. I knew he was longing to sing. So he and P.J. began. They sang alternately, each listening attentively, as if for the very first time, to every line the other man sang.*

Willie Madigan sang this song:
Now Dennis O'Brien had three daughters fine,
The fairest young girls on the block,
And between you and me every night after tea,
To O'Briens the boys they would flock.
When young Mickey Clancey stepped in
to see Nancy,
Sure McClafferty stepped in to see Rose.
And when young Jimmy Kelly stepped in to see Nell,
With a plea to her father she'd go:
"Don't go into the front room, Dad.
Nancy's in there with her caller.
Daddy, dear, won't you stay out here?
Rose has her friend in the parlour.
"Don't go into the kitchen, Dad,
For I'll be out there with my beau."
And since all of those girls have got steady young men,
Sure Daddy has no place to go.
Last Saturday night O'Brien got tight
And he said to himself, "Now, we'll see

If three young galoots dressed up in dud suits,
Can make a wandering Jew out of me."
Out went McClennan, O'Briens and Brogans.
Jimmy Kelly and Clancey felt sore.
He threw them over the stook like an acrobat.
O'Brien will hear this no more:
"Don't go into the front room, Dad.
Nancy's in there with her caller.
Daddy, dear, won't you stay out here?
Rose has her friend in the parlour."
"Don't go into the kitchen, Dad,
For I'll be out there with my beau."
And since all of those girls have got steady young men,
Sure O'Brien has no place to go.

The summer and the winter door on the house of P. J. Ryan at Palmer's Rapids. Above the summer door, to the left, one can see the line going into the house through the square timbers, a power-line whereby that ingenious one runs his televison off his tractor battery.

P. J. Ryan sang the tenderly poignant "One Evening Last June":

> One evening last June and I rambled through the green woods and meadows alone.
> The meadowlark sang so melodious and merrily the whippoorwill's song.
> Though the frogs in the marshes were croaking and the tree toad whistled for rain,
> Partridges all round me were drumming on the banks of the little low plains,
> The sun in the west is declining and shading the treetops with red,
> My wandering feet led me onward, little caring wherever I strayed,
> 'Til by chance I espied a fair schoolmarm who most bitterly did complain,
> It was all for the loss of her lover who was far from the little low plain.
>
> I boldly stepped up to this fair one and these words to her did say:
> "Why are you so sad and so mournful when all nature's so smiling and gay?"
> "Oh! It's all for a jolly young raftsman who I fear I will never see more,
> For he's down on the Wisconsin River a-pulling a fifteen-foot oar."
>
> "If it's all for a jolly young raftsman you're here in such awful despair,
> Pray what was the name of your lover and what kind of clothes did he wear?"
> "Oh! His pants they were made of two mail sacks with a patch a foot wide on each knee,
> And his jacket and shirt were coloured with the bark of the bitter nut tree.
>
> "His hair was inclined to be curly. He has whiskers red as the sun.
> He was tall, square-shouldered, and handsome and his height was six feet and one.
> Oh, his name it was young Johnny Murphy and his equal I ne'er saw before,
> But he's down on the Wisconsin River a-pulling a fifteen-foot oar."
>
> "If Johnny Murphy was the name of your lover, he's a man I knew very well.
> But sad is the tale I must tell you, for Johnny was drowned in the dell.
> We buried him 'neath the scrub Norway. His face you will ne'er see again.
> No stone marks the grave of your lover and he's far from the little old plain."

> When she heard me say this, she fainted and fell at my feet like one dead.
> I scooped up my hat full of water and threw it all over her head.
> She woke and she looked at me so wildly and acted like one that's insane,
> 'Til I thought to myself, "She'd gone crazy on the banks of the little old plain."
>
> "My curse be upon you, Ross Campbell, for taking my Johnny away.
> May the eagles take hold of your body and sink it way down in the clay.
> May your timber all go to the bottom and never rise to the surface no more.
> May all of your creeks and your sandbars go as dry as the log schoolhouse floor.
>
> "So now I will leave this location and I'll teach district school never more.
> I'll go where I'll never, no never, hear the screech of a fifteen-foot oar.
> I'll go to some far-distant country, to England or France or to Spain,
> But I'll never forget Johnny Murphy on the banks of the little old plain."

Ryan's moving rendition led Madigan into a more serious vein and he sang "Now I'm Eighty-four":

> Oh, how I long for days gone by, when we sat beside the mill
> And gazed upon the setting sun as it sank behind the hill.
> I gazed on it once more, sweetheart, it's the very sun we've seen;
> It is just the same now as it was when we were sweet sixteen.
> Oh, how I long for those fond days to come again once more.
> But come again they never will, for now I'm eighty-four.
> The little fish swim in the brook and wander down below.
> They swim until they never will like the dead long, long ago.
> The little meadow by the brook is just as fresh and green;
> It is just the same now as it was when we were sweet sixteen.
>
> Oh, how I long for those fond days to come again once more.
> But come again they never will, for now I'm eighty-four.
> Now the past is past and she is gone. On earth we'll meet no more,

But we will meet in heaven above on that
eternal shore.
And when we meet no more we'll part. In
heaven we both shall reign;
No more I'll sigh for days gone by when
we were sweet sixteen.
Oh, how I long for those fond days to come
again once more.
But come again they never will for now
I'm eighty-four.

Madigan next sang "Robin and Nell":
Come set yourself down and a story I'll tell
About a young couple named Robin and
Nell.
They courted a long time and then Robin
said,
"We've courted a long time; now let us get
wed."
Nellie quickly consented and then Robin
bought
A ring for her finger for to tie up the knot;
Together they went to a neat little home,
For to wait there for the preacher to come.
At last there came a rap on the door.
This was the preacher the fellow was sure
But, when opening the door a note they
obtained:
The preacher would be there the following
day
Said Robin to Nell, "Now what shall we
do?
I've only got one bed and I wish I had
two."
"Oh! I can fix that," Nellie quickly replied.
"Place a chair in the middle, for the bed
is quite wide."
For to show what she meant by what she
had said,
She picked up a chair and she placed it in
bed;
She said to Robin, "Now you sleep over
there,

and I will sleep here — but don't move
the chair."
So, being quite late they started to undress,
And Robin had feelings I cannot express;
The last thing in this world he wanted
to do
Was upset his Nell, but what could he do?
He laid himself down from a long patient
day.
He'd move the darned chair, but what
would Nell say?
Early next morning Nellie quickly arose
And she started at once to pack up her
clothes.
When Robin saw this, he jumped out of
bed
Saying, "Where are you going, sweet
Nellie?" he said.
"I'm going straight home," and she threw
back her hair,
"I won't marry a man that can't move a
chair."
So, come all ye young men, let ye always
beware
The price Robin paid for not moving the
chair.
Remember the saying and it always was
true,
When a woman says, "Don't," they always
mean, "Do"!!!

P. J. Ryan: Yes, my friend Madigan has a friend up
where they let the sun down with a rope and they
raise up the moon with a decking line and a gin
pole.[6] His name is John Foreman from east of Bancroft. That's the gateway to the world, and it's
where you fall off, too. He can play the mouth organ
and he can play the fiddle. He plays the fiddle with
his left hand. He plays for my friend Madigan when
he sings.

8

It's thirty-three miles by snake fence

Ed Hubert's ancestors came out to Canada three generations ago and settled in Alice Township, back of Pembroke, Ontario. His grandfather, a locksmith in Germany, died when Ed Hubert's father, Aldolph, was only two years old. Seeking to escape political upheaval and religious oppression as well to find new opportunities, the Hubert families went first to the United States, where some of them remained. One branch, however, continued their migration up to the Ottawa Valley, where they were fortunate enough to choose some rich farming land on which they prospered.

Ed Hubert was raised on the family farm and at an early age went to work in the Pembroke Shookmills where 300 men then made "everything and anything in wood," cheese boxes, butter boxes, soft-drink cases. As well as farming and working in the shookmills, Ed Hubert acted as a hunting and fishing guide for many seasons of his lifetime. His stories arise indigenously from these varied spheres of activity.

I was first introduced to Ed Hubert by Carl Jennings of Sheenboro, Quebec, who had known Ed for a number of years, had heard his wonderful original stories and knew that I would appreciate Hubert's special brand of humour of exaggeration. Unfortunately, the first time we went to visit the Huberts in Pembroke I did not have my tape-recorder along and that visit, as one might perhaps suspect, was the most spontaneous and richest encounter. Subsequent visits over the next two years never achieved that zenith of spontaneity. Nevertheless, Ed Hubert's stories are outstanding for both the quality of their originality and as prime examples in the tradition of tall tales in the Valley. He can deliver the most outrageous creation absolutely dead-pan.

Like Carl Jennings and Edwin Doyle of Sheenboro, Quebec, Ed Hubert is not just a story-teller and reteller, he is a story-maker. All his life one of his chief delights has been the invention of whoppers or one-liners in which to ensnare his unsuspecting friends, co-workers, hunting camp associates.

As might be expected, Ed Hubert loves to tease and play practical jokes on his friends and acquaintances. Ed lives in Pembroke but has a woodlot out of town. One time recently he phoned up his friend, Carl, in Sheenboro who owns about 400 acres with considerable wood on it, mixed bush and pine.

"Say, Carl," said Ed, "do you have any ironwood back there on your land?"

"Oh, only a little of it," said Carl. "Why do you ask?"

"Well," said Ed, "I just want to warn you to never cut any of it."

"Why's that?"

"Well, last year I cut five or six cord of it on my woodlot and left it to dry. Last week I went back to bring it in. And do you know what had happened to it all?"

"No. What in hell had happened to it?" asked Carl.

"It had all rusted," said Ed.

On the farm where I was raised at Alice, no matter who came my mother would never let them go if it came anyways even close to mealtime. They HAD to stay. But my father had a totally different viewpoint, especially during the Depression years. We often had great big gangs, threshing or haying or milling gangs, at our place for dinner, and they'd all start in to eat, and my dad would let them eat steady for five minutes. And then he'd pass around the toothpicks.

Business section of Pembroke, Ontario, from a postcard in the late twenties or early thirties.

When I was fourteen we always kept sixteen milk cows. And it was so dry that year, the pasture went dead, all brown, and the cows got so thin you could see the hipbones sticking out of them from half a mile away. And my dad said to me, "We'll have to do something. What will we do? If it doesn't rain, we're not going to lose just the milk, we're going to lose the COWS."

And I said, "Don't worry over nothing. I'll fix it up."

Back then we shipped cream to the Pembroke Creamery. Two full cans a week, eh! So, I loaded the cream to take it to the Pembroke Creamery and after I delivered it I went downtown to Canadian Tire and I bought sixteen sets of green glasses and I came home and I put the green glasses on the cows. And that grass, did they ever eat it then! They thought it was green!

This is a true story from the farm. We had the young calves all fenced in behind the barn along the Indian River, which ran through our farm. We had thirty, forty, maybe fifty sheep there and a ram. The sheep all had short tails and the ram — they never cut the tail — so the ram had a long tail. And the bugger was cross. I was five or six and my eldest brother, Albert, he was thirteen years

older than me. And in where the calves were fenced, along the Indian River, we used to go bathing and swimming in the summertimes. It was about seven or eight feet deep — and clear. There used to be whitefish there, the real whitefish that tasted as good as trout.

So my brother Albert got some worms and said we were going to go fishing. The sides were steep in this pasture and the river was deep where we went to fish and the sheep were all in that pasture. Well, anyway, my brother and I, we went to fish and the cross ram was way back there in the pasture. But he seen us coming along the river inside his pasture and he was licking his lips already. He stood and looked at us and I said to my brother, "Watch out! The ram is coming! He's gonna come!"

"Ach!" said my brother. "Never mind the ram. We're here to fish. I'm not afraid of the ram."

So anyway, all at once the ram took off at full gallop and he was licking his lips while he was running. I took off back over the fence but my brother just stood there and watched him. And he was holding his line in and the ram was coming and, just as the ram was about to plough into him full tilt, he jumped back and the ram went straight on by him and sailed out into the river. Way down

78

in the water he went. And then he finally came up and climbed up on the other shore. Oh, it was steep, eh? He couldn't even get up there the first try, and then he went along a little bit further and tried again, and finally he climbed out, shaking his head and the water running off him. And that was the last time the ram ever bothered us when we went fishing.

I can tell you another story about what happened to me on the farm when I was real small. We had all kinds of hens, mixed up like a hound's breakfast. No, no Banties, the eggs were too small — had to eat a dozen to fill up. And we had the grey ones they call Plymouth Rock. I was a little over two years old and the Plymouth Rock rooster was big, so big him and I were the same size in height. But he was cross! That rooster was cross! My dad and mother had a long way to go to get their stuff to the Pembroke market, or to shop there. So, whenever they left, I had to look after the chickens, leave them out in the morning, feed them, put them back in in the evenings. And the chicken yard was all fenced and there was a little gate we went through. When I went to feed them, I had a dish full of grain or whatever we give to them. And I always had everything ready. And the chickens would hear me coming and I could hear the chickens already at the door of the henhouse, and I'd open the little gate and I'd run up and put the dish down and tear back for the gate with the cross rooster chasing me, always chasing me. And I thought to myself, "Someday I am going to get even with you!"

So, it took a whole year to get even with that rooster. The next year I was a little over three years old and I was a little bit bigger than the rooster. Now, my dad used to go in the bedroom in the corner where he had a little knickknack shelf where he always kept a bottle of John de Kuyper's gin in the green bottle. Do you remember that one? Well, he had always had one of those on the shelf. So I figured everything out: I was going to make the rooster drunk. So I went to my mother's cupboard and got some bread, climbed up and got a saucer, climbed up on the bed, reached out and got the gin down, poured the gin on the saucer, put the bread on it.

Now my mother had bought me one of them little velvet corduroy suits with the straps over the shoulders. That suit was a little bit too small for me; I had grown out of it. But then I thought, "Holy gee! That would fit the rooster!" So I went upstairs to the pantry and I got that little pair of velvet corduroy pants. And then to the granary and got a piece of bagstring that they used to use to tie up the potato bags. For, you know, a rooster's shoulders are slanted like a ginger ale bottle. And I knew that the braces on my velvet corduroy pants wouldn't stay up on him.

So I got everything ready, the bread, the gin, the pants, the bagstring — all that would go with it. I didn't let the hens out all together. No. I just opened the door of the henhouse and I let the hens out, one by one, pushing them past the opening, waiting for the rooster to come by me. So finally the rooster came up and I reached in and grabbed him by the neck, pulled him out, closed the door. And did he ever fight! His wings were going! But I held him between my knees with both hands around his neck until he played out a little bit. Then I took some bread off the saucer and soaked it in pure gin. And then I held him and put the bread down his throat. At first, being kind of sober, he didn't want to eat it. But then he got to like it and ate some willingly. Now was the time to put my velvet corduroy pants on the rooster and zip him up.

Now, you know how, in the mornings, the rooster always calls out "took, took, took" to the hens. Well, the rooster called out "took, took, took." But the hens didn't come out. So he picked up the bread and ate it himself. And still the hens didn't come out — they were shut up in the henhouse, you see. So he ate another piece of bread, and another one, and another one. Finally I saw that his neck was getting limp and his wings started to come down. And I thought to myself, "Well, I think I can soon let him go."

There was a big manure pile in front of the stable. I gave him another piece of bread soaked in gin and he ate that. And then the big wings were almost dragging on the ground. And I thought to myself, "Well, now he can do me no harm." And I let him go. He climbed up on top of the manure pile with his wings dragging. And he started to crow. I threw him another piece of bread onto the top of the manure pile. He ate that one. And then he couldn't crow. And I thought to myself, "Now it's time to let the hens out."

So I opened the henhouse door and about ninety hens came cackling out. And the rooster, he was very drunk on top of the manure pile. And he watched the hens coming out and he tried to catch one. He tried to run off the manure pile and catch one but, instead, he rolled down the side of it. He got up and made a dive for another hen. And he missed it. And he fell down again. And he tried the next one. And missed it. I think he caught the ninth or tenth one. He hung on to her with one foot. And with the other one he tried to open his zipper.

I can tell you some stories about how I met and courted my wife, Mabel Rechzin. Our farm at home was fenced in like a cattle ranch and all the big farmers here around Pembroke took their young cattle up there to our farm from summer to fall and they paid us so much a head for pasture. I had to go and watch the fences, see? The neighbour farmers had bulls and sometimes we had ninety or 100 head of cattle in pasturing on our 400 acres, and I had to go in there and fix the fences so that the strange bulls wouldn't get through the fences into the herds. One weekend I came home from the ranch. We lived on Hamilton Street in Pembroke and I walked into the house all black — my hands and face and overalls were all black. My sisters, Hattie and Lydia Hubert — they were twins — were working out in houses for people and Mabel, she was working out in Pembroke, too. So they all got to know one another and my sisters brought Mabel up to our house for the weekend. I was all black and I seen the two sitting there talking and I didn't even know her name then and I didn't even say nothing. I seen a pretty nice-looking lady there and I thought I'd better go and get shaved and cleaned up. I did. And I came down.

Afterwards all winter I walked out to see Mabel in Germanicus. In those days the roads weren't ploughed way back of Lake Doré there and the whole country was filled with them zigzag fences. It's twenty-five miles I walked from Pembroke to her place in Germanicus on the Opeongo Line. But once I got off the highway, holy gee! You couldn't walk on the road it was so drifted and the snow so deep, so I got up on top of the zigzag snake fences. Of course, it was a lot longer by the zigzag. It was twenty-five miles to Mabel's place on the roads. But close to thirty-three miles walking in on top of the zigzag snake fences.

One other weekend I remember I came home to Pembroke from the ranch where I was working. And she was there again with my sisters. Mabel was knitting a sweater and so busy talking I guess you could have clubbed her over the head and she wouldn't even have known that anybody was there. And the ball of yarn was so small, eh! I seen it on the floor when I came down after I was cleaned and dressed up. So I stooped down and I picked up the little ball of yarn and I took the rest apart and I went out the back door. In the drawer we had store string. So I got out the store string and, while Mabel was talking on with my sisters, I tied the store string into the end of her little ball of yarn.

A 1944 postcard view of the Pembroke Shook Mills in the days when it was a thriving industry employing *hundreds of men, including Ed Hubert himself.*

And Mabel and my sisters kept on talking and she kept on knitting. And she came to the place where the store string had been attached to the little ball of yard, but they were so busy talking and gossiping, Mabel didn't even notice that she was knitting the store string into the sweater. She had knit in five inches of it before she ever noticed.

I have some stories of when I was working in the shookmills in Pembroke. This was when the Second World War was on and men were scarce. A lot of the younger ones had joined up and the older ones had left for the deer hunting. Bill Wito, he was the foreman and he had a big mill to keep running and he didn't have enough men. And this young French fellow, he came one morning. Bill Wito was always in bad humour because he didn't have enough men to keep everything going. And the young French fellow came one Monday morning after the whistle blew for work and he called the boss, Bill Wito.

"Mr. Wito," he says, "can I have Wednesday off?"

And Wito got mad right there and he says, "If I have to let another man go, I might as well just close up the damn mill!"

And Wito walked off. He was mad. He walked about ten or fifteen steps and then he stopped and turned back.

"What do you want to get off for?" he snarled at the young French fellow. "Is it very important?"

"Well, not really," said the young fellow. "But Wednesday I'm getting married and I'd like to be there myself."

This is another one from the shookmill. It was Ascension Thursday. Nobody at the mills worked on a holy day but Abby Hoffman, Harold Keel, Lennie Damon and myself had to stay on to repair two tractors that were broken down and had to be fixed for Friday morning. So we had to work, eh? Anyway, break time came. You couldn't smoke on the property after the snow was gone, so they had some benches made for us between the road and the fence. So we're all sitting there with our hands and our faces all black. I wasn't smoking, but the rest were. So up comes this French fellow who works in the shookmills with us. He can hardly talk any English. He's all dressed up, a white shirt and a good suit on.

So he came walking up and he said to me — I was the boss that day — "Are youse working today?"

"Yes. Sure." I said.

So he says again, "Youse are working today?"

"Yes. Can't you see?" I said. "We're working today." I didn't let on I knew it was a holiday.

He said, "Isn't this holiday?"

"No, no," I said, "no holiday."

"Yes, yes," he said. "This is holiday."

"Well then," I said, "if you think it's a holiday, what holiday is it?"

But the French fellow couldn't think of it in English, so he says, "Do you know Jesus Christ?"

I nodded.

"Well, up she goes!" he said.

We all took our lunch and went upstairs to eat at noon. And there was this fellow always sat at our table with us. We sat down and got the lunch pails out and this fellow he opened up his lunch, spread out the waxed paper, took out the sandwich, opened it up, and looked inside it.

"Ah, hell!" he says. "Baloney sandwiches!"

Nobody said nothing. So, anyhow the next day lunchtime comes again and he opens up his lunch pail, opens up the sandwich looks inside it, and says again, "Oh hell! Baloney sandwiches again!"

This kept on for three or four days, eh? Always baloney sandwiches. And he was getting mad about it. So I said to him, "Tell the wife to give you something else if you don't like baloney."

"Ah, but that's just the thing," he says. "I pack my lunch myself."

I have a couple of these lumbercamp stories. My father used to work in the lumbercamps sometimes in the winter. One of them goes like this;

Pat and Mike came out from Ireland and there was no other work except at the lumbercamps. So Pat and Mike went into the bush together working in the same camp for Jake Stewart up there at Rolphton. Pat and Mike were working late in the fall when the snow came. They went out together one morning by the lakes to walk to the place where they were working in the bush. As they were walking along they see there's fresh tracks on the trail of a large animal. Pat stopped and looked and he turned around to Mike and said, "Moose tracks." And Mike stopped and looked and he turned around to Pat and said, "Bear tracks."

They stayed out for a month or so in the bush working cutting the timbers. Finally they got back to the main camp where their stuff was. They had supper and then Mike got out his suitcase and started packing up his things.

"Where are you going? What are you doing?" Pat asks him.

"I'm going out," Mike says.

"Why?" Pat asks.

"Too many arguments," Mike says.

Did I ever tell you about this great big family?

A rare close-up of an old pointer boat used in the lumbering trade. For many years Cockburn and Archer was one of the big businesses established in Pembroke, *employing many men in different plants. They were most famous for manufacturing pointer boats.*

Well, it was all boys, twelve or thirteen or so. This was a long time ago in the olden days when there was only lumbering going on for men to find work. So this big family of boys grew up and when each one was about thirteen or fourteen, he went off into the bush working out for the jobbers and the big lumbermen. One went one way to work and another went another way to work and they wouldn't see each other again for years and years. Or maybe forever. They didn't even know where one another was, you know. But this one brother, Sam, was in this lumber camp working and it just happened one time that one of his brothers, Joe, came in looking for a job. There was no work there. And it was late at night when he walked in and a long way to have to walk out of the camp. So the foreman took pity on Joe and took him into the sleep camp to stay overnight until he walked out the next morning. And, while the foreman was talking to Joe and bedding him down on the floor, Sam, away up on the top bunk, heard them talking. He raised himself up and looked at the newcomer but he didn't know him by looking at him, but he was sure he knew him by his voice.

"By gee!" he said to his chum on the top bunk. "That must be my brother Joe."

So he jumped down and it was. They shook hands and they started to talk, asking each other questions about all the brothers in the big family.

"How's Bill? Where's Bert?"

"Bill's not so good; he got married. I drove with Bert on the Madawaska two years ago ———"

"How's Father? Is he living yet?" Sam finally asked.

"No. Not yet," Joe replied.

I used to work in at the Gatineau Club back there in the Nickabeau on Jim's Lake about fifty miles from Pembroke on the Quebec side. It had about 150 or so members, a mix of Canadians and Americans. In my time I've collected some good hunting and fishing stories from there.

I can tell you the full story of the biggest fish that was ever caught in Jim's Lake. One morning when I was managing there these two vehicles came in, two station wagons full of gear. There was three men and three women. They came from New Jersey and one of the ladies, she was a skinny, tall lady with red hair, and when she got out of the station wagon she was all medallions and chains from her eyeglasses to the ears and all the way down. Gold chains and medallions. And I said to my wife Mabel, "If she's going out on the lake, the first cast they make she'll get tangled up in the medallions and she'll be back."

Sure enough, they were only out about twenty minutes and in comes the boat and she had no more medallions on and the rest was all tangled up, all them beads and pearls, in the fishing lines. And it had started to rain down on the lake and it's seven miles long, so by the time they got in they were not only all tangled up in medallions and fishing lines but they were damn wet as well.

Now the cabins were all heated with oil heaters and the pipelines go underneath the cabins and sometimes air or water gets in and the pipes to the heaters don't go right. So I said to Mabel, "I'd better go over and check on that stove. I bet you it went out again." This was about ten minutes after they got in. And Jeepers Christ! When I opened the door and walked in, never thinking of nothing, there she was bare naked standing — no medallions or gold chains or nothing — right up close to the stove. I only took two steps in and then I said, "Oh, excuse me!" and I took two steps out again.

No, that's not the story of the biggest fish ever caught in Jim's Lake. But we're getting there.

Well, you see, after she changed in rough clothes and a raincoat, they came and got her and they all went out again. At twenty after nine that night they caught this big fish. It took six of them in two boats from twenty after nine to ten minutes to twelve to land this big fish in at the dock at the hunt camp. There were two docks there lined with old tires where the planes with the big Americans came in. So, anyway, they came in with that fish. And you know how the Americans are, how they like to blow about it when they get home — its girth was so much and its length from tail to the head was this many feet and inches, and it weighed so many pounds. So there was this long streaky fellow in the American gang and he came over and he said to me, "We have to weigh that fish." And I said, "No, I don't think so. I don't think we can."

You see, the biggest scales we had in there at the camp was one of them farmer's platform scales that only go up to 300 pounds — even Mabel couldn't weigh herself on them. "You can't weigh that fish here. That fish is too big," I said.

He wouldn't believe me, so I had to take him to the icehouse and show him the scales that only weighed up to 300.

"Well then," he said, "we have to hang it up, for I am going to take photographs of it."

So I said, yes, I think we can do that.

I had some of them double-chain hoists that you take motors out of trucks and cars with. I had a nice long one right at the shore near the dock there. It was nice and clean. So I cut off a twelve-

Vic Doucette of Mattawa, with a trout, caught on Lake Kippewa in 1947.

foot piece, took two ladders, some lengths of chains, and tied them away up a tree, crossways. And I took the chain block and we hoisted the fish up until the tail came off the ground and it could hang straight.

Then this American fellow with one of them Polaroids comes running up with his camera. He took a picture of that fish and the picture alone weighed three pounds.

There was this lake near the club that had never been fished because nobody except me and a couple of others — Roger Degay from Aylmer, Bill Bedard from Ottawa, Eddie Emerson, originally an American but by then an Ottawan — knew about it. They got all excited because I was going to tell them how to get to that little lake.

"But," I said, "there is a drawback. That lake is all minerals, steel or iron, or something."

But nothing would stop them. They went to the little lake and were back in a short while with their limit. Beautiful pickerel. But you couldn't scale them with a knife. That water was so strongly mineral that you couldn't scale those fish. The only way we could scale them was on the grindstone. I would hold them and Mabel would turn the grindstone.

9

The damn best builder from Calabogie to Kaladar

Because of its remoteness and inaccessibility in the early days, the Ottawa Valley established from the very beginning of its history a cavalier attitudes towards the Law of the Land, and a clear tendency for taking the Law into its own hands. It required twenty years of long hard struggle in Renfrew County before the due process of the Law overthrew the feudal system of the Last Laird MacNab. For many years (and who knows, maybe even to this day!) fugitives from justice, outlaws and rogues hid themselves out at Rogues' Harbour on the Madawaska River above Calabogie; if necessary they were outfitted there for a flight to the United States. On numerous occasions the nineteenth century timber trade in the valley has been called "the crookedest business in the world." Certainly cheating, trespassing, illegal cutting was rife and, if the government, and later even the "robber" timber barons themselves, tried to make laws and regulations for the trade, how could laws and regulations be enforced in a vast timbered wilderness? From all the stories I have gathered it would appear that, on one level, the Ottawa Valley was one vast network of illegal stills and outlets. And I have been told stories of revenge castrations, rival clan huntings and killings, unsolved murders that I dare not think about, alone repeat.

Although in a diluted form, this tradition of outlawry is maintained into more modern times in the Valley. It is still told that, during the First and Second World Wars, particularly on the Quebec side of the Valley, whole communities of draft-dodgers were hidden out in the bush. Poaching, hunting and fishing out of season has never ceased as a Valley tradition and is continually played, even today, as a game by "the boys" who will not be men.

Cheating on the government, on insurance claims, unemployment insurance, welfare are everyday occurrences regarded as old stale jokes. I know of people who have never filed an income tax form in their whole lives; others who have run illegal stills for a lifetime. On the roads in the redneck back country I have met characters straight out of the film "Deliverance." Fight-night still exists in the Upper Valley; men are still dreadfully hurt and maimed.

Into this part of the darker scene in the Valley, the image of the sociopathic builder, renovator, developer fits without any real problem. Indeed, just as the image of the hockey hero succeeds from the lumbering hero so the image of the crooked developer may emerge from the earlier "robber" timber baron.

The kernel of the idea for the development of the character of Charlie "Chain-Saw" Channigan was given to me in an interview with some young people in the Valley several years ago. I wore my oral historian-folklorist hat to that interview. But when I got the tape home and listened to it I realized that I had already written about a man just like Channigan. And so I put on my short-story-writer hat, built further the character of Channigan, and added considerable "creative biography" to the original handful of stories. I could not and did not resist the opportunity, in this particular case, to become the story-teller.

Channigan, the amoral builder, may have sprung from the Valley. But his stereotype is national. Readers may well laugh over some of the Channigan stories but also, at one time or another in their lives having been victimized by a man like Channigan, they may contemplate weeping.

Charlie Channigan is now in Fort St. John doing his con jobs. Peter's wife saw him there a year ago. He only stays about five years in one place and then he has to move on. They run him out of town. He was around Carleton Place until about ten years ago. We all worked for him at one time or another when we were in our teens trying to make an extra buck to spend on beer and girls — in that order. I still have nightmares about my part in his con jobs. And I sometimes wonder about the poor people he victimized — yes, sometimes even wonder if they have survived his perfidies!

Charlie was a little guy who always smoked a "cigah" — an expensive "cigah." And he lisped. Lithped. Otherwise Charlie was not at all what you'd expect a businessman to look like. Or even a con man. He was a slob. He bought his clothes at Second Time Round and the Salvation Army. He sucked on his expensive "cigahs" all day long and looked as though he had only half a brain up there. But, all the time, he was taking it in, taking it in. He missed nothing.

I'll tell you right off that Charlie Channigan's gig was that he would buy cheap old houses and do ONLY cosmetic jobs on them before he put them back on the market for sale. And he really did — the rumour is absolutely correct — have T-shirts made for all us lads who worked for him, off and on. On the front of the T-shirts it said "Charlie's Chainsaw Gang" over a drawing of a great big chainsaw.

Charlie was always running ahead of the building inspector. It was like a game of "Cops and Robbers" to watch. Charlie always had five or six houses going at once, being cosmetically transformed, perhaps one or two in town, three or four scattered throughout the surrounding countryside, towards Almonte or maybe even Pakenham. He had to be on so many sites at once, it made it very difficult for a building inspector to catch up with him. He was as elusive as a loup-garou or a will-o'-the-wisp. When a building inspector would finally catch up with him on one of the many scattered old houses he would be working on at the same time with any cheap labour from the area that he could scratch up, Charlie would say to the building inspector, "Excuse me, a moment, I have to go to the bathroom to have a leak." And he would disappear for another three weeks.

Now one of the owners of a major industry in Carleton Place had a really beautiful house, architecturally designed, overlooking the whole countryside in the Almonte Highlands. Charlie bought a strip of land right across from him (can you imagine any council letting that happen? Unless they were bribed, had their palms greased?) and proceeded to put up these cheap pre-fab jerry-built houses. Before they were even halfway finished, Charlie put them up for sale in the hands of one of the real

estate companies in town. What always used to get to me, too, was that the most reputable real estate companies would deal with him.

Anyway, one day one of the real estate men in the company went to Charlie and said to him, "Look, Charlie, this woman is really in a bad way. She had to get out of her house and she has nowhere to go now. She is really going to buy and she wants it by next Saturday".

"No pwoblem. No pwoblem," said Charlie, flicking his "cigah."

"I said she wants it," the real estate man repeated, "but it has to be all finished and landscaped by next Saturday."

"No pwoblem. No pwoblem," said Charlie, flicking his "cigah."

Of course, the whole site was mayhem even as he said this. They were only beginning the finishing carpentry and it was spring and all the lots were a muddy mess with scattered pieces of lumber, cement bags, garbage, strewn around.

But on Saturday the real estate man showed up with his client. Everything was beautiful. New sod. A little rock gaarden in the corner of the lot with a white birch gracefully draped in it. Blue spruce, pine, shrubs around the foundation.

The woman bought immediately for the asking price. But you know what happened in about three weeks, of course. Everything except the sod turned brown and withered down. Charlie Chain-saw Channigan had simply sent his lads out into the bush, had them cut down some small trees and bushes, haul them back to the house, dig holes for them, and stick the trunks in the holes.

Another time I worked for him, he bought an ancient shack of a house in Middleville. There had been an old wood furnace in the basement and the chimney hole — a very large one — came up through the kitchen. Charlie put the kitchen stove in front of the hole and covered it with linoleum. No subflooring, no two-by-fours, no nothing down under it to cover the hole.

"Well, nobody's going to walk behind there anyway," Charlie said to one of his workers who questioned the procedure and who later confessed to me, "My God! I often have visions at night of someone going through that hole with one leg!"

As I said before, Charlie was always two or three steps ahead of the building inspectors. They played games and he almost always won. He would *never* get a building permit. But, he would take — on each site he was working on — a piece of paper, stick it on a piece of cardboard, tear the centre out and leave the four corners hanging, cover it with the usual plastic, and hang it on the wall of the building he was working on. When the building inspector would come and ask for his permit, Charlie would point to his handiwork on the wall.

"Oh yeth," he'd say, "I had one. You can thee what's left of it there on the wall — these damn local kids, you know — vandals, pure vandals."

One time I was working for Charlie on this house he'd bought in Carp. It was the old jail and it had the big thick walls and the bars on the windows and everything, and he was fixing this place up, making it into a house. At the same time he had also bought Scissons Hardware — it had gone out of business there — and he had bought everything. You couldn't believe the stuff there! Been there for a hundred years or more. Charlie gave him $500 and Scissons said, "Take everything." You wouldn't believe the stuff! There was a couple of Rubbermaid display cases, jars and jars of old nails and screws, parts of old machinery. But Charlie thought he would find a use for all of it — someday. So he brought it all over and dumped it in the yard of the house we were making out of the jail. There was also a zillion board feet of old lumber with nails sticking up out of it. When the building inspector told him to get the nails out of it Charlie would always say, "Oh, yeth, yeth, yeth, I'll have to hire some local kids to pull those nails out." But he never did.

As I said before, Charlie was always being hassled by the building inspectors. It was an "in" joke with all of us who ever worked for him. Whenever and wherever we'd meet — on the street, in a bar, at a house — we'd always yell out, "Here comes the building inspector!" and then we'd all run off in different directions, as we had learned to do when working for Charlie.

But finally one day this young building inspector caught up with Charlie in Carp at our building site where we were making the house out of the old jail. Charlie happened to be there, by mistake.

"Let me see your building permit," the young building inspector said to Charlie.

Charlie pointed to the torn and bedraggled piece of paper on the wall, the centre ripped out and just the corners hanging there under the plastic.

"I had one," he said, "but these damn local kids, you know ——"

The building inspector looked out into the yard full of debris and this old lumber with the nails all sticking up out of it. So he invited Charlie to walk out in the yard with him.

"All that lumber has nails sticking up through it," he said to Charlie. "You know that is against the regulations."

"No pwoblem. No pwoblem," Charlie is saying to the young building inspector. "We always keep kids away from the yard."

And Charlie, as he is walking and talking fast to the building inspector, he steps on a piece of old lumber and the nail goes right up through his foot. And he's trying to shake the nail out of his foot without the building inspector seeing it. And we're all stopped work and standing watching this. And Charlie's really in pain. You can see it on his face. But he's trying not to show it.

"No pwoblem. No pwoblem," Charlie keeps saying over and over again, shaking his foot with the nail sticking into it and the piece of lumber attached to him, and trying to hide the pain.

And the young building inspector continues his inspection, never stops walking and keeps pretending he doesn't see a thing.

Another one of Charlie's renovation secrets was wallpaper. If a wall was defective in any way, he would just say to his men, "Wallpaper. Just wallpaper the whole thing over."

He was always making deals that were just short of very crooked. That's how he got his houses. I heard about one time he made five thousand dollars without crossing the room. That was one night at the Newborne in Arnprior. Charlie used to sit in a corner and smoke his "cigahs." And he'd be talking there. And he'd know all the "fahmers." And this one night he bought this farmer's place at eight o'clock in the evening. They had worked at it, and drank at it all day long, and at eight o'clock the farmer signed his place over to Charlie. For about $12,000 dollars. The guy left pissed. But Charlie had the deed. By the time the farmer left, Charlie crossed the room and sold it to another "fahmer" he knew for $17,000, a "fahmer" he knew beforehand who really badly wanted the property. Charlie knew it and he wheeled and dealed all day and made himself a neat $5,000.

Charlie owned and still owns a lot of property around Manotick. Don't think he didn't have any money, lots of it. He was making a thousand here and two thousand there all the time.

One time he bought this huge big lakefront and landlocked a local lawyer who owned property on the same lake. Charlie knew this, of course. And he waited. When the lawyer came to him complaining about the situation, Charlie just said (the way he always said) with a shrug of his shoulders, "Well, it's for sale."

So the big small-town lawyer had to buy the

whole huge lakefront property from Charlie who, naturally enough, charged him enough to make it worth his while, being as he had the guy over a barrel and knew he would pay almost anything. Charlie charged the lawyer so much money on the deal that the lawyer had to divide the piece up and develop it in order to survive financially.

Nobody knows, as I said before, where Charlie comes from or where he is going. But everybody is curious, mighty curious. One day when we were working on a shack at Oompah I asked him, "Charlie, where do you come from?"

"I grew up up North," he said.

"Come on, Charlie, " I said, "that's a big place."

"Well, yeth it was," he agreed. And that's all he would say about it.

"What's Channigan?" I asked him, not giving up so easily.

"Irish-Chinese," he replied. "Way back in the Ping Dynasty, B.C. The Chinese invaded Ireland. A very ancient family we are."

People always wonder how Charlie gets away with his scams. But, to my knowledge, back in those days in the boondocks, he was never sued for all his deceits and deals during the time I knew him in Carleton Place and environs. But, oh my God, he should have been!

Like the time this elderly gentleman, a retired farmer, was going to buy one of Charlie's "castles."

"Does it have running water?" he asked Charlie. This was pretty important to the old man. He was coming in off the farm and, after using the pump and the backhouse for fifty years, he wanted all the luxuries.

"Running water? Sure thing," said Charlie.

Of course, the old house didn't have any more running water in it than the farmer's old house back on the homestead. But right away, Charlie got two fifty-gallon drums, put them in the attic, filled them with water, attached a hose down through the wall into the kitchen taps. So, when the elderly farmer retiring to town came to see the house and tried the taps there was, indeed, "running water."

One thing I should like to mention here because it is one thing that always puzzled me. Charlie Chain-saw Channigan got away with a lot of his scams because he was associated with reputable mortgage and real estate men in Carleton Place. So, some people trusted him because of his association with the reputable. And I guess even the most reputable real estate companies in town dealt with him because they knew they would make money. He turned over houses as fast as pancakes on Shrove Tuesday. And that was enough. And Angus Mac-

Donald was backing him with good mortgages. Charlie would buy a place for $2,000, mortgage it for $6,000, use $2,000 of the $6,000 to fix it up — cosmetically, of course — put $2,000 in his pocket, sell it to somebody for $1,000 down, ask $1,000 down in cash payment, and they take over the existing mortgage. He walks away with $3,000 cash. And he wasn't the only one who functioned that way in the Ottawa Valley building business.

He always had a dozen scams going at once, making one or two thousand here and there. I worked on two or three places for him in one week, one near Clayton, in Lanark, in Scotch Corners.

Shortly before he left Carleton Place, one of the real estate men in town said to him, "Charlie you'd get $1,500 more, maybe $2,000 more for that lot on Easy Street if it were treed."

"No pwoblem. No pwoblem," said Charlie. And sent some of us chain-saw boys out to the bush to cut some trees and "transplant" them to the lot on Easy Street.

The night before Charlie Chain-saw Channigan left Carleton Place, his big place in town where he lived was struck by Jewish lightning and mysteriously burned to the ground.

Nobody knew where he came from and, when he left Carleton Place in the middle of the night, nobody knew where he had gone. A lot of people knew they had been left with substandard housing, bills they couldn't collect and a number of impossible second mortgages. The boys who worked for him — well, we had our T-shirts.

We thought we had heard the last of Charlie Chain-saw Channigan in Carleton Place and we settled down to a quiet uneventful life again. We heard he had moved to Moosonee to work amongst the Indians there; someone else said they had seen him in North Battleford, putting up substandard shacks for an oil company; he had been sighted in Newfoundland. But all the rumours, as it turned out, were false. Charlie had done his apprenticeship in the boondocks and he had decided he was ready for the big-time operations in the capital city of Canada. Either he was ready for it, or it was ready for him. Looking back, I've never been sure which it was.

Anyhow, one night I got this phone call from Charlie in Ottawa. He was into a big housing development there and he wanted me to come and be his "kitchen cupboard man."

"The rest of the house can be klutz," he said, "but it's the kitchen that wins the little woman. In these days of militant women's lib, the men are scared to death to say 'no'. They're scared shitless, to put it plainly," Charlie said. "You're a good kitchen cupboard man," he went on. "I want you to come. I'll pay you well." He offered me double what I was making.

I listened. Because things were really getting tough in Carleton Place. Half the town was on welfare or pogey. In the meantime, I had married, had a couple of kids.

"But Charlie," I said, "what about the building inspectors in Ottawa? I hear they're really tough."

"No pwoblem. No pwoblem," Charlie said. "I've learned what ones can be bought and what ones can't. You have to get a building inspector who is older, corrupted and whose palm twitches. I've got one."

So I went down to Ottawa to see Charlie. He had done the impossible. In the fashionable West End he had bought the tail ends of some of those older lots that were real long, put them all together and created a new cul-de-sac circle, which he called Greenwoods. There wasn't a tree in sight, but I already knew his skill at landscaping.

Yes, by buying up the butt ends of long lots on the periphery of his intended circle, he had invented a new street, had the "minimum requirement" of footage to present the city with a subdivision plan. He had even been lucky enough to have some of his new lots on the north side abutt onto the Ottawa Parkway and overlook the Ottawa River. He had promised to build there only "quality expensive housing" and the city council, dreaming of high taxes on a very small piece of land — indeed, of high where no taxes before had even existed — gave immediate approval to the plan, zoned it A-1 single-family, had the city engineers juggle up plans for a totally inadequate road area.

"What did you have to promise in return?" I asked Charlie.

"I promised them I'd put up a street lamp," he said.

Charlie had also learned a few other lessons, particularly in the advertising field. He had himself billed as "The Best Damn Builder from Kanata to Carlsbad Springs" and he was running ads on both radio and television. He had hired the advertising company that does a famous fast-food-chain ad and convinces the whole world that a mix of sawdust and bad meat makes the greatest hamburger in the world. In no time at all, it seemed Charlie Chainsaw Channigan was recognized as The Best Builder from Kanata to Carlsbad Springs. By buyers, by other developers, even by architects. It was something like the Emperor's New Clothes illusion.

I commuted for a few months and started to work for Charlie on Greenwoods. Oh God, those houses looked good on the outside! But those of us who worked for him looked down at the ground and around and about or disappeared into the park on the west side when the buyers and the real estate men came by. We knew all about the timber so green that it was moulding and the cinder blocks below regulations, and no insulation, and the garage doors and the landscaping.

I was working on the kitchen cupboards in one of the unfinished houses on the cul-de-sac Channigan made for himself out of nothing when the first house buyer came home with a new Gran Torino. He got it into the garage but, once in there, he found he couldn't open the doors of his new machine to get out of it. He could get his Gran Torino in but, when he got it in, he couldn't get out.

He backed it out of the garage and yelled for his wife like a bull moose in rutting season. His wife, who was always on the phone, was on the phone and did not hear immediately his cries of rage and frustration. We saw him heading towards us and we quietly laid down our tools and disappeared into the park behind the houses. Needless to say, one of the second things which the Gran Torino owner did was phone Charlie, the Best Builder between Kanata and Carlsbad Springs. Naturally, Charlie was out of town. The case dragged through the courts for months and finally the *Monopoly News* stopped covering the proceedings. The strange thing about the whole case was that Charlie continued to be acknowledged as the Best Builder from Kanata to Carlsbad Springs. Not only did people continue to say it, but his ads on radio and television continued to say it as well.

Even I got sucked in eventually. It was wintertime and the houses were going slowly — only three had been sold to date — and Charlie needed the cash for another scam he was involved in in Brockville. So he offered me one of his houses at almost cost price. I knew all about the insulation, the green lumber, the below-standard construction. But I knew I could correct most of it. And at that price! I was tired of commuting and my wife was hankering for a fancy-looking house on a cul-de-sac with a low number on it — like 17 Greenwoods. Say, you can think you've moved into society with a number like that one! My reasoning was that I would like to humour the little woman, for a while at least. And since Charlie had established a reputation as the Best Builder from Kanata to Carlsbad Springs, I was pretty sure I could sell the house at a good profit, if we had to.

So we moved in. Right off, the Gran Torino guy never spoke to me. And he had his wife never speak to my wife. But the other houses were selling and we had a variety of neighbours.

I'm no great hand at what makes people tick. All that psychology stuff. But there was something working in Charlie that made him a two-story man. He wouldn't allow anything except a two-story to be built on his cul-de-sac. But since the cul-de-sac was so small — some houses on the circle had frontages on their pie-shaped lots amounting to twelve feet — you got the effect of too-high houses perched on little rises of landfill, leaning over into the tiny circle below. On windy days in the winter, my wife said, you got the effect of toppling. After she said this to me I thought about it a lot and I decided that on very windy days you got the feeling that, only owing to the genius of Charlie Chainsaw Channigan, did your great hulking two-story house stay hooked into its windowwells. Our next-door neighbour, Ferris Fotheringham from the Philosophy Department at Carleton University, dubbed the circle "the amphitheatre." My wife and I didn't make the Roman-Greco connection, as he called it, so he showed us pictures in books on Greece. And then we could see what he meant all right.

I remember the first time Ferris Fotheringham's en suite bathroom off the master bedroom froze solid in the first winter. He knew I had the biggest plunger on the street and he came rushing over to me. "Please come and bring your plunger," he begged. "Our upstairs bathroom is plugged solid."

I got my plunger out of the basement and went over. It was a terrible spot for me to be in. I looked into his toilet. It was as I already suspected.

"Professor," I said, "I hate to tell you this, but your toilet isn't plugged. It's frozen."

"But," he cried out, "this can't be! This is a Channigan House. This is a Centennial House. This house was built by the Best Builder from Kanata to Carlsbad Springs!"

It was six months before Professor Fotheringham got Charlie on the phone — by mistake. And the court case dragged on for months.

Charlie's little cul-de-sac was so well situated in Ottawa and his houses looked so good on the outside — he was a master of cosmetics by now — that his houses were bought by very choosy buyers — by small businessmen, professionals, university people. Babe and I, out of the boondocks in Carleton Place, were very definitely the outsiders or lowlifers. Professor Fotheringham next door described Greenwoods as a "very conservative establishment upper-middle class type of street or community."

Well, it may have been all of that, Babe and I weren't sure. And didn't really care.

But we definitely learned there wasn't very much difference between what went on with those folks and the folks back home in Carleton Place. There was a *ménage à trois* in Number 9 Greenwoods. Mrs. Weatherall's redheaded toddler was probably best explained by the redheaded man who came every Wednesday afternoon in a white convertible. Arnie Askwith, the computer man, really did break his leg when he was throwing his Weight-Watcher wife over their patio railing after a New Year's Eve party on the circle.

It is also quite quite true that Dodie Denton, the dentist's wife, one Hallowe'en got all masqueraded up in a black coat and face mask with nothing, absolutely nothing, on underneath, and came to his door as a caller. When Denton answered the door, she threw open her black coat and said, "Trick or treat!" Doc Denton laughed so hard he fell off the porch, landed on a concrete planter and broke three ribs. When the ambulance came to take him away he was still laughing so hard that Dodie had a hard time keeping the attendants from certifying him on the spot.

And it is also quite true that Chris Cane, the one-cent candy man from 11 Greenwoods goes to Florida every year on the money he made on the stock market. He got a hot tip from a candy-bar salesman that Neilsons were going to put nuts in Sweet Marie. He bought the stock and it went straight up.

We stayed on Greenwoods. Charlie was developing in Smith's Falls and he wanted me to be his kitchen cupboard man there — for the same reasons — and Babe and the kids had got attached to Greenwoods, so I commuted again. For five years or so everybody stayed — all the original buyers in their houses keeping their secrets, the Gran Torino man with the two-by-four garage, Professor Fotheringham with his upstairs en suite toilet that froze every time the east wind blew in the wintertime. Those we all knew about. But when Harvie Garvie, the government man, was moved to the UIC offices in Sudbury he sold to Peter Pontillo, the Portuguese decorator. What was going on in all those cosmetic houses on Greenwoods that Charlie had built finally leaked out. No pun intended.

None of us will ever forget the shock of that night when Pontillo, shortly after he had moved in, blind drunk and looking very much like a Christian who had been thrown to the lions, ran around the "amphitheatre" yelling up at all the darkened windows, "You bastards! You knew it leaked!"

Truth to tell, Harvie Garvie had kept the secret well — who wants everybody to know they have been taken? For six years, as it turned out, the Garvies had run around the family room when it rained and put pails under the leaks to catch the Channigan run-off. When we learned about all this, we finally understood why it had been that sometimes Garvie was seen crawling alone along the eaves at night with a flashlight. Why they had ripped off their brand-new roof, torn apart their upstairs dormer windows. They had never found the source of the leak and they managed — after greasing the palm of their real estate agent — to sell the house on a sunny day to Pontillo the decorator. He put it back on the market in December in preparation for the spring rains.

The house was next bought by Dan Daily, a draftsman for a drainpipe manufacturer. That April everyone on the Greenwoods circle discovered that the house leaked in more places than one. One rainy night when I was watching our basement fill up with water and was running around by flashlight in the dark trying to put things up on boxes and blocks and wondering if the furnace would be drowned in the night, Dan Daily came to my door. He was dripping rain.

"My God!" he said. "Is your basement flooding?"

"Heavens, no," I replied, "dry as a bone."

He turned and fled, yelling backwards as he ran.

"I have to keep bailing her out!"

Randy Robertson, the Fire Chief, was the next purchaser and he, in time, solved the leak problem. He heard from an ancient clairvoyant the house was actually built on limestone caves through which ran an underground river. He tore up the entire back garden to get at it and then, when the underground river couldn't be found, he put a sump pump in the basement. Rain still leaked into pails in the family room on bad days, so Robertson devised a cosmetically disguised run-off pipe — it was an exact replica of the fireman's pole in the firehall — which ran through the outer wall and into the swimming pool which he had had built in the backyard to catch the overflow from the house.

Well, the job we were working on in Smith's Falls was coming to an end, and me and the boys were getting a little worried about what next. Was Charlie moving on? Would we all be out of work? We heard he had gone to Florida for a vacation to look over the deluxe condominium situation there. Then somebody said no, he was going into Quebec where there were very lax building and zoning by-laws and building inspectors were as rare there as an honest politician. Pierre Picard, a guy I worked with who came from Quebec, said to me, "Shit, yes, Quebec! That's where you can still build a cottage on a lakefront with the backhouse on the beach and the water supply to the family sink running through it".

But then one day all our worries were over. There was a big announcement in the paper that Belleville was to have the largest covered mall in North America built at its north end, right on 401, and that the OMB, after sixty-three hearings at an estimated cost of $33,674,123.29 to the taxpayer, had chosen the plan submitted by none other than Charlie Channigan, the Best Damn Builder from Kanata to Carlsbad Springs.

Charlie turned up on the Smith's Falls site one day when we were just putting in the finishing touches on some of the landscaping. I was getting scared about my mortgage payments and their relationship to my not having a job any longer. So I said to Charlie, "Well Charlie I hear the big news about the mall in Belleville. Good going. Good going."

"Yeth", Charlie mused, flicking his "cigah." "Good news travels fast these days."

"I don't suppose you'll be needing me on that site," I said.

"Why not? Why not?" Charlie asked.

"Seems to me that you won't be needing a kitchen cupboard man on that job."

"No, that's true, that's true," Charlie mused, "But stick with me anyhow. I want you to do the plumbing."

Built in the days of the Klondike gold rush, and once one of the grandest inns along old Highway 17, the Klondike Hotel at the village corners in South March has fallen into the ignominious position of being used for storage.

10

Strike again, you son of a bitch

WILBERT IVES, DUNROBIN, ONTARIO

When I taped Wilbert Ives at South March, in October, 1983, he had been living on his farm for sixty-six years. Many years before that, his grandfather, Joseph Ives, had emigrated from England with two motherless sons, Wilbert's father William and his uncle Joe. Grandfather Ives had been a butcher in England but there was no work for him in Canada, probably because at that early stage of settlement people still butchered their own meat every fall and salted it down themselves. The result was that the immigrant Ives family followed a very thorny trail as the grandfather moved from place to place looking for work. When he was only ten years of age Wilbert's father William decided to go out into the world and seek his fortune. He made his way to Torbolton and hired on with a man by the name of Bill Major, who was an auctioneer and cattle dealer. At seventeen Ives found his way "home" to South March, married Evelina Graham there, and went to work for Wentworth Monk, who ranched 1,360 acres at the river front. William Ives rose to become superintendent of the Monk ranch and saved enough to buy his own 170-acre farm.

"So we've been here since 1917," says Wilbert Ives. "Our neighbours at South March were Grahams, Gowells, Monks, Armstrongs, Morgans, Riddells, Smiths, Boweses, Scissons, Logans. At Dunrobin there were Carrolls, Monahans, Murphys, Hogans, Brennans, Reids, Davises. Mostly English in the first place, a lot of Irish in the Dunrobin place."

Mr. Ives's down-to-earth and of-the-earth stories prove that the Irish in the Valley do not have a monopoly on storytelling. Neither do they have a monopoly on the humorous story.

You want some stories about the old Klondike Hotel at South March? Well, it was quite the stopping-place. I haven't got too many. But when you mentioned the Klondike it reminded me that that's where my dad first stopped in after he left Majors. He stopped in at the Klondike and there was a man there by the name of Joe Smith and my dad asked Mr. Smith if he wanted to hire a young lad. Now the old gentleman had a way of saying "By hang this" and "By hang that." So he said, "By hang, I'll have to ask Annie." That was his wife. So he told my father to come up to the house and they went up to the house and Annie decided yes. Now the reason that my dad was upset about asking anybody for work was that he had got an overheat running after cattle and he took some kind of a heat rash out of it and he lost most of his hair over it, and it was at its worst then. But old Mrs. Smith was — well, I guess you'd call her a kind of quack doctor — she could mix up all kinds of stuff for cures. So she took my dad in and cleared it all up. And my dad always said that was the first real home he ever had. Did Mrs. Smith grow back his hair? No. The hair didn't grow back, but she cleaned up what was left of it.

This is a Klondike Hotel story that old Mr. Smith told. Anyhow, this one very dark night it was going pretty high at the Klondike. And there was a pump in the middle of the yard, eh? And so this old Kennedy gentleman walked out into the middle of the hotel yard — and I guess he was very tight — and the pump handle was sticking straight out and he ran right into the pump handle. It knocked him down. So he got up and he stepped up a little closer and he said, "Strike again, you son of a bitch, 'til I find out where you are".

And I'll tell you how that part of the Third Concession of March came to be called Purgatory. There was no roads there then — just trails through the bush you could walk or go on horseback. And the priest must have come across at Quyon on the old ferry to Fitzroy Harbour and then he'd come from Fitzroy Harbour down to South March here. It was a long, hard trip in those days. And after he got to South March somebody there asked him, "What road did you come, Father?"

"Well," he said, "I don't know what road I came on, but I am real damn sure that I came through purgatory."

There was an old fellow around here by the name of Whalen and he stuttered a bit, you know? He and his wife were one time taking a child to be baptized. She was hard of hearing. When they were about to christen the baby she had it on the wrong arm, eh? And the priest asked her to change it on to the right arm but she didn't hear him. So her husband nudged her and said, "Mary, Father Sloan says would you change that baby end for end?"[1]

There was another story often told about Mr. Whalen. He liked a drink, you know. And, when he'd get pretty well on, one of his favourite recitations in the Klondike was:

When I die bury me deep
Make it simple and make it cheap.
On my tombstone I want it wrote
A million drinks went down my throat.
And should you pass by where I lie
Pour some water on me, for I'm always dry.

This is a story about Mr. and Mrs. Hogan that used to live right up the road here. They always kept a cow and a couple of pigs and, come the fall of the year, Eddie Kennedy and I used to go and help Mr. Hogan butcher the pigs. Mrs. Hogan was a real genuine housekeeper. Everything was shining. And Johnny Hogan was a kind of quiet, dry old fellow. Anyway, we had the water boiling in the house to scald the pig. So we went and got the first pig and butchered it and then took the water back into the Hogan kitchen to reheat it for scalding of the next one. Mrs. Hogan was having trouble with the stove and the water wasn't boiling and she was fiery — a nice person, but fiery. And Johnny always smoked a pipe and we stood around in the kitchen for a while and Johnny had the tobacco out and she was poking away at the stove, getting crosser all the time. And Johnny said to Eddie and I, he said, "You know, I never saw anybody that could boil water for scalding pigs like Tess Carroll" — that was a neighbour. And Mrs. Hogan hopped about three feet off the floor and said, "You can go to hell, Johnny, and get Tess Carroll to boil your damned water!"

Old William Penny was a very gentlemanly

old lad. And a bit religious, too, you know? This story is about way back when he was driving a 1927 Chev. They used to go in from here all the time to the Ottawa market to sell their produce. William was a very witty man. Anyway, he was going down to the market with some produce from his farm. Down at the corner of Rideau and Sussex Streets there always used to be a great big policeman there with the white gloves on giving the hand signals — there were no lights then. And this morning that old William Penny went down there was a great big Irish policeman at the intersection directing traffic. The traffic was a bit thick on market morning. And William didn't understand the hand signals and he done the wrong thing. And the policeman put his big white hand up and stopped Penny. And he strode over to Penny's car and Penny rolled down his window. "And gracious!" Penny said later. "That great big fellow just run his head right into my car right up to the shoulders and he yelled at me, 'Are you stone blind? Can you not read signals?'" So Will straightened himself up in the car and said, "Gracious! If I was stone blind do you think I could drive all the way down from Woodlawn and get into a damned mess like this?"

And the big Irish policeman laughed and pulled himself back and said, "Get the hell out of the road! You're blocking the traffic!"

This really happened one day at Dunrobin. There were two families; one was Mr. Ray and the other was Mr. Kennedy. Both of them were bald. But Mr. Ray had a wig and Mr. Kennedy didn't have one. So this one day Mr. Ray went up to the store at Dunrobin. It was a very windy spot around Dunrobin anyway. But this day it was very windy. And Mr. Ray went up to the store and tied his horse to the hitching post and, as he was going around the corner, there came a big blow of wind and it took off Ray's hat and his hair went with it. And Mr. Kennedy was across the road watching all this and he couldn't let it go at that, so he shouts over: "It's a pretty windy day, Mr. Ray, when the hair is flying."

"Yes," Mr. Ray yelled back, "and there'd be a hell of a lot more hair flying today if some people could afford it!"

Old Mrs. Cunningham in here — she was quite the character. And quite the tongue. Of course, she was an R.C. And they'd have threshing bees and so on, in those days. And this happened at a threshing bee at the Cunninghams. The men would all come in at lunchtime and they'd wash their hands, but that was it. Just in to the table fast and reach. So this day they were all in for lunch and they got in around the table and some of them made to reach for something, and Mrs. Cunningham said, "Just a minute. We always say Grace here before we eat." Of course, in a house like that they always crossed and blessed themselves and, of course, they pulled back and she stood up at the end of the table and recited:

> "Oh God of Love look down from above
> With eyes as sharp as sickles,
> And cut the throats of the hungry folks
> That come to eat our vittles."

This is a story about a long train. It's about a fellow from around here, too, by the name of George Brennan. In my younger days I worked on the railroad for five and a half years on the section and this Brennan fellow was on, too. And there was a fellow by the name of Cunningham working on the gang. Sometimes we'd have twelve men and then maybe they'd bring along an extra gang

and there'd be fifty. But Brennan and Cunningham one time got talking about long trains. They wouldn't tell any lies to do anybody any harm, you know, but they could stretch it, oh!

Anyhow, this Cunningham fellow was a fireman on the old Grand Trunk that run through Carp and Arnprior for a few years, but he quit and then he was working on the section. And one noontime they got to telling yarns about long trains and, of course, one was trying to beat the other. Cunningham told about the log trains on the old Grand Trunk that had about seventy-five or eighty carloads of logs — which was impossible for an engine to pull at that time.

George listened and then he said, "By Moses, I saw a longer train than that. I was up in the Mattawa area in the shanty and it was back about twenty miles from the railroad and I got word that they wanted me at home — someone was very sick — and I came out to the station there and a freight

Kitty-corner from the Klondike Hotel at the village corners in South March is another abandoned heritage treasure of the Ottawa Valley, Armstrong's General Store. The store still contains the furnishings and artifacts of its early years of operation.

train came in and it was doing sixty miles an hour and the engine was on time, but the van was an hour late!"

This old couple at Dunrobin were getting quite old, and they were sitting out on their verandah, rocking away in the rocking chairs and reminiscing about different things. And the old lady said to the old man, "John, whatever happened to our sexual relations?"

And John said, "You know, I don't know. We never even had a card from them at Christmas."

_____

After we had talked for an hour or two and Mr. Ives had told many fine stories, which re-created the Dunrobin – South March area in early times, he went to a drawer somewhere and pulled out some dog-eared sheets of paper on which were written two hitherto-unpublished folk-poems, long treasured by the old-timers of the community. They were an integral part of his repertoire because, like most folk-poems, they had been written about real people, many of whom Mr. Ives had known and some of whom appear in the preceding stories. The untitled one about the big woolly ram has some interesting juxtapositions and parallels with the Old Nero folk-poem of the Sheenboro area. Perhaps, just as "Bear" runs through the Canadian psyche, so "Ram" runs through the rural psyche.

Untitled Folk-Poem from Wilbert Ives

Two farmers went sailing along the Third
Line,
Along the Third Line where the wind blows
cold.
They thought of a prize ram so fat and so fine
As they felt in their pockets and fingered
their gold.
"We'll have him," said they, "let him cost
what he may,
If he won't live on straw, we can feed him on
hay."
So they bought that prize ram with his fleece
long and woolly,
And one of them said, "Now, don't he look
bully."
Into a sleigh with a rope round his neck,
They tied that ram fast to keep him in check.
And on the road home they whistled a song,
And cracked a long whip as the sleigh slid
along.

They came to Woodlawn, at the blacksmith's
did stop
As they had some small business to do in the
shop.
The ram gave a "Ba-a," and jumped up at the
sky,
And the horses unattended 'way homeward
did fly.
The blacksmith came out and winked his left
eye.
Said he, "There'll soon be lamb chops for to
fry."
But his father said, "Son, you talk very rash,
There'll be nothing left but soft woolly hash."
Mr. La Furrier, the carpenter, stood at his
bench.
He's a jolly old man, talks nothing but French.
He say, "My, look dat ram, she jump very
tall,
She sure break his neck all de time dat she
fall."
Jack Vance, the sawyer, stood in his yard,
And as the show passed he stared very hard
To see the long bounds the horses did take,
And the big woolly ram trailing far in their
wake.
William James Moore, he twinkled his eyes,
And smiled through his whiskers. Said he,
"There's a prize
For the racing of horses and the improvement
of sheep,
But the two combined makes me laugh till I
weep."
Young Wilson said slyly as it flashed by his
gate,
"If that mutton's for dinner, it's not going to
be late."
And Tom, the bold butcher, so smart and so
fat,
He lifted his hair and scratched his old hat.
Said he, "I can smell fresh meat in the air,
And if it comes quicker it will soon be here."
His father said, "Tom, don't talk like a fool,
Have some sense like a man or else go back
to school."
His sweet sister Jenny said, "Tom's right this
time,
For a streak of fresh mutton just passed up
the line."
When the horses were safely back home with
that ram
It resembled not much but hash-mutton-jam.

Mrs. Weatherdon said, as she scratched her
wise head,
"I truly believe that that sheep is dead."
Mrs. Gray said so calmly, "Oh my, what a
pity,
For that fool of a poet will make a great ditty
About horses and rams and other wild things
'Til the walls of the houses with laughter do
ring."
The neighbours all gathered to have a big
feast,
There was skin, wool, flesh and bone, it was
a great treat.
Now no cash goes for yarn, they have gold in
blocks,
And pick wool from their teeth to darn their
old socks.

---

*Mr. Ives, as it turned out, had another unpublished
folk-poem tucked away in a drawer which he also,
in time, drew out for me to see. This was titled
"The Doctor, the Farmer and the Bullfrog." Mr.
Ives's interview and taping included two snippets of
doggerel and two folk-poems, so we might have
to conclude that either he was very inclined to collecting such rhymes or the South March – Dunrobin – Woodlawn area was very given to the poetic
muse.*

The Doctor, the Farmer and the Bullfrog

A good and honest farmer who near the creek
did reside
Was tortured, cramped and twisted with a
pain in his inside.
So up he got and started for the doctor's abode
Said he, "My dear, good doctor, with death's
shadow I'm bestowed.
I hear you can detect with your instruments
so clever
The slightest cause of any sickness from the
palate to the liver.
And when it goes below that there's not the
slightest doubt
With your stethoscope you'll find it and fly-
blister it right out."
Said the learned and clever doctor, "Carp
village is cleaned out
Of all windy colic, spasms, sciatica and gout,
So now I am quite ready to attend you. Let
me hear the

Latitude and longtitude of what makes you
feel so blue."
Said the good and honest farmer, "I have a
pain right here
And, when I explain, the cause will be quite
clear.
For you see, when I was drinking at the
Constance muddy creek
A lump of something slippery went down me
like a streak."
When the doctor heard this he his stethoscope
did take
And clapped it on his belly and his hand began
to shake.
Said he, "My dear, good patient, your life is
now at stake
If you without my orders any movement now
do make.
There's a bullfrog in your belly and his mind
is fully bent
On tearing out your gizzard or some other bad
intent.
He has one paw on your kidneys and the other
in your maw
And if I do not get him, your insides out
he'll claw.
Now take this little opiate and oblivion will
rest
Upon your mental faculties, which will do
the job the best.
No pain you'll suffer when we get a hitch on
him
And jerk through your oesophagus this big
and slippery thing."
The oblivion it rested upon the farmer's mind
so strong
The learned and clever doctor said unto his
partner young,
"We'll go down to the creek and sit upon a
log
And wait until we catch a thumping big
bullfrog."
They caught a big bullfrog. It had an awful
tail.
The body of the horrid brute would fill a ten-
quart pail.
Away they went back to the house and the
bullfrog they did take
And set him on the table till the patient did
awake.
Then the patient did awake and open both
his eyes

This big and burly bullfrog he quickly espies.
Said he, "My dear, good doctor, you must
be very smart
To extract that big bullfrog without injuring
my heart."
The patient then got up and walked around
unto the door
Said he, "My dear, good doctor, my insides
yet are sore."
Said the learned and clever doctor, "Of course,
it must be so,
For we had an awful job to make the brute
let go.
No pain will you suffer. A week or so 'twill
take.
A puncheon of good medicine I skilfully will
make.
I'll visit you quite often, just seven times a
week
Until I get you strong enough to stand upon
your feet.
My fee for the operation of course 'twill be
quite small
In fact, you'll hardly notice or think of it at
all.
It's seventy-five dollars — a trifle you'll admit
When you look at that big bullfrog of which
you now are quit."
Said the good and honest farmer, "Your fortune
you will make
If you can persuade the people to drink from
Constance Lake
And then charge them so quietly with just
such little bills
For jerking out the bullfrogs that slip down
between their gills."

11

Late leaves and bran baths

FROM THE NICELY PSEUDONYMED NELLIE FINNUKEN

Back in the Fifties in the Ottawa Valley, there was a little string of small-town hospitals where girls could take their nurses' training and garner, after three years of hard, hard work, their coveted RN. Nowadays, of course, nurses in training work out of large and very sophisticated metropolitan hospitals, earn money as they go, and have total liberated movement in their private lives, usually living out in the community. But back in earlier times nurses in training had to be kept by their families while they trained, and therefore usually had very little money; they lived in cloistered nurses' residences where the strictest of rules were enforced — no smoking, no drinking, no "all-nights." The superintendent of the hospital presided over her "girls" like a headmistress in a private boarding school, saw that the rules were strictly abided by, and meted out the punishments when the rules were broken. A "late pass" was until twelve o'clock and expulsion was not an infrequent punishment. It is not surprising, therefore, that many of the nurses in training and, in particular, the more spirited ones, espoused the old dictum that "rules are made to be broken." And, as might be expected, the three-year autocracy in which they had to work and survive melded the nurses in training into a kind of camaraderie and esprit de corps that bound them for the rest of their lives. This is one RN's story of her three years of training in a small hospital in the Ottawa Valley. The names of the people involved and the name of the hospital have been changed in order to protect the innocent — and the guilty.

Nellie Finnuken, the nurse-in-training heroine (or anti-heroine, if you will) of this series of stories, actually began her working career in a bank where she hoped to make enough money to be able to pay for her nursing training. Her banking career, brief as it was, was a sort of rehearsal for her time in training. For these reasons, some of the best of her banking-career stories have been included here as a prelude.

When I first went to work in the bank I was about seventeen and the majority of the women there were a lot older than I was, and a lot of them were old maids, and they had been at the job a long time. And they were very critical of the young girls and they picked on them a lot. My name was Irish Roman Catholic but I was raised Protestant. So one of them asked me one day at coffee break when they were all sitting around if I was related to Father Finnuken of St. Joseph's and I said, "Oh yes. He's my father." Oh, they were mad about that! They didn't like my poking fun at their religion. So I cooled quite a few of them off. But I still had a couple of friends at the bank.

I didn't like the work there at all, so I never pushed myself to do what was called "our daily quota." I was always leaning over my desk talking to somebody, or telling the latest joke, or passing around notes more than I was ever sitting at my desk doing the work. It was War Savings Certificates then and it was all mostly numbers and it was really boring. Miss Methantha Murphy was our section supervisor and she came charging down the aisle at me one day and said, "Miss Finnuken, I don't think I have ever looked down here that I haven't seen your rear up in the air."

Oh, it was boring in the bank! So boring that I decided I had to liven things up. So one time I went to the joke shop and I bought false faces. One was a rubber mask of Mortimer Snerd. Of course, I had been relegated to the back seat in Miss Murphy's section in the bank. And I put on the Mortimer Snerd mask and just sat there. And somebody would turn around to say something to someone and they'd see Mortimer sitting there smiling and they'd just go into splits. Everybody was chuckling and laughing and leaving for the washroom all day long. Yes, we had a good day with the false faces all day long.

At the joke shop I had also bought this little bottle of chemicals that smell like rotten eggs. I always went home on the same streetcar with a lot of the girls from the bank, but then I had to transfer at Queen and go on my way, leaving some of them behind on the first streetcar. So when I got off I left the bottle behind on a seat. They came to work at the bank the next day and told about the terrible thing that had happened on the crowded streetcar. They were all nearly gassed. It was a small bottle, but oh, it was powerful!

Miss Veronica Chisholm was one of the bank old maids who really rode me hard. She was due for retirement — overdue, I guess now, looking back. On Valentine's Day I decided to send her a rotten Valentine. And I did. It had something to do with this old maid praying for a man to be found under her bed — and that *she'd* find him. I carefully mailed it from some remote place in the Ottawa Valley. When Miss Chisholm got it, she just about went wild. She checked everybody on it, and said she was going to have the handwriting checked. She came to my desk and she said she was getting the police on it, they were going to take fingerprints and all that. Nobody in the bank could keep a straight face, and there was once again a terrible run on the washrooms, and some even had to rush into the vaults to break up.

But getting near the end of my banking career — I'd had it — Miss Priscilla Boland, the manager, called me down to her office and had a chat with me. She wanted to know what my plans were for my banking career, and all that. I told her quite frankly that I didn't think that banking was for me. And she said that was good because the banking higher-ups had decided that I wasn't for banking.

"In that case, Miss Finnuken," she snapped, "we have other people we can train in your position on the floor. We will have to put you down in filing."

Now, filing was in the basement, so I went down there. It was cool and nice and there was nobody to watch you. Right off the start I got it into my head that, yes, I would file, but I would make the files more interesting with my own inserts. I was only marking time at the bank until I got accepted into training. I was always a great one for collecting jokes, all kinds of them. So I started typing them up every night at home and filing them in every file I touched at the bank during the day. I filed jokes with the bank's files every day until the day I left. Years later at the bank they were still

pulling them out because eventually everybody cashed in their War Savings Certificates. For thirty-five years the bank was laughing. I know because I have a cousin who stayed and went way up in the bank. She said that, until the day she retired, they still hadn't been able to pull all of Nellie Finnuken's banking-career jokes out of the files.

I saved enough from my banking career to get myself ready for my first year as a nurse in training. We were required to have a steamer trunk, a good watch and an alarm clock. We were measured for our shoes and uniforms, which were provided by the hospital. There were twenty of us in my class to begin with and we were each given an allowance of fifteen dollars a month for sundries.

On the first day we met the Nursing Superintendent, Miss Harkness, who gave us a lecture on the Responsibilities and Rewards, Ethics and Morals, of Nursing. We had a tour of the hospital, met some of the doctors and then were assigned to various wards and nursing stations. And so, shaking at the knees, we began our nursing careers.

Dr. Mosie Hill was a real grouchy old dictator and all the student nurses were terrified of him if they had to work with him. They would stand around, shaking at the knees, waiting for his orders. This one day he was examining a patient and all of a sudden he yelled out, "Get me the head mirror! Get me the head mirror!" So away ran the little student nurse at full tilt. In a little while she came back with the superintendent of nurses, Miss Harkness, in tow.

Dr. Hill took one look at Miss Harkness, threw down his instruments, and roared out, "What the hell do I want her for? I said 'head mirror' – not 'head mare'."

The first time you are in the O.R. you go in and you're very nervous and you try to do everything just right. One of the first jobs given to a student nurse was to sterilize the instruments. You put them all into this big sterilizer full of boiling water and you turn it on. Well, the first time I was getting ready for the O.R. I thought I was doing everything just right. I thought I'd get everything done before the supervisor of the O.R. came in. So I went in and got the sterilizer ready, full of instruments, and went into the next room, busying myself so that when she came she would see that I was not idle. Then all of a sudden I heard her start yelling, "What's going on here! What's going on here?"

I went in in front of her. "I was just getting everything ready for my first scrub . . . ." But behind her I could see — even though she was over six

"The Angels in White" enjoying a tea party in the nurses' residence in a small Ontario training hospital about the turn of the century. Nellie Finnuken and her cohorts may have appeared as "Angels in White" during their daytime duties, but they certainly changed hats for their night-time escapades. Nellie Finnuken, it was said, always preferred Bloody Marys as her beverage. "It's such a sensible drink, because while the vodka is breaking you down, the tomato juice is building you up."

feet tall — that the sterilizer had boiled over and the water was running all over the floor.

"Your first scrub, eh?" she fired at me. "Well, your first scrub will be this." And she handed me the mop.

Fannie Foster and I were a terrible combination. We worked together often. I was on this day with Fanny when a new doctor came to town, Dr. Ambrose West. He had all these newfangled ideas and he had left orders for us to compress this guy's leg, and he wanted it done every so often, and he wanted wax paper wound around it, and he wanted it left so long, and then taken off and more put on. And, oh God! We were busy that night and, along with everything else, we had to do these compresses for West. So we pulled the old standing folding floor screen around the patient — they didn't have these easy flowing ones they have now — and we started doing him. And Fanny started cursing Dr. West to the very lowest. She'd call him every four-letter word in the book and then she'd say to me, "Hand me some more wax paper," and I'd just rip some more off. And she'd say, "Holy God! We're using a lot of this stuff!" And she'd laugh. And I'd say, "Who cares! The hospital's paying for it!" So we got him all done up, and all the other patients bedded down, and we went out to our desks and were sitting making out reports when the bell rings in

The inscription on the back of this rare and beautiful old photograph reads, "Marjorie Johnson (1870) R. N. Bill Johnson's daughter. Lived at Tupper Lake (N. S.) and married Dr. Thessel. No children." Marjorie Johnson must have been one of the first R. N.'s to emerge from the Opeongo Line settlements.

one of the rooms again. There's about five men in this room and one of them beckons us over to his bedside and says, "I have something here you might like to listen to, you girls." So he puts this tape he had done of us putting the wax paper and compresses on the man behind the screen, Fanny cursing and swearing and me saying, "Who gives a shit? The hospital's paying for it." We were scared shitless and we didn't sleep at night waiting for word of that tape, a summons from Miss Harkness. But it never came.

The supervisors would go off and then another girl would come on for the three-to-eleven shift. She wasn't really a supervisor; they just had to put someone in charge. But we knew we could put things over her more easily. Something was on, a big dance somewhere or a party, and we all wanted to get off early. We used to have to work from seven to seven all the time. So I devised a ruse to get us off early. I went upstairs and then I came down on the elevator and I said to the supervisor in charge of our floor, "How come the girls upstairs are getting off early and we aren't?" "Oh," she said, "I didn't know that. If they're being let off early, I guess you girls can get off, too. But I want you to do that bran bath before you leave."

Now to do a proper bran bath, you should mix up bran and honey in careful proportions, apply it to cut-up pieces of gauze, and then carefully place it on the skin of the patient. It's for an itchy skin rash. And the procedure is done in the bath.

Well, I knew I didn't have time for all that, so I just grabbed the bran and I ran into the bathroom where the patient was already in the tub. And I sprinkled it all over her and took off. Well, the bran plugged the drain and stuck to the skin of the patient and the whole scene was just terrible, and the nurses who had to clean up afterwards were torn between cursing and laughing. I was hauled up on the carpet in front of Miss Harkness and everybody thought I was going to be expelled.

And then one day I was uptown shopping and I was just about at the Bank of Montreal corner when this woman stopped me and said, "Hello, Miss Finnuken." And I didn't know her. People look so different, you know, when they're all dressed up in their good clothes after you've seen them stripped down and sick. And the woman said, "Do you not remember me? I'll never forget you. You once gave me a bran bath." And she started to laugh.

We were always short of money. Our fifteen-dollar-a-month allowance was scarcely enough to cover all our "high living" and "sporting events." We finally devised a scheme which I might describe as a stroke of genius on my part. In my year there was a lovely Lithuanian girl named Luvina — she was actually in the end one of the four who managed to graduate. And I had read somewhere about a Landed Immigrant Grant given by the government. So we talked Luvina into getting the application forms. She finally agreed to fill them out — with our help — and sign them and send them off. Can you imagine our surprise when the first cheque for twenty dollars came through? From then on until we all graduated we had a twenty-dollar-a-month allowance for our booze and beer. For three years it was kept hidden in my laundry bag.

At the hospital I trained in when you were in your first year you had a senior nurse in training who was your "big sister." We decided that we were going to give our big sisters a party. There were four big sisters and ten of us. One of the girls was going with a Lynch lad who had a cottage and it was decided that we'd have the party there. We had to get some food and we didn't know how we were going to get it because none of us had any money. We knew that the cupboard at the hospital was always full. It was a big walk-in pantry and it had a screen at the bottom to let the air in. We cased the kitchen and planned our job just like a bank robbery. We thought we had everything down just pat and it had been agreed beforehand that all ten of us had to be in on it — or none at all — because if we got caught, Miss Harkness couldn't expel all of us or the hospital would collapse.

So one night we went over to the kitchen and we loosened the screen. And we thought we had chosen the right one to go through — Hodgins because she was the smallest in the bust and we could get her through the little opening and she could reach up and unlock the door from the inside. But it ended up she wasn't long enough in the arm and the lock was too far up for her. So we got Phillips and we had to put her through. We wiggled her in all right, but she had a big bust and when we got her in we couldn't get her back out again.

We didn't panic. She unlocked the door and we pushed the door open with her in it — she said we nearly broke her back. We had an A & P grocery basket with wheels on it at the ready and, while some of us kept on working to get Phillips back through the screen, the rest ran around and filled up the grocery basket.

Well, we did finally get Phillips back through the hole, but she always claimed her bust was never the same afterwards. And there we were with all this stolen food outside the kitchen door. We put it in baskets and put towels over and tried to figure out our next step. And then we saw Will Burwick there. He was an intern at the hospital. We asked him if he would do us a big favour and carry these baskets for us up to the residence — they were so heavy. And he very gallantly carried all those baskets for us up to the nurses' residence — and he never knew what he'd done. We stashed all the stolen food away in cupboards and under beds. And that night we headed for the chicken farm in the back country. We had cased all the chicken farms and picked out this one that had fat pedigreed chickens, all leg-tagged. And we went in and stole the chickens and put them in the back of — I don't remember now whose car it was — I think it was a Hodgins lad. And we drove up to Holden's Hill. At that time there was an old wooden bridge across it and it was dangerously decrepit and everybody was warned not to cross it. But we crossed it and went up the hill because we figured nobody would follow us there. And the boys killed the chickens right there by slamming the trunk lid down on them.

And then we took them, fresh-killed, to Barry Lynches' cottage. His mother was away at choir practice and we plucked all the chickens in the cottage. Oh, it was just wild! Feathers everywhere! And I guess we were drinking a bit while we did it. And Mrs. Lynch came home and she went wild — she was hyper anyhow — but all those feathers everywhere. She was screaming and yelling about the mess the house was in. So we took the chickens off to somebody else's mother — they were looking quiet and respectable now — and got her to cook them for us. And the party boasted the best chicken bouillion and the best accompaniments that ever were known in that whole country. We got Angela Larose to be our chaperone — we always had to have a chaperone — but she was a good head, and we knew that. So we all had quite a party — Angela Larose as well.

The next day on duty Miss Harkness stopped me in the hall. "I hear you had quite a party last night at Lynches' cottage," she said.

"Oh, just a small quiet party," I said.

"And what did you do for food?" she asked me.

"Oh," I said, "we had donations. Everything was donated."

We used to have one late leave a month — twelve o'clock — and two semi-late leaves — eleven o'clock. It obviously wasn't enough, so I became quite expert at coming in various windows. I wasn't very big then and I could squeeze through half a pane of glass. Stan Marker, the maintenance man at the hospital, was always astonished by how small a space I could get through. He used to shake his head on the mornings after the nights before and say to me, "I don't know how you do it. I don't know how you do it." So I showed him one day. Before he took the storm windows off I showed him how I got in. The ledge sloped and I could walk along it and then I'd just put one leg in and then sit down and get the rest in. He couldn't get over that.

In order to keep me on the straight and narrow, Miss Harkness moved me out of my room with Fanny Foster, tried me around with several other roommates. Maybe Harkness was looking for a stoolpigeon, I don't know. But anyhow I ended up with Hodgins, and Hodgins was a bugger for going to bed early. She'd go to bed so early that she would have to get up and go to the bathroom during the night. So I trained her. You had to go downstairs to the bathroom, so I trained her to go ahead and unlock the side door and then go back to her room. It worked very well. Not all the time. But most of the time.

One morning I had to come in the basement window into one of the student nurses' bathrooms. One of the girls in my class, Richardson, was for-ever taking her baths late at night. She would fill the tup up to the top and lie and soak so she could live through another day as a nurse in training. So this night I came in late, late, late, with my shoes in my hand and crawled through the basement window, and Richardson had left the tub full and I slid right in and went under water immediately. When I surfaced and climbed out of the tub, in my haste to get to my room before discovery, I left my shoes behind in the tub. They were my very best high-heeled shoes, my dating shoes. They were discovered the next morning floating in the bathtub by a cleaning lady, who delivered them to Miss Harkness.

I have very tiny feet, size three, so I was called up on the carpet immediately before Miss Harkness.

She had my shoes in her hand, still wet.

"Miss Finnuken," she said, "a very peculiar thing has happened here. These shoes were found floating in the water in the downstairs tub. I believe them to be your size."

"Oh no, Miss Harkness," I said, my heart sinking at having to deny my only good pair of dating shoes. "Not mine."

The whole affair became a variation on the Cinderella theme as each member of my class was summoned in before Miss Harkness to explain the shoes. But nobody knew anything. And the mystery was never solved.

Yes, lots of things went on, some bad, some

not so bad. But, my God, it was a tough life and hard work and long hours! And you had to have some fun sometime. Sometimes you'd be dead beat, and you'd get off duty, and you'd get all the ice you could lay your hands on and put it in your sink and drop a couple of beers into it. And one day Fanny Foster and I had done this and, my God, who should come into our room but Miss Harkness! Just out on a little spot check! Just my luck! We were as good as caught breaking the "No Drinking" one. But I sprung into action and, quick as a wink, grabbed some towels and walked them over and dropped them all accidentally into the sink. Once more saved from expulsion.

Once a month we got a weekender to go home and see our parents, visit our families and boyfriends — if we had any or many — stock up on some good home cooking after the institutional. One of the rules of the hospital was "no hitchhiking." But we never had any money, so we had to hitchhike. We wouldn't hitchhike outright, but Fanny and I would go along the street of the little town where the hospital was, and we would look in the parked cars and we got we could tell the travellers from their sample boxes in their cars and from where they were parked. So this day we looked at one of the cars parked along the main street and I said to Fanny, "This guy's a shoe salesman." And she said, "How can you be so sure?" And I said, "Well he's parked in front of Reward Shoes and he's got shoeboxes in the back seat." Sure enough, out he came, a shoe salesman going back to our home town. So we hit him up for a drive, and it ended up he lived only a few blocks from where we lived in the city. He said, "I come through every month at such and such a time." So over a period of time we worked out a schedule with the salesmen. The shoe guy came this day, and the chocolate bar man came this day, and the ice cream man another day, and the Coca-Cola guy another.

So along came this weekender on a real cold day in wintertime. As usual, Miss Harkness was at the door to see us off for our weekender. But this time she says, "Are you girls dressed warmly enough?" "Oh yes, Miss Harkness," we chimed. But we were definitely puzzled at this concern.

"Let me see what you have on," she said.

So we showed her. We thought it was getting very peculiar, but we didn't want to ask what was up.

"I'm just asking you," she said, "because I was talking to one of the drug salesmen the other day, and he told me about picking up a couple of student nurses hitchhiking."

Our hearts sank. Oh my God, that guy we hit up for a ride in front of the drugstore had been a drug salesman! Most of *them* kept everything locked in the trunk, so you couldn't tell.

We stood at attention waiting for the blow to fall. But she didn't say anything more. And ever after that we made damn sure our ride to the city was not a drug salesman.

And then there was one time we had this patient — I can't remember his name but he was from Buritt's Rapids — and he had parked his old T Ford out on the hospital parking lot, and when I was in his room I used to look longingly out on his "wheels" parked out here. He'd had this big operation and I knew he would be in for several weeks. I used to joke and kid with him and we got along really well. So one day when I was looking out at his Model T he said, "If you want to take it to get to town sometime, I'll give you the keys." So he gave me the keys and the first day off I got three other girls and I took off in the Model T, headed for town and a day of joyriding.

It started well. We're driving along having a time and, just before we got to the main highway, I started to put on the brakes. But there weren't any. I didn't know what I was going to do. I knew if we got out on the main highway there would be a disaster. So I pulled to the right where Camerons owned this eating place and service station and they had ornamental cedar trees planted there, big ones, and there was a phone booth. To this day I don't know how I did it, but I went right in between the cedar trees and came to a halt. The only thing that was damaged was the runningboards, which were pushed in on each side by contact with the cedar trunks. Well, we went in and told Mr. Cameron what had happened and he got a big laugh out of it. "Just leave it and I'll look after it," he said. "I don't know how in hell you ever got in there. But it should be easy to fix." He took it to Bennett's Body Shop and they started fixing it.

That problem seemed solved, but what was I going to tell the patient who owned the car? I came pretty close to the truth: I told him the brakes had failed and I was getting them fixed. Then I realized that he was due to be discharged. His doctor was a Dr. Robson, a stout, jolly fellow whom everybody liked and who had a real sense of humour. When I told him the story of our predicament, he rolled in the aisle. "OK," he said, "you tell me when the car is ready and I'll discharge him." Everybody on staff wondered why this patient was being kept in so long, and everybody kept asking Dr. Robson, "When are you sending Mr. So-and-So home?" And

he made excuses until one morning the Model T was back on the parking lot. I saw him that morning on rounds with Miss Harkness and he said, "Well, Miss Finnuken, I guess it is time." And I gulped and said yes and Miss Harkness glared.

Another time, Fanny and I had another kind of ride. It was springtime and the end of the second year and we had a day off and I wanted to burst out. So I said to Fanny, "Have you ever driven in the engine of a train?" She allowed that she never had. "I haven't either," I said, "but I think we will today."

Now just on the edge of town near the hospital there was a railway crossing with the big old-fashioned wooden arms, and the trains came through very slow. So we went down to the crossing and waited for a train. We didn't have to wait long before one appeared and slowed almost to a halt. We put our thumbs out to the engineer and he said, "How far are you going, girls?" And we said, "Oh, just up the line." And he said, "OK, hop on."

It was that easy. There we were sailing away with the engineer, hitchhiking on a train.

He asked us where we were from and we told him we were nurses in training on a holiday. Pretty close to the truth again. He asked us where we wanted off and we said we weren't sure yet. The truth was, we didn't know where his train was going, but we were enjoying the ride, our heads out the window, hooting along through the countryside in an engine.

After a while, since we didn't know where we were going or where we wanted off, I thought I'd try him out and ask him where *he* was going.

"How far does this train go up the line?" I asked him.

"Oh, a fair piece," he said, "this is the Transcontinental to Vancouver."

We nearly fainted.

"I think we had better get off at the next stop," I said weakly.

"I'm afraid we don't stop again until Mattawa," he said.

We had to get off a long piece "up the line," I tell you, and we had to hitchhike all the way back, and we didn't get anywhere near the hospital town until near dark. And then we couldn't hitchhike anymore, so Fanny had to phone her father to come and get us and drive us back to the residence. At first he refused. But she told him it was that or we'd be expelled. So he came. Oh, that was a close call!

Sometimes Miss Harkness would punish me by putting me on a long run of the three-to-eleven shift. But this time, just before Christmas, she came up to me and said, "Finnuken, you are going to be on the nursery for another month."

The nursery shift was a lot of responsibility and it was hard work, too, with a whole lot of babies to make formulas for and bathe and change, and then get them to the nursing mothers on time as well. I used to have some fun with the other nurses in maternity. I used to put a girl, a boy, a girl, a boy alternately in the nursery cots. I would look them over and pair them off. "This girl looks good with this guy and this one matches this one." And I'd change them around all the time. And the nurses and students would come into the nursery in the usual rush and they'd just go along and pick up what they thought was baby So-and-So. And they'd get out in the hall and they'd look at the baby's tag and they'd have to go and hand it to another mother, and it made them look sort of crazy, and they'd be ready to kill me. After about two months of this game the nurses would come on at night and they'd pick the babies up and check the tags and say, "Oh, she's been at it again." And they got in the habit of reading all the tags before they took the babies out. They were all tagged, but you got that you knew all the babies anyhow. You'd look at them and they're all different and you could always tell.

But anyhow, Benson and myself, and Supervisor Angela Larose, who had grown to be a good friend of mine, ended up in the nursery on duty for Christmas. There weren't that many babies at Christmastime. It seemed to be a slack time, as though some planning had gone on. And we just were using one nursery and the other was empty. So I brought a little mickey of rye in and put it in the back of the formula fridge and got some ginger ale and mixed the drinks and had them all ready. I called in Angela. "Come on in here," I said, beckoning her into the empty nursery. "I have some soft drinks." So both of us were small and we plopped down beside each other in two of the nursery cots right in front of the big nursery window where you looked in to see the babies and which was covered by a drawn Venetian blind. And I gave her a drink and she then into the laughing. She knew what it was. So we sat there plopped in the two nursery cots, two nurses on duty on Christmas Day having a little Christmas cheer. And I guess we finished it all off.

And all of a sudden Angela reaches out and pulls the cord on the Venetian blind. And Benson was coming out of this big maternity ward — there must have been six to eight women in there — and

in those days you always gave the nursing mothers water, water, water — and Benson's tray was loaded with big water jugs and glasses. And Angela lets fly with the Venetian blind just as Benson is coming out of this room loaded with a tray full of glass. And she sees the two of us sitting in the nursery cots with our glasses and our bottle. And she let fly with everything. Her mouth fell open and she let fly with everything. And there was glass everywhere. And Angela and I just lay there laughing hysterically in the nursery cots on Christmas duty.

The hospital where we trained was an old hospital. Today it's been all renovated and updated, filled with new technology. But in my time there were boxes up on the wall near the nurse's station and the bells from the different rooms rang in there to summon the nurse to come. I was short and I had always to stand up on a chair with a ruler in my hand to reach up and turn the number off. This time I remember so well, this woman was in labour and she was ringing and ringing. We had already called her doctor, Dr. Ford Hanna, to come, and we couldn't do any more. She was an old patient of his, and she had had four babies before this one, and doctors get to feel that they know a patient like that so well that they can time pretty well when they should arrive on the scene. So they just come when they think the time is ripe, and not before it. And I got up on my chair with my ruler in my hand and I'm clicking the number off and at the same time I'm saying to the other nurses, "I wonder where that old son of a bitch is." And all of a sudden, Dr. Ford Hanna, with both hands, went right up my legs and said, "The old son of a bitch is right here."

Miss Harkness allowed us in our first year to have a Hallowe'en party, so we decided that we would get guys for all the ones that didn't have any — blind dates — and we'd all come in costume. In the end everybody had a date through somebody else; we got quite a few of the lads from ———— to come, and they could always be counted on for a good time. There was a punch bowl allowed and, of course, there was nothing in it — to begin with. And Miss Harkness was there with another older woman as chaperones. But we were all dressed up in costume and I mean really dressed up, a lot of us unrecognizable — especially to the two chaperones. And everybody who passed the punch bowl spiked it. And Miss Harkness began to get suspicious but she couldn't finger anybody behind the masks. And we all began to feel really good; I remember they began to walk across the back of the chesterfield on their way to the punch bowl. And Miss Harkness had figured two people would be enough to chaperone the party. But it definitely wasn't enough that night!

And finally Miss Harkness said, "That's it. It's all over. Girls to bed. Guys to home."

But the next morning out on the lawn were piled all these empty liquor bottles.

"No more Hallowe'en parties for the class of '53," said Miss Harkness.

Macpherson was the hospital dietitian. She was quite stout and she thumped. When she walked she went "boom, boom, boom" and we christened her "Thumper." Or, at least I did, and the rest followed. Maybe that's why she disliked me so much. We all had to do our stint in the diet kitchen and one time I was working in the diet kitchen doing my stint when I did something that really upset her — I can't remember what it was now — but she was cutting something with a butcher knife at the time and she took after me with the knife and we whipped around the kitchen a few times. And then she began to gain on me and I was really rather frightened by the look in her eyes and the sharpness and length of the knife. So I went shooting out the diet kitchen door and into the dining room where everybody on staff was eating at the time, including Miss Harkness. I ran past the tables with Macpherson in pursuit with the butcher knife. But then I guess she realized where she was and how she looked, so she calmed down and retreated, and I escaped to my room.

When I went on duty at night the night supervisor said to me, "Oh my God, I'll never forget the day that Macpherson chased you through the dining room with the butcher knife. Do you know that everyone was in splits — including Miss Harkness?"

The following weekend Miss Harkness had off — when I look back now I think how badly that poor woman must have needed time off! — and I decided it was time to get even with Macpherson of the diet kitchen. I got out my Mortimer Snerd face, which I had kept from my banking-career days and I put it on and went into Macpherson's bedroom when she was sleeping at night. She was sleeping on about five pillows and she was snoring loudly. And I had to shake her and shake her until she woke up. And she woke up to the Mortimer Snerd face and started screaming, "Get out of here! Get out of here! I know who you are. I know who you are!" I just kept saying "Ahaaaaaa-ha." Everybody was out in the hall listening to the performance. We had quite a night of it with Miss Harkness away for the weekend. Macpherson, of course, reported

us as soon as Miss Harkness came back, and Harkness had me up on the carpet wanting to know what had happened while she was away. I said I had no idea what had happened; I had been resting all weekend. As it turned out, nobody knew anything.

We had this nursing teacher named Radford. She was really quite clever, but she couldn't teach. She read everything from her notes and she'd put us all to sleep and we could hardly wait to be let out of her class. Now, in my day we had to wear these great big wide starched white belts and a great big starched white bib apron, and it was all tight and hot and uncomfortable. So what we used to do in Radford's class, the last one of the day, was unbutton all this stuff and be at the ready to run because the doctors or somebody on staff would be going downtown — there was no bus service — and they'd give us a ride. Well, this day unexpectedly she told me to stand up and answer a question and I stood up and my whole uniform fell off. She was hopping mad and she asked somebody else to stand up and answer the question. She did and her whole uniform fell off. I guess she couldn't believe it all because she tried a third student. When *she* stood up her whole uniform fell off, Radford fled the room like a hornet. She was always reporting us to Miss Harkness anyhow for something or other. But after this affair she decided she was quitting our class completely. She was not going to teach us anymore. She had had it. We could get our exams any way we wanted because she was finished. And Harkness came to us and said, "I don't know what happened, but you don't have a teacher anymore." And then she came to me — she quizzed us all — and she said, "What do you think happened to Radford?" And I said, "I don't know. But I think we might have laughed in class." We did laugh a lot, you know. And Miss Harkness said, "Well, you've just laughed yourselves out of an instructress." So we never had Radford for the rest of the time, but we all got our RN's anyhow. We had doctors and pharmacists who came in to teach us, and we could learn more from the books than we ever did from Miss Radford's boring classes.

Late in my second year of training I did something terrible — I can't remember what it was now — but Miss Harkness took away *all* my late leaves and she said to me, "If you're late once coming in, you're expelled." I was doing very well at nursing and after two years of the sweat shop I didn't want to get expelled. So I really buckled down and I always made it in on time. And then, my God, this night I was out on a date and we parked and turned the radio on for baffle, and didn't the battery run

In early days in the rural hinterland communities of the Ottawa Valley, the priest and the doctor were of such singular importance that they were simply referred to by their surnames. The parochial inference was that only a dummy would need a given name as well to identify him. These two photographs beautifully document this fact. Simply inscribed on the back of these photographs are the names, Doctor Connelly and Father *Dowdall. Little is known about Doctor Connelly except that he practised in the Mount St. Patrick area. Father Dowdall, born in Perth, Ontario in 1855, was one of the outstanding priests in the Roman Catholic history of the Valley. His first parish was Mount St. Patrick. He then went to Eganville for twenty-two years. At the time of his death in 1927, he was rector of St. Columba's Cathedral in Pembroke.*

down? By the time my date got help and got the battery started, I was very late in. By the time I arrived, all the girls were sitting up waiting for me because they knew about the threat. Miss Harkness had already been in to my room several times and as much as told them all, "This is it! She will be expelled." When the door finally opened, they knew it was me and they all went back to their rooms. Miss Harkness met me in the hall.

"I told you not to be late again," she snapped. "What's your excuse?"

And I said, "Well, I hate to tell you, Miss Harkness, but we were parked and the battery got run down because the radio was on and we had to go for help — and that's why I'm late."

So she just got a sort of big grin on her face — I guess she had had some fun when she was younger, and remembered it — and she didn't say anything more. And I went to my room.

There was total silence in the residence. They were all up but they were afraid to come and ask me what had happened because it was after hours anyhow, lights out. They all thought I had been expelled that night.

They were dumfounded to see me in uniform at breakfast the next morning. They all crowded around and asked me what had happened.

"It was the only time I ever told her the truth," I said, "and I guess she recognized it."

So I made it in to my third and final year. There were only five left in my class. But we all felt that, having made it so far, it wasn't likely now that we would be expelled — unless for some mortal sin, like getting pregnant.

The Women's Auxiliary of the Hospital had fixed up and furnished this lovely new sunroom for the patients and they had put new lockers in it and everything. And one day we're all out there having a smoke — which was forbidden — and all of a sudden word shot down the hall to the sunroom, which was on the very end, that Harkness was coming with a bunch of the Women's Auxiliary to show them the new sunroom. Well, some of the girls got out all right. But everybody couldn't rush out the door at once, so I just stepped into one of the lockers and closed the door. And Jesus! Didn't Miss Harkness choose that very locker to open to show the ladies! And there I was standing in a wreath of smoke. And she was so dumbfounded she never said a word, just went white and shut the door of the locker.

In our third year we were sent to Brockville OH for a month to do our psychiatric training. We got pretty frisky there, being away from home base and the eagle eye of Miss Harkness. Across the border there were all sorts of boys' schools and they used to invite the nurses over all the time to their parties. We had late leaves until twelve o'clock and we'd go across on the ferry, crossing at Prescott. That ferry was a wonderful excuse because we could always say, "Oh, we missed the ferry by a few minutes!" And what could they say? Well anyhow, we had gone to this big do in the States and, as usual, we missed the ferry and we had to drive around by Gananoque. Even when we got in we were all still pretty well loaded, but the other girls signed in and I signed in, and everything seemed fine. Nothing was said. So I was really surprised when I got the summons next morning to report to the supervisor's office. So I went down. I can't remember the supervisor's name now. But she was young.

"You were out pretty late last night?" she said.

"Well yes, that's true," I said, "but we missed the ferry."

"As long as you're in and on time to go on duty," she said, "that's what counts. But you're going to have to keep an eye on the time better from now on."

And she hummed and hawed and was so nice about it all that I began to wonder why on earth she had called me down to her office. And then she sort of started to chuckle and she had the nurses' ledger in front of her where you sign in. And she opened it up to the last page and turned it towards me.

"I have something I want to show you here, Miss Finnuken," she said.

And I looked down to where I had signed in the night before. And there was my name, Nellie Finnuken, scrawled drunkenly across the whole two pages of the ledger in letters about four inches high!

"I think you will agree," she said, "that the only thing we can do in this case is tear both pages out."

We went back to our own hospital, then, for another round of duty there. But we had had such a good time in the States and the ferry had provided such an effective excuse that we were all in the habit of staying out late. And, of course, Miss Harkness and I were into it again over my evening hours. Finally she met me in the hall one day and she said, "Finnuken, I'm not burning the candle at both ends any more waiting up for you."

We were sent to do a special training stint in the Ottawa Civic Hospital. It was pretty wild there, too. One of the greatest things about the Civic was the tunnel that ran underground from the hospital to the nurses' residence. They stored extra mattresses and bedding down there. If you were rushing in late, you could meet your friends who were coming off duty there at, say, seven o'clock in the morning and you could do a quick change of clothes behind the mattresses and go up to the floor and sign in in a fresh uniform as though nothing had happened. There were some pretty funny-looking apparitions on floor duty in the Civic in those days, I remember, like size-eighteen girls in size-twelve uniforms, and size-thirty-six busts in size-thirty bras.

Some of the grads lived in residence and in those days they wore these huge capes over their uniforms when going on and off duty. And lots of them were really good heads who remembered their days as student nurses very well. And there was this really stout girl named Doreen Wallace, and if you were late and waited outside the door and she came along she'd open up her cape and you'd hang onto her waist hidden under her cape and walk up the stairs with her to your room. She was so funny. She'd always say, "Well, just this once. But I'm not going to do it again." But she would always do it again.

In my final year there was a big nurse-in-training

conference and I was chosen to go. You well might wonder why Miss Harkness would choose me. But out of ten trainees who began the programme, only four were left. So we all, by default, went. The conference was held at the Royal York in Toronto, all expenses paid, for three to four days, with the drug companies hosting the hospitality suites. It promised to be the big event of our training period.

On the very first day I was crossing the corner of Yonge and Bay when I heard this voice roaring behind me, "Cousin Nellie! Cousin Nellie!" I turned around and there splendiferous in his RCMP uniform was my cousin Rob! He was with two other RCMP lads. I told him about all the nurses at the conference and he made a date right there and then; said he'd go back and get the RCMP. I gave cousin Rob our room numbers — 812 and 814 — at the Royal York. On Saturday afternoon a battalion of RCMP lads, out of uniform of course, began arriving at the Royal York and passing through the lobby with cases of beer and liquor on their shoulders, taking in supplies for Rooms 812 and 814. Of course, while all this was going on, the girls and I were stuck with attendance at the conference and, worse still, the possibility of a conference dinner that evening. So Marg got sick, and I had to help her out and back to her room. Of course, word had spread like wildfire amongst the nurses that the RCMP was in attendance. And little by little, and one by one, the nurses faded from the conference rooms.

In Room 812 the bathtub was full of beer and ice and in Room 814 the bathtub was full of liquor, soft drinks, and ice. The party began about six o'clock and by ten the complaints began coming in from other guests at the hotel. By eleven the house detective was at our doors. Some of the RCMP lads just lifted him right into the bathroom and began to put the drinks to him. It turned out, of course, that he was from the Ottawa Valley and related to half of us at the party! By twelve the house detective was playing Chug-a-lug with Cousin Rob, for many years the Chug-a-lug champion of the Upper Ottawa Valley. By four o'clock the bathtubs were empty and the house detective was sleeping in one of them. There was no further attendance at the Nurse-in-Training Conference.

I don't know why, but it was the tradition in those days in that hospital to tear the uniforms off the nurses on their last day of duty before graduation day when they got their coveted RN's. Within a few hours on duty after everybody, doctors included, had grabbed me and taken a hunk out of my uniform, I was pretty well in shreds. Now, I had always told them that on my last day I was

going to fly my uniform from the flagpole of the hospital. And they were all waiting, the whole staff, nurses, doctors, everybody, to see if I would really do it. So I went over to the residence and I took my uniform off. And I went up to the attic floor of the hospital with some of the girls along to help me and I got an old table and put a chair on it and I climbed up, with everyone holding the chair, and got out onto the roof through a trapdoor and lowered the flag. And flew my tattered white uniform.

Everyone went outside to look and laugh. Miss Harkness told me to take it down.

"Oh no," I said, "I had too much trouble to get it up there. Somebody else can take it down."

So my uniform flew there on the flagpole for half a day or so before they got a maintenance man to go up and take it down. But by then we were gone.

I went to a big city hospital and got a job. About a year later Miss Harkness sent me a message through a mutual friend of ours.

"Please tell Nellie Finnuken," she said, "that the hollyhocks are growing under her window for the first time in three years."

110

12

The big moose in the mash

ALPHONSE CLOUTHIER, PEMBROKE AND IVERY NEWTON, SHAWVILLE

Since the beginning of the twentieth century, Algonquin Park has been renowned as a recreational wilderness, and the reaches of the Upper Pontiac have been the hunting preserve of both Canadians and Americans. In my travels through the Ottawa Valley over the past five years to record on tape the stories and reminiscences of the old-timers, certain names have recurred as a theme throughout the tapes, indicating to me that I am on the trail of a legendary figure. One of these names was that of Alphonse Clouthier[1], a trapper (illegal) in the park for forty years. I was repeatedly told by old-timers that one time he escaped the game wardens of Algonquin by wearing his snowshoes backwards and walking out to safety at Mattawa while the game wardens pursued him in the opposite direction into the heart of the park.

The trapping and hunting stories of the past eighty-three years in Algonquin Park and Pontiac County, if recorded, would no doubt fill a book and move the readers to both tears and laughter. I have collected only a few here from trapper Clouthier and hunting guide Ivery Newton. When I spoke with them, both men were looking back over some sixty-odd years in the bush; they were then in their older years and when they were only thirteen had gone into the lumber camps for the Pembroke Lumber Company and the Gillies Lumber Company respectively.

Born at Black Bay on the Petawawa River in 1896, the eldest son of Jane Pouquette and Alphonse Clouthier, trapper Clouthier has lived his sixty-five years of married life in Barry's Bay and Pembroke.

I trapped all through Algonquin Park over as far as Opeongo Lake. I knew the whole park like the back of my hand. When I was trapping in the park there was lumbermen's roads. Gillies had the limits then. I met the old Buck Beaver, the old fellow blazing the main road for Gillies then. I said to him I wanted to see So-and-So, but I was just working my way to get past the Gillies men and on my way. These were the lumbermen that I had to go round. The lumbering road was part of the Opeongo Line and we called it the Opeongo Line. It went right through to Bark Lake. I could make you a map of the park out of my head — and my feet. I knew where every beaver pond was, and every lake. I was smart. I trapped one year in one part of the park. And the next year in another part.

No, there's nothing in the park now. Why, there's hardly any beaver in the park now. What happened to them? The bush is all dead. No more swamp or anything. They damned that all up. And all the trees died. And so many roads through now, too. The deer was the same thing. That's why all the deer got to hell out of the park. There's no swamp for them to stay in in the winter.

I'm eighty-six years old. I trapped for forty-five years illegally in Algonquin Park. They only caught me three times. I could outrun any game warden in Algonquin Park. It's twenty-five years or more now since I was last caught trapping illegally in the park so the RCMP granted me amnesty for life. Yes, I knew John Joe Turner[2]. I have a knife here that he gave me as a present.

I'll tell you about one of the three times them wardens caught me. I used to trap for Tommy Skuce, who worked at Murray's store in Barry's Bay. He was no trapper himself, so he wanted to come with me, so sometimes I took him along with me. But there came a year when my oldest son was big enough to come with me, so I took him. I didn't take Tommy. He was no use anyway — all he did was follow me. Anyway, Tommy got mad because I wouldn't take him with me and he reported me to the Forestry. He even sent them a map of where my camp was at Lake Lavoie. I kind of figured he would have reported me, so we waited and we got

111

Spoils of the traplines, Pontiac County, 1935.

to the camp after nine at night. The camp rangers had already found my camp. They had been watching it for a week before we ever got there.

Well, it was the good trapping season, just before Christmas, so we had to make our way. We had a hundred-pound bag of flour and we carried that divided up into four packsacks. Now, at Lake Lavoie I had a canoe hidden. I used to guide there all the time in the summer, and I had this old canoe I always left there to use on Lake Lavoie and on the big lake, Clear Lake. The two lakes were very close. So I said to my son, "By gee, we better not go into our camp by daylight. They're looking for us. I can smell them." So we pulled out across the bay to make the short portage between the two lakes and, as we came along the shoreline, I said to my son, "I think we'll stop and make a cup of tea." And it was a good thing we did because if we had gone over that portage, they were there waiting for us — Iz Dorchurka, Stewart Edie and my uncle, Jack Pouquette. But Uncle Jack wasn't doing anything. He just had to go along. We watched them disappear.

So when we got to the camp that night I said to my son, "I'm going in to set some traps and we need some bait. I think I'll just take the rifle and we'll go up the side of the hill, and we might see a deer or a moose and kill him and get some bait for our traps." So we went there and we shot a moose and we cut up two bags of meat off of it and we portaged it over the bay into Lake Lavoie — it was about a mile — and we carried the bait bags back to a shack we had in the swamp there. There was a kind of trail in — it wasn't blazed or anything — just the odd tree blaze here and there — but they had found our camp anyway. We could tell by the fire and the grub they'd taken. We had killed fourteen beaver on the way in and a couple of otters: shot them with a twenty-two. We cleaned all them beaver and otters and stretched the skins in the shack. But I was uneasy and I said to my lad, "By gee, something tells me they're still watching for us". So we didn't go back into the cabin. We stayed out that night and set more traps. All we took along was a couple of sandwiches. So I says to my son, "I think we'll go back around along Lake Lavoie and we'll come up by the river there where we left that canoe, you know." So we came up. We hit the trail just about 100 yards from the lake and holy jumpin'! They have a path laid down in the snow two feet wide. And they're waiting for us. And I can tell by the tracks they are headed back to my camp for the night. "They'll be getting low on grub," I said to my son, "They've stolen every-

thing I have there, but I think they have some for one more night." It was getting near dusk and we were soaking wet and the kid was getting really tired. And it was travelling in the heavy wet snow and the trees were loaded with wet snow falling on you every step you took — and we're hauling these heavy backpacks. So I said to my son, "Stay here. I'm going to sneak up and see what they're up to." I took the trail and I sneaked up easy and there was two of them standing outside looking around. And they were lighting their pipes. And I was standing there watching them. And they were watching for me. If I had been alone, I guess I would have shot them.

So they stayed there and Stewart Edie said to my uncle Jack Pouquette — one of them was my uncle, you know, and he had trapped with me before he got that job of park ranger. He had learned everything he knew about trapping from me. So Stewart Edie says to my uncle Jack, "We've been a long time trying to catch Alphonse, but I think we've got him this time." And Uncle Jack says to him, "We haven't got him yet."

So I turned around and I says to myself, "They must have a canoe or a boat here someplace down by the lake." And the young lad, this was his first trip in the bush with me, and he was tired. By gee, we went down and the canoe was there, but so was one of the game wardens, Jack McIntyre. They had me pinned and they gave me the summons.

Jack McIntyre, he was a hellion in the park. It was him that caught me. We came out with him, but we didn't give them nothing — no furs, no backpacks, no rifles, nothing. They were supposed to take everything, but I wouldn't give it to them. I says to them, "You're getting nothing. Be glad you're alive. I could have shot you all back there."

By gee, we went over to my mother's place in Barry's Bay and left my gun and packsack there. And I said to Mother, "Phone Edelman the Jew to come and get that packsack right away." They drove us, the game wardens did, down the street to pay our fine, and in the meantime Edelman the Jew, who always bought my furs, he came and got the packsack while we were out paying our fines. They came back to search my mother's for the furs, but I was smart and the furs were gone.

I have a brother that looks just like me, and one time the game wardens chased him all over Algonquin Park thinking they were going to catch me.

Another time, I was making maple syrup at home and they came to pick me up for illegal trapping in the park — three of them, including the

Mountie named Storie that shot that old bugger trapper at North Bay, that Rogers.

I was coming up from the barn with all the kids and Storie slips out from behind the barn and he says, "I've got a summons here for you, Klukee." And I said, "Good." And I slid into the house. I had a bunch of rifles there, well-loaded. And McNeil, the policeman from Pembroke, was there, too. And I pointed the rifle at the Mountie and I said, "Are you the bugger that shot that trapper at North Bay?" I scared him. "Well, don't try to shoot me now," I yelled. And McNeil warned the Mountie: "Don't mess around with Klukee," he said. "I'm telling you, he'll shoot!"

So anyway, they took me. The Mountie was going to take me with him to Barry's Bay by train that day to appear in court. But I said I wouldn't go any damn place with any damn one of them. "Tomorrow," I says, "I'll take the car and I'll go down to the track here at the next siding, and I'll take the train there." So I did. And the next day we're going up on the train when the Mountie says to me, "Are you hungry?" At Madawaska he says, "Johnny Borchat will get off with you and he'll pay for your meal." So I says, "I wouldn't be caught dead outside with you or Johnny Borchat." Johnny Borchat was another game warden. He's still living.

So we went up to the Highland Inn in Barry's Bay which was the headquarters where the trappers had to go who were caught. There was a bunch of game wardens there and I knew them all. So they gave me a room at the top of the stairs, and I was sitting at the top after supper and I could hear a bunch of them talking downstairs and I knew them all. They were saying they weren't strict enough with the trappers. I knew damn well they had all been trappers themselves, but they couldn't catch enough to make a living, so they got in as game wardens. Anyways, I got mad listening to them, so I went down there and I went right up to them and I said, "You, you and you! You were all poor turns in the park, couldn't make a living." None of them even opened a mouth.

Well, the next morning Johnny Borchat was taking old John Yakabuski, an old Polish fellow from Barry's Bay, up for a witness. The Pole hadn't seen me trap, but he saw my brother and his chum crossing the track at the Aylen Lake siding. So they brought me up in front of this judge and asked me all these questions and cross-examined me and all that nonsense. They asked me if I had crossed the tracks at the Aylen Lake siding, but I told them I was at home. The truth. And then the judge turned to old Yakabuski and said, "Is this the man

that crossed the track at the Aylen Lake siding?" And old Yakabuski says, "No. That's not the man." And the judge just put his head down on his arms on the desk and then he slowly raised his head and said, "This case is dismissed." That was poor Judge MacDougall. He was a travelling judge and he travelled through the park.

In those days I used to trap with the Indians in the park. The Lavalees and the White Ducks. The Indians were our allies. We were all the good guys against the game wardens. The money for trapping was much more than the money for working in the lumber camps. I seen me going trapping for three weeks and come back with 2,600 – 2,700 dollars.

Well, anyway, after the case was dismissed, we all went to the station at Barry's Bay — me, Storie the Mountie and Johnny Borchat. I gave Borchat a few slaps that put him in the hospital for three weeks, and I went home that night and I got my packsack and I left early the next morning and went and stayed in the park ranger's cabin on the Bonnechere that night. I broke the lock and I stayed in his cabin for a week. I could see he was illegal trapping himself, for he had traps hanging up in the cabin all over. I used his traps. I made 900 dollars in six days. And I slept pretty good. Right in his cabin. Then when I was leaving, I put his blankets outside and I cut them all into little tiny pieces and I took his traps and I broke them all. And after that we became best friends. He used to beg me to come and stay with him on the Bonnechere and trap, even although he was a game warden. "I have about two bags of traps," he said. "You can use them." I had a notion to tell him that some of them were mine. He used to steal my traps, you know, when he was trailing me as a game warden. "Yes," I laughs to myself, "maybe half his traps are really mine." But I said nothing.

Periodically, when I tape old-timers, I ask them, "What is the most beautiful thing that ever happened to you in your life?" Almost invariably the women reply, "The time I met Joe," or, "The time Bill and I were married." And almost as consistently the men would begin to tell me fishing and hunting stories. Proving once again that

> *Love to a man is a thing apart,*
> *'Tis a woman's whole existence.*

Ivery Newton was born at Otter Lake, Quebec, the son of Eddie Newton and Wanda Rebertz

Many of the lads in the lumber camps were very young indeed.

from Waterloo, Quebec. Both Ivery's father and his grandfather before that, Eddie Newton also, were Gillies men. Mr. Newton's tragi-comic tales begin in the lumber camp but move on to the love of his life: hunting–fishing–guiding.

I was a young gaffer just fourteen years old walking to Dan O'Leary's camp 105 miles in. I was hired by Bill McNeil, who was the clerk at the John Bow Depot. He didn't come into town to hire men; you had to go up there to be hired. And then I walked from there to the East Branch Depot and stayed there overnight, the first night. At Bartrand Lake I rapped on the door and the old boy says, "Come on in. What's the matter with you? Where the hell do you think you're going?"

"I'm going up to the John Bow," I says.

"Well, you'd better have something to eat," he says. "It's a long piece over that mountain."

So I got some tea there and some salted pork, which I couldn't eat it was so fat. The bread was so hard it would knock a bull down easily and the tea was so strong it would twist a wrench. The old

boy's name was Billy Baker and God only knows where he was from.

Well, anyway, I landed in at the O'Leary camp about four o'clock in the afternoon and there was about ninety men in the camp and they were all old boys. The chore boy says, "You'll have to wait now till we get a table for you." You didn't change places at table, you know. Everybody had their own place. So I got me in a corner with this old guy — he had whiskers down to his knees — and I slept with him the first night. The first night it was all right. But the next night I kept scratching and he kept jabbing me in the ribs. I got up — it must have been about twelve — we never had a watch, so I can't tell you what time it was — and I pulled my underwear off and I put on a clean suit. And in two more days I was as bad as ever. But the old fellows there, they'd be crawling along the backs of their necks and they wouldn't even feel them!

I buried my clothes in the snow because I thought I'd freeze the lice to death. The third or fourth night in Dan O'Leary's camp I was as bad as ever, so I thought I'd get my clothes out of the snow. I didn't want anybody to see me or hear me

Caesar Paul, a renowned fishing and hunting guide of the Pontiac. When he died in Fort Coulogne, a few years ago, he was over a hundred years old.

And I can tell you a couple of other funny stories about that camp. Harry Lance from Bryson was making white pine logs and I was rolling them. One time we're going up this long hill when we met this young fellow.

"How do I get out of here?" he said.

"Walk," I said. "That's the only way out of here".

"I've only been here three weeks," he said, "and it will cost me fifteen dollars for a jump."[3]

So he passed by. This was about nine or ten in the morning. Harry starts yelling at me, "Come here, quick, quick!" So we go up and here is Harry Lance holding this young fellow by the hand.

"What the hell happened?" we asked.

"He cut his finger off," said Harry.

"Well, that's one way of getting home," I said. "He sure must have wanted out badly."

So we tied him up with a swifter[4] — I had a red handkerchief — and put him on a horse's back — there was no sleigh — and sent him on the trail through the bush. Later on, we found his finger back on the stump.

You've heard tell of Joe Fly? He was one of Gillies camp cooks and we christened him Joe Fly because no matter what you ate there were flies in it. He was the dirtiest bastard I ever knew and he starved us because he was on a budget and if he saved a buck on our food, he got it. Anyway, years later I was up in the mines and I was in this hotel and this lad came in and I thought I knew him. So I says to him, "Sit down and I'll buy you a beer." And he started to tell me about being a cook in the lumber camps and then about being a cook in the Gillies camp. And I jumped three feet in the air and I yelled, "I know you! I think you're Joe Fly!" And he jumped three feet in the air and took off.

The Algonquin, they were all wonderful guys, pure-bred Indians. Faithful. Honest. I can't say a bad word about any of them. My first year in the lumber camp I was eleven months before I came out of the bush. I came down as far as Jim's Lake with Louis Montroid and Mike Zahodnic, and we came around this lake and went into this shack to visit Caesar Paul, the Algonquin everybody knew from far and wide. The Paul cabin was very small and he had two girls and one boy of a family. Caesar Paul was only a small guy. Louis had known him from before in Maniwaki. We used to go and visit him then every year after that when we'd come down from the bush. So finally I said to Louis, "How come you got to Paul's place in the first place?" And he told me this story:

because the old lads would make fun of me. No light or anything, I dug up the clothes and pulled them on and went back to bed again. Well! Once they warmed up a bit in the camp they were twice as bad — and twice as big!

A Miller lad hurt his back and they asked me if I could sand his logs, so I stayed all winter. You got more money for that — thirty dollars a month — and then we were hired for the spring cutting and we stayed for the drive to Fort Coulonge. Harry Frost, related to the great Larry Frost, was on the drive with us, and when we come to Labine's Hotel in Fort Coulonge he had his caulk boots on and he kicked the boots right to the beams of the ceiling. We looked at that for years and years afterwards, until the hotel burned down. I was there the whole first winter, even for Christmas. The only thing different about Christmastime in the camp was that a priest or minister came in to collect from us for the poor!

There was two tribes of Indians around here back some time ago, the Algonquin and another tribe. And Caesar Paul fell in love with this Indian girl, but she was not of his tribe, so they refused to let them get married at Maniwaki. So they ran away through the bush by canoe, the two of them, and they went until they landed in at Jim's Lake. And that's where they lived the rest of their lives together; raised a lovely family, too. Old Caesar Paul lived to be one hundred and four, but I don't know when she died.

When I was only a kid about fifteen, sixteen years old, one time Joe Mayhew comes to me and he says to me, "Would you like to cook for eight or ten Americans back in the bush for a few weeks?" I says, "OK." So I cooked for them for about a month. The stove was old and the camp was cold — you could see through the walls. I got thirty dollars a month. "Now," Joe says, "I've got another job for you." I said, "OK, what is it?" And he said, "Poaching." Of course, it was the Americans' private preserve.

So we took the canoe down and we set out nets in front of their camp only about 100 yards out from their verandah on the spawning bed. We picked up in the nets in about an hour or so about 100 pounds of bass and pickerel, and we cleaned them up on the shore and carried them out to Harry Wade's old fishing wagon about four miles away. He'd meet us there and he gave us about fifty cents a pound and he took them off to the Ottawa restaurants. He got the revenue, but I was paid by the month, thirty dollars for poaching — out of season. So Joe and I decided to cut Harry out and have the revenue for ourselves and we went back and we made three 100-pound catches of fish on three different nights. Then the Americans' caretaker man, Felix Lance, turned up, so we disappeared. About a week later Joe says to me, "We'll go out and see old Felix at the camp." So we went out there and Felix came out and told us that somebody had been poaching — they'd found the pickets and the nets. "Somebody went into the lake right in front of us," he says, "and I never seen them. Now wouldn't it take a dirty son of a bitch to do a trick like that?" And we agreed.

Archie Oscavell was a trapper up by Jim's Lake. He was from Campbell's Bay. Anyway, he came to me and he says to me, "Would you like a couple of really big moose?" And I said, "I dunno, I'd have to see what my chums say first."

I knew I couldn't pick up two really big moose by myself. Besides, it was out of season and the country was full of game wardens. It was 1,200 dollars

a shot at that time. Archie told me that moose were in the mash[5] back of Jim's Lake about seventy-five or 100 miles away. So I went to see my three friends, Ernie Klukee, Mike Zahodnic and Bob Hornigan, and we decided to do it. We hated to see all that moose meat go to waste.

So we took two vehicles and our liquor and we went to a place on the Coulonge River and we put in our canoes and got the moose. We cut them all up, no bones or anything, and paddled back to the banks of the Coulonge below our cars. But the banks there were fifty feet high and we were half-drunk by then, so we couldn't pack the meat up the banks. We pulled it all up by ropes and it was covered with sand and pine needles and all kinds of stuff.

Then we discussed who was going to take the shot if we got caught. "OK, I'll take the shot but everybody pays." So the other three agreed to pay their share, too, about 300 dollars each.

Well, we're coming down the Black River road with all this moose meat. And we come to Dempsey's Stopping-Place. It's still there and it's on a hill and you have to go up to park, and we saw the game wardens' cars parked there — Bert Horner and Jim Quinn and Leo Bertrand. And my three friends went up to have a drink with the game wardens and keep them busy while I slipped by in my car with the moose meat, and went on home. But somebody squealed on us and my three friends caught up to me and told me the game wardens were on our trail. So the four of us, we took the moose meat and we hung it on the trees. From Fort Coulonge to Campbell's Bay, from Shawville to Otter Lake, the trees were hung with pieces of those two really big moose.

Forty years ago me and my friend, Mike Zahodnick from Bryson, decided that we would go up and fish in Gillies's preserve. That was forbidden. You weren't allowed to hunt or fish on the Gillies, and there was a gate there with a caretaker who checked out everybody who went through. This was in the hunting season, so they were being even more careful. The caretaker was Bill Butler from Buckingham, Quebec — he knew me because I'd worked with him in the camp — and Harry Nelson, the foreman, was from Buckingham, too. So Butler says at the gate to Mike and me, "Where are you guys going?" And I said, "This is a fur buyer from Aylmer and we're going up to see Archie Oscavell, the trapper, to buy his furs." "Well," says Butler, "I can't stop a fur buyer from going in to buy his furs." So we went up as far as we could in the old car and Harry Nelson, the foreman, comes along and he says, "Where are you guys going?" "We're going in to buy Archie Oscavell's furs," we tell him. So he asks us into the camp and we sit around the table and killed a bottle and had supper with him. We shot the line there all night. Harry asked me about my friend the fur buyer and I told him he was Mr. Edelman from Aylmer — and poor Mike could hardly keep a straight face there, especially because of all the liquor we had drunk. And the next day we killed a deer, shot some partridge, caught some fish, and came back down to the gate. "Well," Butler says, "did you find Archie?"

I says, "Yes."

He looks at our bags in the car, full of Gillies's preserve game. "It looks like your trapper friend had a pretty good catch of furs," he says.

"Yes," I says, "he had a lot of fur and we had a good trip out of it."

And we did.

I'll never forget this as long as I live. When I was only a kid about so high and Bob Simpson was a very old man, he came into our lake — Otter Lake — on his wagon, and my dad says to him, "Did you do any fishing at Indian Lake, Bob?" It's called Vennard Lake now and it's about 100 miles from Shawville. "Yes," Bob says to my dad, "some real good fishing there. I backed the horses up and I backed the wagon up right into the water. And I tied them up to a tree and I threw a line in. And the first thing I seen the wagon was up to the hubs in water. It was full of pike! So I turned and hitched the horses to a whippletree and I pulled fish out 'til four o'clock. And then I tied the wagon to a tree and I came back and pulled the rest of the fish out the next day."

Some pretty funny things have happened with me and the American hunters in the bush. I was at Campbell's Bay this time in the moose season and the wife and I, we had got our moose and we were in the restaurant at Campbell's Bay when these two Americans tracked me down. They wanted a moose. They talked me into it. Anyway, we went up to the camp at the Hog's Back Bay. I thought I saw this moose, so I went to tell the Americans. "There

A ghostly hunter of the past posed on another ghost of the past — an old stump fence.

118

may be a moose over there. I'm not promising it, but you stay here." I wanted to see what the moose was up to because they were a bit scared of it. Anyway, I wasn't away five minutes until I heard "bang, bang!" And about ten minutes later I see this damn moose coming through the bush with this red jacket swinging from a horn.

These crazy Americans! They'd knocked the moose down, but they hadn't killed him. And one of them had a movie camera and they wanted to take a picture of their moose. So one fellow, he got on the moose's back and the other fellow takes off his red jacket and puts it on one horn and his rifle on the other horn. And the moose comes to and takes off! And the moose comes down to me and I could see this red jacket swinging. "Jesus!" I thought. "We've got a dead man!" So I had to wait until the moose got in range and then I shot him. And I thought, "If I ever get out of this jam, never, never again Americans."

I ran into the bush to where I thought they were, shouting to them and nobody answered. And I ran back to the camp, shouting, but nobody answered. I went back to the bush to look for them. Nobody answered. By that time it was starting to get dusk. I went back to the camp. This time I could hear something upstairs going bump, bump, bump. I said, "Is there somebody there?" "Is that you, Newton?" the voice came back. "Yes, what in hell happened? What in hell are you upstairs for?" I shouted at them. "We're afraid of the moose," they said. After a while they came downstairs, "What the hell happened?" I asked. One of them said, "I'll tell you what happened. We knocked the moose out with the first shot and I got on its back so we could take a nice movie picture. The moose got up and we ran."

They never found the camera or the rifle and they never came back — never.

Well, I've had some lovely times in my life fishing for trout and hunting for moose. One time Joe Mayhew and I went up — you know, Joe Mayhew? You must know Joe Mayhew — he was half Indian and half French but always one of the boys and a good friend of mine. He was a good poacher, too, and I used to love that, you understand? Anyway, Joe Mayhew and I went up and got our moose this year and came down and we were in the restaurant in Campbell's Bay and Bob Horty said to us that two American doctors had been in, dying for a moose, and where did we get ours? So I'm sitting there and the two American doctors come in, all dressed up and everything and they say to me, "Do you know Bob Killer?" And I say, "Yes,

he's a good friend of mine for twenty years." And they say, "Well, he promised us that you would get us a moose. We want to hunt moose. We can't go back without a moose." "Well," I says, "I've just come down from moose hunting for two weeks and I'm tired."

They begged and they had money, and I didn't want to let Bob Killer down. So I went to see my friend, Joe Mayhew. "Come on," I said to him, "they want to go. We'll go along and have some fun."

I sent the two Americans up to Fort Coulonge to get their licences and we left Friday about four for Gale Lake. There was a bunch of French guys working in there; they wouldn't speak English, but they told me that there was about three big moose in the mash. And it's a rainy evening.

I lay down to catch up on my sleep but the Americans kept at me: "When are we going to hunt? When are we going to hunt?" So finally I got up and had some tea and said to the two Americans, "Let's go!" And we started off on the craziest goddam hunting expedition I ever was on. We drove about a mile and a half down the road to where the French guys had told us there were three moose in the mash. And I said to Joe Mayhew, "I'm not going in there. You go in with the guys." So the three of them went in behind a pulp pile right on the side of the lake and I stayed behind with the flashlight on the water. These two Americans, they were going to do the shooting. Joe left his rifle in the trunk of the car. So Joe made a moose call and I heard the moose coming down through the swamp, bawling and howling. And I'm waiting for some shooting and waiting for some shooting. "Jesus! What the hell's going on?" I thought to myself. So anyway, I hear the plinks and plonks in the water of the moose coming closer and closer and still no shots from the Americans. And then all of a sudden, there is one at my elbow. "Would you turn down the flashlight," he says. So I turned down the flash. And then the other American is there beside me, "Would you turn up the lights on the car?" he says. So I pulled the lights on. They are both standing there shaking. All right there and then, they stripped off their pants and threw them into the bush. Instead of shooting, they had both shit their pants when they seen that moose come through the mash and right up to them!

So they washed themselves off and put on a change of some kind of clothes and came back. "Aha," one of them says, "we'll pull out the bottle now and have a good drink. We've had a good hunt and now we're going home." They were both still shaking. "Oh no," I says, "we came here for a moose. And we're going to get one."

Now, I knew Ivan Harris of Shawville was coming into the lake the next morning with his plane. It was heavy fog, but right on time about nine o'clock he came in and landed. I says to him, "Do you want to take me up for about five minutes?" He says, "Sure." It was about thirty-five dollars for five minutes. He took me up the creek at Gale Lake and there, sure enough, was a great big bull moose. So we came back down and the Americans were still shaking. So I says to them, "Well, I've found your moose." "Oh, no," says one of the Americans, "I don't think we're going hunting any more. We're going home to New York City."

But one American does decide to stay with it. We drive about twenty miles to the other side of the lake. And the American says, "What'll I do if a moose comes out here? What's it going to do to me?" And I said to him, "Shoot the goddam thing! Christ! You've got a gun!"

So we pulled out the canoe and I got into the bow and Joe got into the back and we put the American in the middle. And I had my rifle there. "Look," I said to the American, "don't you move until I make the sign. Then you do it. It's your moose!" So we're paddling and paddling through the mash and through the fog — can't see a thing. And all of a sudden the sun breaks through and there he is right in front of us, eating the lily pads, and his head came up, and when I seen the size of those horns my stomach turned over. I said to myself, "If I lose that fellow, I'll shoot myself!"

We stopped paddling and stayed quiet. The moose's head goes down again into the lily pads. We start the paddling again but the moose's head goes up. He senses something. "Joe", I whispered, "you can't go no further." So we pulled into shore and we're about 300 yards from the moose and I give the signal. The American had a .306, and all I had was my 30-30. So he started shooting and every bullet was hitting the ground. And I yells at him, "Jesus! All your bullets are hitting the ground!" "They are not," he says. "They are so!" I says.

So the moose was going to get away on us. So I say to Joe, "Joe, I'm going to try him with my rifle!" I got him in the front shoulder but he didn't even flinch. Then Joe fired and I fired again, and the moose went down. We got the moose. He was in the mud. We paddled up to him. We couldn't budge him.

The American, still shaking, says, "Can I have a smoke?" "You can shout, cheer, have a smoke, do whatever you want to do," I says to him. "It's all

over." So he went to put his cigar in his mouth and I noticed he had no teeth. "What the hell happened to all your teeth?" I asked him. And he says, "I lost my plates when I was shooting back there." So we paddled back and tried to find the American's teeth in the mash, but we couldn't. And he'd lost one rubber boot, too. And we tried to find that, but we couldn't. And we tried to raise the moose out of the mash again, but we couldn't.

There was a timber jack working at the top of the mountain there that day about two miles back. I could hear him, but I'd never been through that part of the country before. So I says to Joe, "You go back to the truck — and take this hunter with you — and I'll get to the timber jack." I figured I could hit him if he didn't quit on me. Joe says, "I'll wait here in case something happens. I'll keep shooting and, if you think you're going to get lost, it will bring you back here." So I trudged through the swamp and about an hour and a half going up to where the timber jack was working. So I says to him, "Have you got a horse up here?" He says to me, "Was that you and your friends doing all the shooting down there?" I says, "Yeah, and we have this moose stuck in the mash."

Well, the timber jack has better than a horse; he has a skidder. He says, sure, he'll go and get the moose out of the mash for us. "Hop on," he says to me. So I jumped on his skidder. Jesus! He was going straight through that bush, knocking down trees that size! I couldn't stay on, so I jumped off the skidder. He went ahead and strung a cable and pulled out the moose. Seventy-two and a half spread! He weighed around 1,800 pounds and the timber jack brought him right out to where we had my truck.

So the Americans finally got their moose!

The real hunting lads from Shawville! They are posed in front of their rough-and-ready hunt camp on the Pickanock River in the 1920s. From left to right: Bill Elliott, some Klukees (Clouthiers) and Lepaques and Ned Finnigan.

1. Throughout the Pembroke area the French name "Cloutier" has been anglicized to "Klukee."
2. John Joe Turner was one of the most famous of the Algonquin Park guides.
3. To "jump camp" is to leave camp before one's contract is completed.
4. A "swifter" is a tourniquet.
5. "Mash" is a Pontiac County colloquialism for "swamp."

Along its seven hundred and fifty mile course from Lake Capimichigama in Northern Quebec, through the mining north, down to its entry into the St. Lawrence near Montreal, the Ottawa River Valley in both Ontario and Quebec was the cradle of hockey for North America. Judging by the trophies in front of the group, this is obviously a photograph of a collection of winners taken in Fort Coulonge, Quebec, 1930's. Three of the team were Davis brothers.

13

Disturbing the piece

I maintain that the Ottawa Valley is one of the last great seeding grounds of the storytelling tradition in Canada. I am sure, too, that the tale-bearers, chroniclers and legend-makers still survive in staunch numbers in remote places such as Cape Breton Island, Newfoundland and the Klondike. But in the Valley during my tapings and interviews over the past five years, I can honestly say that I have very rarely gone into a rural kitchen where the people there have not been quick to turn off the radio or the television. I consider this proof that many country people would still rather talk face to face to someone they know, about someone they know, or even to someone they don't know, rather than sit in the sealed tomb of silence that is the spectator role.

In the spring of 1983 I spent several Saturday afternoons around a kitchen table with Pierre, Jean-Paul and Hank, all young raconteurs of Renfrew County.

For me they were an exciting discovery, for they were maintaining a story-making tradition handed down from their grandfathers and great-grandfathers, while the patterning of Hank's story-telling expertise winds itself back into ancestors untold.

The stories of Pierre, Jean-Paul and Hank all tend to be true slapstick-type tales, situational humour spun out of their memories, out of exaggerations of their own experiences in growing up in the Valley, and out of their inherited ability to laugh at themselves. These young people are a different generation from most of the other storytellers in this book. Although they were all into their third decade of life in the Valley, in their adolescence they had belonged to the guitar-playing, hitchhiking, grass-addicted, anti-money, anti-work, protesting, sexually liberated, wildly experimental inheritors of the Sixties.

To make matters more complex and to widen the generation gap, there was a new language to go with the new lifestyle. "Aw shucks" and "Gee whiz" of the older generations had given way to constant everyday usage of explicit four-letter words and formerly prohibited cursing and swearing — in the Anglo-Saxons all related to sexual repression, and in the Canadians of French descent all related to the holy sacraments of the Roman Catholic Church.

Apart from youthful enthusiasm, the tempo of the language is much speeded up from that, let me say, of the gentle tongue-in-cheek stories of Billy James, aged ninety, of Carleton Place; or of P.J. Ryan of Palmer's Rapids, who still chews snuff and has no electricity in his log house. One is still horse-and-buggy language while Pierre, Jean-Paul and Hank's lingo is of young people coming out of drugs and headed into space.

The generation of the Fat Sixties was able to be constantly "on the move." Many of the young people of that generation had seen the whole of Canada before they were twenty and long before many of their parents got as far as Toronto. It is not accidental that the settings for this trio's stories range from Kaladar to Fort St. John, from Calabogie to Timmins.

Sociologically, these stories reveal the strong tendency to clear, clean (as against fuzzied) role-playing still prevalent in the Valley, of the retained so-called "macho" values, of the ancient male initiation rites into the tribe.

On another level, more personal, these stories will bring empathetic tears — as well as laughter — to the parents who lived through with their own children the tragedies and tomfooleries of Pierre, Jean-Paul and Hank's generation.

Jean Paul: I was coming up Number 7 from Kaladar. I was hitchhiking with my pack and violin and I saw this van coming and it didn't look like it was going to stop. It goes by and then it comes to this howling stop and the guy says, "Get in, get in and get that fiddle out!" And one guy's got a guitar and a mouth organ and there were harmonicas all over the dash, all the chords you could think of all over the dash, eh? The guy's driving this van with his elbow and playing the harmonica. The other guy's on the guitar. And I tried to tune my violin too quick and we played a few tunes and then I broke a string.

"Don't worry," he says, "We've got a set of spoons[1] in the guitar case."

He gets out the set of spoons. I say, "I think you guys are crazy." Like this is right out of the book. Every hitchhiker's dream. Whiskey and the whole bit. I happened to have some in my pack. But they said, "Listen, when you ride with us, you drink our liquor." These guys were great. They had obviously done this before all the time. We played and played and played for hours, driving along. Well from Norwood to Dacre, right through to Dacre. They were going to Pembroke, but they went out of their way. They were about forty years old, these guys, and they were having a great time. And I couldn't find the right harmonic at one point and the guy says, "Never mind," and downs his scotch with one gulp and slips the glass over the harmonica to change the key.

Hank: He's a legend in his spare time — Brian Slavinsky. We invented the term "scobaphobia" for him — fear of being well dressed. He used to play hockey for us in Renfrew and we used to call him "the league's best-dressed player." He doesn't like to wear traditional hockey equipment, eh? He wears sweat pants and he wears his shin pads on the outside of them. His ankle guards, he wears them backwards because, like he says, "Christ! When the guys shoot, I always turn around and go like this, eh?" He's a sight to see on the ice.

Norm Bujold, the famous bouncer from the White House[2] (and his own legend), was telling us that when Brian was about fifteen he went to Toronto and he was waiting on a bus. He didn't know anything about the big city or big-city buses. He was smoking a cigarette, so right away the bus driver says to him, "No smoking on the bus." So Brian looks around and, you know the holes where the tickets go in? Well, Brian thinks it's a big ashtray, so he goes "pow" and throws his cigarette in there and the whole thing goes on fire, and the bus driver has to get the fire extinguisher and put it

out. And the bus driver says, "I guess you're not from Toronto, eh?" It's like me standing on downtown Yonge Street one time in a pair of old torn-down moccasins and asking this city slicker, "Am I going the right way to Aurora?" And this guy looks at my boots and says, "I don't think you'll make it in those. It's about thirty miles." Anyway, after they get the fire out, the bus driver says to Brian, "Five for a dollar." So Brian forks over his money. But he didn't know it only took one ticket, and he puts all five tickets in the hole, and then he realizes his mistake and puts his hand in to try to get them out, and it gets stuck there. . . . Not long off the boat, eh?

The first time Brian went to Montreal he must have been about seventeen or eighteen and he's going to see Expo. He parked his car and he asked somebody how he would get to Expo. "No problem," they said, "you're right at the Metro here and you get on the Metro and you just go, and it's clearly marked at the exit." So Brian says OK and he parks his car and gets on the Metro. And it's about nine stops or something and they finally get there but he's at the tail end of the train, right? So he sees everybody getting off and he figures it'll go "sweeeeet," and everybody'll get off. So most people get off but he stays on. And he's waiting and waiting. Then he gets so disgusted that he figures he'll never find Expo anyway. So he starts back, but he forgot where his car was. So he had to get off at every Metro stop, run up the stairs, look to see if his car was there and run back down again. Twenty-nine stops before he found his car! Brian never got to Expo.

Pierre: A bunch of us boys in Renfrew, a wild bunch, we have this "gentleman's club" called Club 500, a private club, you see. It's just a he-man, woman-hater club. There are no fees, just BFFI — Brute Force and Fucking Ignorance — required for entrance. The boys have this store mannequin hanging there and they've got her hanging by the neck and they've got blood coming out of her nose. It's just a little room at the back of a house and they've a bar set up and a TV and video games, and they play 500, and they've got a dart board. You have to be able to buy at least one round a night. They're always testing to see who's the toughest, who can take the most shit and abuse. The aftermath of the Grey Cup, the place looked like a cyclone had been through.

I'll tell you about some of the games we play at Club 500. Norm Bujold is a sort of legend in the Valley. He finished third or fourth in the world in wrestling. He was the bouncer at the White House

124

for years. He's a character. Everybody knows him
and everybody respects him. Some nights at the
Club 500 we play this little game where you lie out
prone and put your head on one chair and your
heels on another and see who you can hold up for
how long on your belly. One night Big Norm held
Cory Leblanc and myself — I weigh 174 pounds and
Cory weighs 240 — for the count of four, eh?
Then I tried to hold Norm — he's 270 pounds —
and I held him for the count of four. Once I said,
"That's it," he was supposed to jump off. But he got
to laughing so hard — because he didn't think I
was going to be able to hold him for that long —
that he couldn't get off. So I came down and my
neck was still on the chair — it was an upholstered
chair — and I had burns on the back of my neck
for weeks and a disabled back.

The great dart tournament, eh? What we do
at the club is you put the safety glasses on and one
guy stands in front of the dart board and the closest
shot to his head wins a beer. Cory Leblanc one
night wanted Norm Bujold to get up there and be
shot at with the darts. So Norm Bujold puts on the
safety glasses and goes up to the board. No one
else wanted to shoot because they were all afraid of
hitting Norm, so Cory had to get up and shoot.
He shot and got Norm right on the end of the beak.
The dart just kind of hit and hung there on the
end of his nose and then dropped slowly down. And
Cory goes up to Norm and says, "You owe me a
beer."

Hank: Cory and Norm! You should have seen those
two guys last Hallowe'en at the club. They were
the prisoner and the cop. Cory was dressed up like
the cop. Cory's a big guy too, a real big guy, and
Norm's built like a bowling ball. He's five-foot-
six or five-foot-seven and 270 pounds. He's really a
powerful guy. What they used to do when they
were young and couldn't get money from their old
man — Norm had a brother built like him — they
used to pick him up, turn him upside down and
shake him. Whatever money fell out of his pockets,
they took.

Pierre: Contrary to local legend, Norm Bujold was
not the guy the pipeliners[3] pounded to a pulp
when they were here last year. That was Bob Bennett. At the White House. I got sent over there
that night. I was working at Butson's Motel bar but
they asked me over. I thought it must be pretty
wild there for them to ask me over. So I went
scooting down in my wee Toyota and when I got
there, you could actually feel it in the air. But he was
pretty near pounded to a pulp. The guy took a beer
bottle and slashed his jugular and then he pounded

him to a pulp. Just before he passed out, they rushed
him to the hospital. He was lucky he was that
close to the hospital, eh? So I got there (to the
White House) and I went up to the till and said,
"Where's Big Bob?" And they said, "He's in hospital. He got his jugular vein cut and they took him
away in an ambulance." So right away, I had a
herd of butterflies in my stomach and I went up to
the bar and I said, "Could I have a double rum
and is there a baseball bat anyplace?" I was Big Bob's
replacement.

So I went and sat at the door and I was kind
of watching around, and at this one table there was
about eight guys sitting and there was this one big
guy and he had a six-inch tattoo on his arm and he
had room for about a three-inch border around it.
He wasn't doing anything. Just sitting there big and
ugly, you know. He's with his friends and they're
all little jerks. Finish their drinks and smash the
glasses on the wall, you know. So Peter Aikenhead,
he's all zipped up, and he comes over to me and he
says, "Christ! Look at the size of that big Amazon."
And I said, "Keep quiet, Peter. He'll hear you." So
Peter keeps coming over to me and he says,
"They're breaking an awful pile of glasses." So I
said, "Don't worry about it. I'll pay for them." So
then I thought to myself, "They're going to wonder
what kind of a person I am. I wonder if I should
go over and see them, take the bat." I finished my
drink and had another double rum and Coke and
then I thought to myself, "Well, I'll just leave the
bat because if I go over with the bat they'll think
I'm being aggressive." I knew the big guy could
have shoved it up my arse and turned me into a
popsicle. So I never did anything. I just left the bat
there, eh?

So I just went up and I said to the big guy,
"Hi. See this here? Very fragile. It breaks when it's
hit." I thought that would be a good opening line,
eh? His eyes were just charcoal black, and he looked
at me. So I put my hand on his shoulder and I
said, "I don't know if you were here and seen what
happened here tonight but, you know, I don't work
at this hotel. I work at the quiet place up the road,
and they sent me down here tonight. It's none of
my doing and it's going to get pretty hairy around
here tonight, and I've got butterflies bad, and you
guys are breaking a lot of glasses here. So what
I want to ask you is, if there are any more problems
here tonight, will you give me a hand? You look
like you could probably give me a hand, eh?"

"Holy sheet!" the big guy says, "Is that what
you want?" He stood up and shook my hand. I'm six-
one-and-a-half but the son-of-a-bitch was six inches

bigger, higher than me. And he shook my hand and I disappeared from about there down, eh? And he says, "Got a name, kid?" And I says, "Pierre, Pierre," like this, eh? And he says, "Just call me Bear." I could relate to that. So I said, "Could you kind of quiet your animals down here?" And he turns to his friends and he says, "The next one of you fuskers that lets a peep out is in the fuskin' parking lot on his head."

So the whole rest of the night it was nice and quiet at the White House. So it comes around to about one o'clock and he's ready to leave. He got up and started to walk out and you could just see everybody kind of move back — like a boat going through water, eh? So he just walks over to me and he says, "I'm going home now." And I didn't want him to leave because all the fights start up after one o'clock when everybody has to leave, so I says to him, "Are you sure you don't want to sit down and have another drink? Double scotch, double rum, on me. What are you drinking?"

"No, I gotta go," he says. "It was nice meeting you."

And you should have seen his eight little followers going out behind him, eh? It was like Chester and Spike[4]. He was a pipeliner. I think he lifted those pipes or changed the tracks[5] on the bulldozers — no, he probably held up the bulldozers while they changed the tracks on them. He was awesome. You should have seen the arms on that guy! I couldn't say what nationality he was, but he had a great deep raspy voice and he had a set of shoulders! Well, I've never seen a guy that big!

Jean Paul: There was these two girls. Pierre and I met them on the road when we were coming from work. We were in northern B.C. Couple of damsels in distress, eh? We thought maybe we might help them out and then make time with them. The muffler had come off their car — a small one — and it was hooked over the rear end so they wouldn't have been able to go anywhere. So we stopped our car and Pierre says, "OK, girls, we'll fix that." Then he winked at me. The big impression. "I'll pick it up, Jean Paul, and you get underneath and take the muffler off." We both knew he could pick up cars — and easily Toyotas — and the girls' eyes pop a little and their mouths drop open, so we figure they are impressed. So I get underneath and I start trying to get the muffler off, but I'm having a little trouble and, Jesus, it feels like he is going to let the car down! He starts shouting, "Hurry up! Hurry up! Jesus! This is heavy! It's the most I've ever picked up!" And I'm shouting from underneath, "Hold it up! Hold it up!" And I'm underneath this

damn car and these two damsels in distress are watching, eh? and I think they're smiling a little and I'm wondering what's going on. So finally I get out from under the car with the muffler and Pierre puts the car back down and he says, "Jesus! That was heavy!" and he opens the trunk of the girls' car to put the old muffler in it. And here's these four tires and rims! No wonder the girls kept smiling to themselves!

Pierre: One of the funniest things I remember about Fort St. John was that the motto of the town up on big banners on the main street was "Fort St. John, Land of the New Totem," which everybody had translated into "Foreskin John, Land of the New Scrotum."

Hank: I could tell you a million funny stories about that place. It's a wild town. One night I picked my girl, Sherry, up at Casey's Pub where she worked. And I went out to get something out of my car and here was two of the natives from the north going at it right on the hood of my car. They do it on the grass all the time, and it's cold. It was warmer on the hood of the car — the engine was still warm. But can't you just imagine it? Walking around the car park looking for warm cars, saying to your girl, "What do you think of this one, baby? Never mind the hood ornament. Just get the feel of it, eh?"

Which reminds me of another wild town: Detroit. One time I was in Detroit. I went to see a baseball game there alone and when I came out of the stadium it was dark, twilight. I walked way back to where my car was parked, and I had this old '63 Pontiac, and when I got there there was this couple in the back seat of my car. They were having a great time. So I didn't say anything — just thought I'd take a little walk. How long can they be there, eh? So I went and checked around the neighbourhood of Tiger Stadium and came back. They were still there. I wanted to get back home. I didn't like being in Detroit all by myself, especially being a Canadian from across the border, and an Indian at that. So I knocked on the window of my car. The guy was quite rude. "Fuck off!" he said. "This happens to be my car," I say. But the guy got very hostile, "Look," I said, "I'm a reasonable guy but I have to get back. I'm a Canadian, eh? I'll go for another walk and I'll come back in ten minutes but, when I come back, I expect to see you gone." So I disappeared again and when I came back the guy was still there and now he was really abusive, threatening me and everything. So I said, "Look! If you don't get out of my car, I'm going to have to call a cop."

"Call a cop," he said, "I don't care." So I went

A "gentleman" fisherman obviously from some strange and foreign parts, either American or 'terribly British, my dear', posed in a photographer's studio with his trophy trout.

she thought that would be a good spot to have a holiday. But things couldn't have been working out to her expectations, because I was in the big bar in Fort MacMurray one night when this woman comes in. She got up on a barstool and announced in a very loud voice, "Any man in this place that can guess my weight can have me for the night."

There was a deathly silence amongst the 200 men in the bar. Then my friend, Joe, being a bit of a wise guy, pipes up. "One hundred and fifteen pounds."

And the lady from Calabogie roars out, "That's close enough!"

And I remember another night I was sitting in the Fort MacMurray bar. There was a bunch of us sitting around one table, chewing the rag, about girls we'd met and places we'd been — even some of the work we'd done — when this guy suddenly pipes up: "Yah shit! the only good things that ever came out of Timmins was whores and hockey players."

So I said, "Hey, watch that! My mother's from Timmins."

And quick as a wink, he snapped back, "What position does she play?"

Jean Paul: Oh, the Americans! In the summertimes they were all around Calabogie and the area in droves. And if you caught a big fish, they bought it. They wanted to take it home and say, "Look what I caught in Canada!" And then it's not a wasted vacation, eh? I can remember how it was when I was a kid. I can remember this one instance when it was a big catfish, big sucker — caught him in the middle of the day when the river's wide open. I caught this rock bass, beat him all up, cut him into pieces, put a piece on the hook, threw it in, and let it go with the current. I thought I was stuck on bottom! You know, there's a really slow flow in the river and they don't move much. I could of swore I was stuck on bottom! And I had one of these Canadian Tire $2.99 reels — well, it wouldn't even have cost $2.99 then — and I'm reeling it in, and the gears start to really go once the fish started to move and it starts to move upstream. And I've got this cheap little nylon line and I'd move it a little bit, not much drag on it, but I finally get it almost to the shore and my poor little rod is starting to die on me. Like the gears, you know. Anyway, I get this sucker in and the Americans, they all fish around the bridge in the village — Calabogie — and they see this and it looks like a monster. And these two Americans, they're watching this. And I'm only ten years old but it looks like they're going to bargain. And I'm thinking, "If I can only

and I found this security guard and I asked him to call the cops because this guy wouldn't get out of my car and let me go home to Canada. So the cops come along and who do they arrest? Me. I spent the night in jail in Detroit, for Christ's sake! And do you know what the goddam charge was? Disturbing the "piece."

Pierre: There was this very heavy lady from Calabogie — she weighed in at about 400 pounds — who one time decided to go up to Fort MacMurray to have a good time. She had heard that there were twenty men to every woman in the place and

get them up to five bucks, it's a whole new fishing reel." And they bought it off me for five dollars and off I went. So then you catch on, and anything big after that, you just take it and sell it to an American.

Pierre: I had a paper route. I used to do the village paper route. I'd come around by the dam in the village and there's the channel iron that skirted the dam and I'd just hide the spear up under there. And there's a backwash just beside the dam and, in about half an hour, I could fill this paper bag, take them home, clean them up and sell them to the Americans as pickerel. Perch, bass, pike — but I said everything was pickerel because for some reason the Americans were nuts about pickerel. Once you cleaned them all up, they all looked the same to the Americans. They're still good. But they're not pickerel.

Jean Paul: One time we were down at McGonigal's Bay snorkeling and I'm snorkeling along and it was fairly deep in a few places, eh? And I go down and I see this big catfish. You know how your mask makes things look really massive? I had to come up for air and I'm wondering if he had moved. I go down again and he's still hanging on the bottom. It's pretty dark down there and I'm getting all hyperventilated. So I go down again and I lay the spear into the back of his head. But I couldn't get him up. I didn't have fins on — that was part of my problem — and I just couldn't get him up. And I'm running out of air. Gasp. Gasp. Gasp. Turning purple, but still hanging on, I had to let him go. I was in the bay, so it took me about fifteen or twenty minutes to track down my spear. I mean like, it had slowed him down for sure. So when I finally tracked him down, he's getting to the tripping-over stage. So, I get him to shore and, even dead weight for my age, it was really hard to swim with this thing in my hand. I get him to shore. He's something like eighteen pounds.

Sure, I sold him to an American! He was so proud of it! And, of course, the story I used for him was that I caught it on a fishing rod — I couldn't say I speared it, eh?[6] — I told him I caught it on a fishing rod but had to use the spear to get him to shore, and then I got him close enough to the shore, and held him with one hand, and nailed him with the spear. And the Yank, well, he's really getting onto this story. The bigger the story, the better. The wild North of Canada, eh? I got seven bucks for that one and I think the spear marks were worth even more because I'm sure, when that Yank got back, what he did was tell them all back home about how *he* got the big fish to shore and how

he had to spear it.

Pierre: You can call this one, "How I Got Taken by a Big American from Sioux City, Iowa." We had been hunting bear and Dennis finally shot one and he says, "Do you guys want the skin?" So Dennis and I went at it and we made one helluva mess of that bearskin. We'd never skinned a bear before and we scored it in about twenty places. But we were really proud of it. I was about eighteen at the time and Dennis was sixteen. We built a frame and we stretched it out and we pounded in rock salt.

Now down at the farm about fifteen miles away there was a lake, eh? And there was a fish tank there and you had to fly in. This was up at Red Lake and there was no road or nothing and all these Americans had to fly in. I remember this one guy there. He used to say, "I'm Big Bob from Sioux City, Iowa. I'm a tool-and-die maker. You know that part in your grandmother's fire — I make that." Well, Big Bob wanted to buy this bearskin from us. But Dennis and I were so proud of it that money couldn't buy it. He offered us 200 dollars for it and that was in 1969. But there was no way we would sell it. Anyhow, we were away the day the gang of Americans left, and when we got back that night our bearskin was cut right out of its frame. All we had there was canoes, so Dennis and I booted down to the lakeshore — we figured we could catch him before he got away with it. He had his own plane, this guy. And he was gone.

So we asked Mr. Swain if Big Bob from Sioux City, Iowa, had left that day. Mr. Swain said yes. And we said, "Did he leave with our bearskin?" Mr. Swain said yes. "And did he tell you where he got it?" we asked. "Yes," said Mr. Swain, "He told me he paid you guys 200 dollars for it." I can just picture Big Bob in Sioux City, Iowa, telling everybody he knows, and lots he doesn't, how he fought this bear, bare-handed, you know, with only a knife, a little penknife.

Jean Paul: I remember one night when we were spearing fish on the Madawaska. That was when they were doing construction on the bridge. We used to go downriver to the bend. They were still using the old train trestles, so you could drive across. It was in the spring of the year and that's spearing season, and that's when they're on the lookout for you, the cops and the game wardens. So they came by. And all of a sudden there's this spotlight like the light from a cigarette lighter lights up the whole shore and we squeeze down onto the rocks and think we are hidden. But I didn't know they had already seen us. I was with my cousin and we had a case of twenty-four — neither of us of age — and I had borrowed the spear from a guy who lived nearby. The cops were in on this because what we found out later was they had stopped this guy I borrowed the spear from and asked him to help them get through the bush to where we were spearing. But the guy had just lent me the spear, so he's no fool, eh? He says to himself, "If they are trying to catch young lads who are only trying to catch a snack of fish, they can figure their own way through the bush."

So anyway, we're sitting there having a few beers and, of course, after you spear, you have to wait a few moments for a new flock of fish to come in. So I'm sitting there and we're having another beer and all of a sudden we think we can hear this racket behind us. Not very well, though, because of the roar of the river, eh? So I didn't pay any attention and I had the spear set aside, and all of a sudden this light comes on. But you don't hear anything coming behind because of the roar of the river. So I naturally assumed it was the guy I had borrowed the spear from, eh? So I swing around with my light and say, "Would you shut that fucking light off! We're trying to spear-fish here." And just at that point my light glances off his badge, eh? Me, like a fool, here I'm sitting on a twenty-four and I toss my beer over my shoulder — like what a waste of a beer, eh? The cop he comes up and he asks us, "Are you boys spearing fish?" "Oh no!" we say. "We're just sitting here having a beer." "Got IDs?" they ask. "No, no IDs, officer, but we're of age, that's for sure."

Now the game warden's waiting up at the new construction bridge. It was Jack Stewart at that time. He was the game warden and he was getting up in years, and he had to pant to even get out of the car. So we're coming up from the shore at this time and, on the way, we're showing the cops all the nice fish. And Jack Stewart's standing up on the bridge figuring, "Hey, we've caught these guys spearing." But the cops never did look for the spear. But Jack Stewart, he's sure of his bust this time. We get up to the bridge and Jack's looking for this spear, and the cops say, "Well, they don't have a spear. They weren't spearing." Well, the game warden knows more about what's going on in the spearing season than the cops do. So Stewart goes phew, phew, phew — he's hyperventilating — and he says to the cops, "Jesus! You didn't look for the spear?" And the cops say, "No. They told us they didn't have a spear." Phew, phew, phew. Stewart goes on hyperventilating — only worse now. We had told the cops that my cousin was getting married

and there was a big commotion at the house, and we just couldn't handle all the commotion, and that was to explain why we were down on the river, eh? Phew, phew, phew. Jack Stewart's really upset that he didn't get a bust. And the cops, they're so taken by our story and all the nice fish we showed them, they give us back our beer and say, "You boys go straight home, now." And the game warden is still standing there, phew, phew, phew, watching us take our beer and go off.

Hank: Talking about cops, I was just thinking about this story. We were all about fifteen at the time, in Timmins, and there must have been about ten of us. We used to rent motel rooms for parties. We'd get one guy, whoever looked the oldest, to rent the room. And we ten guys, we'd party all weekend. It used to be then you'd get a room for about seventeen bucks for a double, and we'd all pitch in and we'd get one of the old winos to get us beer or wine, or whatever we were drinking in return for some for himself.

One night Dennis Mussell — he's a character you've got to meet — was there and well, he was the only virgin amongst us. He was the only guy that had never got laid. Dennis was fourteen then, well, maybe not quite fourteen, but anyway we decided we were going to get Dennis laid. Donny Colaminkle — he was probably the coolest of all of us and he looked the oldest and he knew all these hookers — he said. So he calls up this taxi — and I think there were eight of us in the room that time — and we're going to hide and the hooker's going to come into the room and Donny's — well, he knows how the ladies work and everything, eh? — and he's going to have his way with her and then Dennis. Dennis is waiting in the bathroom, stark naked, and Donny's going to slip out and Dennis is going to get in at the other side of the bed. Well, the hookers charge so much per time, he says, and it's gonna be fifteen bucks a throw, but we're all chipping in for Dennis. We're all standing up in the bathroom and Dennis is standing there, too, stark naked. Donny's in the bedroom in his T shirt and jeans looking really cool, eh? Waiting there. This car pulls up outside and we're just killing ourselves laughing in the bathroom and Donny's trying to quieten us down. He's going sh-shh-shh. And Dennis is stark naked. And Donny says, "Be quiet! The car's here!" And the door opens and who walks in but the morality squad — Timmins Police Department — morality squad. Alan Cool, he's one of the guys standing in the bathroom with us, and that's his father out there, Maurice Cool, head of the Timmins Police Department Morality Squad.

So its, "OK, you guys, everyone out of the bathroom." And Dennis, he couldn't find his clothes, and the cop turns on the bathroom light and says, "Everybody out." And we all come out, with Dennis stark naked. The cops have seen a lot of kooky things, you know, but they are looking around wondering what's going on here, eh? I don't think anybody was of age.

And the cop says, "Who rented the room?" Nobody knew.

And the cop says, "Whose is the beer?" Nobody knew.

So he starts taking down names. He knew most of us. "Don't have to ask you your name," he says, looking around at Alan, his son, you know.

But they were very good to us. They said, "If this beer doesn't belong to anybody and nobody rented the room, then you guys had better get out of here real quick."

So zoooom, zooooom, everybody's gone, eh?
Pierre: The Williamses are noted in Calabogie for red-necking and big mouths. So we were all sitting around the dam. We're all in our teens and one guy has the wheels — that's all you need. One set of wheels. So it's in the summertime, in the morning, and the sun's coming up and it's coming up time to think about going home and going to bed. And we're sitting in the car and there's a last little bit of a case of beer, so we figure we'd finish that up. We see a police cruiser come round by Billy Dobbs's store, so there is no point in starting the car because you're the only car on the road, and they're going to follow you, eh? Might as well save your gas. So the cop pulls in behind the car and, of course, everybody's ready for the questions — like who's going to claim the beer. It doesn't matter much because everybody chipped in, right?

Well, I'm sitting with it under my feet, so it seems reasonable that I should claim it. The cop comes over and he's really decent about it, looks at the licence of the guy that has the wheels, asks, "Who owns the beer?" "I own the beer," I say, so he takes my name, Such-and-Such, and all the details. Things are working out really OK until Williams gets mouthy. Has to walk over to the cruiser and starts coming on to this cop. He's only getting back his licence and stuff — the cop hadn't even made out a ticket at this point. He's just doing a standard check on the radio. He was really polite and we were really polite — up to this point, eh? So the cop takes a little bit of this for a little while.

But then Williams starts: "If you'd like to get out of that car, we could settle this another way." And of course, quick as a flash, it's just reach for the dash, the ticket book and all. And then he just humiliated Williams so bad, right in front of everybody. The cop was Big Ronald MacDonald from the OPP in Renfrew and he's a big man. He's about six-foot-four and about 230 pounds and Williams keeps coming on to him with, "If you'd like to step out of that car," and "Sure you're brave. You've got your uniform on." And finally MacDonald looks at him and laughs and says, "Williams! You're all the same. You're with your gang here, eh? And you think you're impressing somebody. Let me tell them a few good stories about the times we've had you in jail and you've cried like a baby."

And Williams is going red in the face — he's just raging — and the cop's just coolly delivering all these little stories to us, and we're just sitting back there snickering because he's the asshole that got us the ticket, eh? I'm pretty sure, except for dumb Williams, it would have ended up the cop would have just confiscated the beer. To me that was just a fine example of how giving the cops a hard time just isn't the way to go.

Jean Paul: I remember the crazy time we rented the boat from Jocko's Motel on Golden Lake, my brother-in-law and I. Three-horse motors. We're going to go over to Grassie Bay to fish bass. So we got over there and neither of us had played around too much with motors, eh? So we got over there and we fished and we caught a few bass and then we run out of gas. So we started to fill her up with gas and the gas spills all over the place and, at one point it touched the sparkplug. Whoops! The cord was started and of course the whole back end of the boat catches on fire and, like with gas on water, there's nothing much you can do. And we're trying to beat it out with life jackets and stuff, and we can hear these guys in the background screaming, "We're coming! We're coming!" But they're coming with battery-operated eggbeaters — gneerm! gneerm! You can hear them coming. But it seems like forever. I'm starting to panic and I'm standing on the boat and I am not about to go down with the ship, right? I've my lifejacket on. I could swim but it's still Panic City mainly because we're on the bay side, and the problem is that you really don't have much water to swim in. It's mainly that loonshit. And you can't stand up because you have about this much mud up to your neck. Well, these guys come in with the eggbeater but, by the time they get there, we've got the fire under control. We take the boat back, eh? We pull into Jocko's. Maybe we'll just pay the rental and scram. But Johnny Jocko knew where I lived, so it was going to be easy to track me down. So we explained to Johnny Jocko and he was pretty sympathetic. We'd pretty well charred up the back of the boat, so to speak. But he kind of sanded it down and repainted it and it was OK.

Hank: Reminds me of a funny story about Fort Chippewan. The Indians up there are called "Chips" by the locals. And there is a big fish camp about sixty miles from Fort Chip. This pilot used to stop all the time and pick up the fish and fly it out to Edmonton. At the same time, he'd pick up any Indians that were going out to the big city. And they used to ask the pilot what he flew in his plane and he always used to say, "Fish and Chips."

Noël and I and Luke — he's a guy from Timmins, his father was one of the guys that was killed when they were drilling the tunnel under Niagara Falls when there were sixteen guys killed. Anyway, we were out canoeing and fishing and photographing on Lake Athabaska — really big lake there — and Noël was staying at the cabin of this old Indian trapper — Noël knew this guy, eh? There was this old boat there. I was pretty certain it wasn't seaworthy, but the girls were out in the canoe and us guys were back in the cabin, drinking beer and guffing around and stuff. And Noël says, "Let's have a little fun with the girls. We'll take this boat out and chase them around the lake." So we got out in this boat and I said, "Noël, I don't like the look of this boat." "Oh, it'll be good enough," Noël said.

So we took off in this thing and we have this little tobacco can with us to bail, and as we're going out, we're taking on more water and the boat's filling up. And I'm rowing and my end's going down and Noël's yelling at me, "Get up to this end! Get up to this end!" And I'm trying to bail the boat with this little tobacco can, and the girls are circling

us in their canoe, just killing themselves laughing, and Donna's taking pictures as fast as she can. And we're standing up in the boat and the boat starts to go down. You know that sinking feeling as the water comes in over the gunwales. And we stand up tall, like this, and we're holding our watches and wallets way up in the air, like this, over our heads. And we just keep sinking and sinking until all that's left of us is our hands up against the sky, holding our watches and our money and our precious ID cards up there — and we can hear the girls still laughing — and Donna took pictures of it all.

Pierre: This young guy from Renfrew went up to Toronto to get this job driving a bus for the TTC. First day on the job he is driving up Yonge Street there, and he spies this guy standing at the bus stop with only one leg and two heads. And this young guy from Renfrew, he wheels the big TTC bus right over to the bus stop, opens up the door, and yells out, "Gidday, Gidday! Hop in!"

---

1. When all else fails, a true Valley musician can take an ordinary pair of spoons and make music with them.
2. The White House is a Renfrew Hotel, formerly the mansion of MP Tom Low.
3. Pipeliners laying pipes for natural gas came through the Renfrew area in 1982.
4. Chester and Spike are Bugs Bunny cartoon characters, Spike being the huge bulldog and Chester the little terrier.
5. Different sets of tracks are used on big bulldozers for different kinds of terrain and construction.
6. It has been for a long time, and still is, illegal to spear fish.

Both Joseph Montferrand and Harry McLean were renowned as high-kickers. In the lumbering era in the nineteenth century, Montferrand was reputed to have kicked the ceiling of every inn from Quebec City to Temiskaming. As a teenager during the forties, I can remember Harry McLean coming into the kitchen of the hotel in Merrickville on his birthday in a celebrant mood and yelling out, "Look at me! I'm seventy-nine today and I can still kick my own ass!" He then proceeded to demonstrate his feat. In this drawing, Montferrand in a shantyman's bar demonstrates his agility and suppleness.

14

He done a lot for the town

I find similarities between the legend of Joseph Montferrand and the legend of Harry McLean. Both were huge men physically, probably pituitary giants, and outstanding leaders in their specific fields, Montferrand in the lumbering era of the nineteenth century and McLean in the construction era of the first half of the twentieth century. Both during their working years were based in the Ottawa Valley and so belong to the Valley region; but both were larger-than-life men of national scope and, in the final analysis, belong to the whole country.

Rupert Brooke once described Canada as a country without heroes — and therefore a country without an identity. When he wrote his provocative lines, most of our legends were still circulating in the oral tradition. True, Benjamin Sulte had written his account of the life of Joseph Montferrand in the year 1899. But, until a decade or so ago, both legendary men were still incipient fires in the imaginations of the shantymen and the construction men who had known and worked for them both. Then suddenly, as though we had been signalled by some national subconscious, the oral traditions shifted to written traditions. In Giants of Canada's Ottawa Valley (General Store Publishing, Burnstown, Ontario, 1981) I researched and integrated into the written tradition everything I could find at that time to document my accounts of the lives of Montferrand and McLean, extending the legend of Montferrand through taping in the Ottawa Valley, and putting into written tradition for the first time an account of the life of Harry McLean of Merrickville. I knew Harry McLean first when I was a young girl of nineteen intent upon working my way through university. My parents had sold our house in Ottawa and moved to Merrickville, where my father had bought the hotel. There, of course, he and Harry McLean resumed

an old friendship that had begun when they both lived "high on the hog" at the Royal York Hotel, my father as a Toronto Maple Leaf and Harry McLean as one of the biggest construction men in North America.

Home one weekend to visit my family I observed that Harry McLean employed an entourage of retainers. "Do you think you could get me a summer job there?" I asked my father. And it was no sooner said than done. I was hired on at 100 dollars a week as the "house secretary" for Harry McLean. This was an over-refinement of language. In actual fact, I was a typer of obscene and libelous letters dictated to me by McLean when in his cups, and directed towards people like Mitch Hepburn, Mackenzie King, Duplessis, Jewish merchants in Toronto — people for whom McLean seemed to have an overwhelming antipathy, which his daily alcohol intake incised. All these letters were censored by his housekeeper. I assume they were burned or put in the garbage.

As a nineteen-year-old girl my observations of Harry McLean would probably be described as simplistic. I saw clearly that it was, indeed, "Lonely at the Top," and "Lonely at the End"; that his money had alienated him and that he found he could not trust people; that he could (and would under the influence) "use" and "buy" people so that he could laugh at them. I was aware, from some very few conversations that we had when he was early-morning sober, that he was intellectually starved in Merrickville; its provincialism offered him lots of hail-fellow-well-mets but no real companionship.

Following the publication of Giants of Canada's Ottawa Valley, I went on the usual rounds of publicity and promotion associated with writing a book in this country. Amongst other things, I went

on the *Hal Anthony* open line radio programme
on CFRA in Ottawa. This was then a very popular
two-hour radio show beamed throughout the whole
Ottawa Valley to which people could phone in
their opinions, ideas and stories. When my turn
came up Hal Anthony invited his audience to phone
in and contribute their stories about the six legendary giants in my new book. The switchboard lit
up; there was never a pause; people who couldn't
get through on the lines left memos and phone
numbers; and almost 99 percent of the callers
wanted to tell stories about one particular giant:
Harry McLean! Many of them illuminated his
life and character. The following stories were collected from Hal Anthony's programme that day.

Hello, I'm a Merrickville girl and I heard you talking about Harry McLean. They say he
started his career as a water boy with the CPR —
at least that's what we were told when we were
young. One of the things I remember was that he
had all kinds of animals on his land and we used to
come from Smiths Falls to see that. And we were
told that he threw money out of hotel windows and
that he tipped waitresses twenty dollars — that
was a huge amount of money in those days. One of
the things I recall myself was Hallowe'en at his
house. I'm sure every kid in Merrickville went to
his house. And when you walked in the front door
of the house into the foyer — which was the size
of my own house right now — there would be a big
tub in the foyer and he made us bob for apples
before he would give us candy. And that candy
wouldn't be in bowls; it would be in bushel baskets.
And that is what stands out in my memory the
most.

---

*In his later years, his dams and railways and
aqueducts all built, Harry McLean returned to live
in his favourite place — Merrickville, Ontario.
Generally, the town was divided into two camps:
those who enjoyed his madcap antics and eccen-
tricities and opened their doors to his night prowlings,
and those who regarded him as a form of outland-
ish outlawry, and locked their doors upon him. A
handful of people knew his abilities — and his real
generosity.*

I'm not as old as Mr. McLean, but my dad was
growing up in Merrickville and was a teenager when

H.F. was in his prime there. My uncle, my cousin,
my dad and myself were swimming at the fairgrounds
outside of Merrickville when H.F. came down with
his pilot to get into his seaplane to have a little
fly around the country. He had with him his pet cat
— a bobcat or a lynx or something like that. And
he had this cat under one arm and he had a bottle
of whiskey under the other arm, and between taking
swigs himself and trying to get the cat a little bit
intoxicated, the cat had managed to claw him
completely. He was blood from head to toe.

We looked around for a place to go. My dad
and my uncle hauled my cousin and myself out into
the water, as this was the only place they figured
we could all be safe from McLean. Yes, all the stories
about his drinking capacity, they seem to be 100
percent true.

McLean seemed to have a very close rapport
with the children of Merrickville. Or so my dad
tells me. I think the only people who didn't like him
were the ladies of the town because they were
afraid that their husbands were going to get too
closely involved with him. I remember my dad telling
me that he and his brother had done something
one time for Mr. McLean, something quite incon-
sequential, and he gave them each 100 dollars.
Dad still rues the day that he went home and told
my grandmother that Mr. McLean had given them
this big sum of money. Why? Because my grandmother promptly grabbed them both by the ears and
marched them across town and made them give
it all back. She did not like the man.

My name is Kelso. I remember in 1932 H.F.
opened the quarry at the end of our property. The
men were all out of work at that time, so he
opened it up to give the boys work. And then he
stockpiled it and sold it later. There is a cairn built
at the foot of the hill just as you go up to our place
put there by McLean. I've been in Harry McLean's
private railway car many a time. It's not there now.
Even the tracks are not there now. What
happened? A lot of that stuff was taken out at the
time of the last war for salvage. I don't remember
what it was like inside, but I remember it used to
be shunted off at Deek's Quarry. There were a lot
of other railway cars used to be burned in there
during the Depression. We didn't know anything
about his accomplishments when he opened the
quarry at the end of our property, but we later
thought of him as a great man. He done a lot for
the town and for the entire community of Merrickville.

McLean had a '42 Chev car that he had bought

in Nova Scotia. He had it shipped down here. He had a special feeling for that '42 Chev for some reason or other. Anyway, it was a little bit different at the front end and I bought it a long time after and the bugger knew it. And if he got on a big spree and he saw that old car of his, it was "look out!" because he'd try to steal it back. One night I was taking my sister back to Kemptville to catch a bus and he was driving in another car with a guy from Merrickville. And he spied the Chev and he says to the guy, "Stop! There's my car!" And he stopped in the middle of the road and I couldn't get by. So I stopped and he leaned in and says, "Where are you going?" I said, "I'm going to Kemptville." And he said, "So am I." And he just got in and there was the three of us on the front seat and we couldn't breath because he was so big and he kept calling my sister "Mother Superior," and we took her and got her on the bus finally. He had a nice place at Merrickville and I've been there a few times at night. When you went in at night, it was pretty hard to get out before daylight. He was a nice man and a good man and he enjoyed fun and he liked to pay for it.

This is Bill Willis calling. I can give you a short story about Harry McLean. When I was a boy growing up in Lanark village I used to hang around Noonan's store after school. I had always heard a lot of stories about Harry McLean giving money away. So one day I'm standing in Noonan's store and Mr. Noonan says, "Here comes Harry McLean!" A car pulled up and this great big man got out. He looked to me to be about seven feet tall. He walked in. In those days the bananas hung in stalks from the ceiling and I suppose there'd be about four or five dozen bananas on a stock at about twenty-five cents a dozen in those days. And Harry just walked up to that thing and lifted it onto his shoulder and went over to the counter and threw a hundred-dollar bill at Mr. Noonan. "Thank you very much," he said. "Keep the change." And out the door he went. Apparently after that he went into his brother's house in Perth and knocked down every dish in the cupboards. Then he set down a thousand-dollar bill and said, "I think you need new dishes."

About Mr. McLean. I was in Ottawa here in the forties in the air force and I remember him throwing money out of the Lord Elgin and the Chateau Laurier. And I mean hundreds of dollars. And I knew a guy in the air force who had his car damaged by McLean. McLean left him a note with his name and address on it, and when the air force guy went around to see him about the damage, McLean gave him the money for a new car. I remember the time, too, that he sent a ton of seafood to Uplands for the mess hall. A ton. Oysters, lobsters, everything flown in fresh was there on the pile on the table, and you could go in there and help yourself and take it to the cook and he'd cook it for you. All the oysters you wanted! We used to take them back to our section and sit there all night and drink beer and eat oysters. Yes, we all knew it was Harry McLean that sent the seafood in.

Another time for the air force lads at Uplands base he sent out 1,500 dollars to put on a dance there. A guy from Dominion Command in Montreal — Raymond I think his name was — he was the squadron leader or something and he turned McLean down and wouldn't allow the dance. So McLean sent a taxi out to Uplands to pick up the 1,500 dollars, and said he would have no more to do with the air force again.

One time Mr. McLean came down to the woollen mill that was owned by Mr. McCarney at Burritt's Rapids. He was paying a bill. And a whole lot of we younger people were in a boat by the dam there at Burritt's Rapids. And Mr. McLean got mad at Mr. McCarney — I think Mr. McLean was feeling no pain — and he got mad and, instead of paying the bill to McCarney he just took out a handful of bills from his pocket and threw them out the window onto the water. Imagine sitting in a boat and being rained on with bills! There was a scramble to catch the bills before they all sank. I got a dollar out of it.

I'm one of the waiters that used to look after Harry McLean at the Chateau Laurier. I remember him coming in at night with his private plane and he always had a nurse with him — I don't know whether he was sick or not — and there was always a man with him. It was his agent, I believe.[1] I was working on Room Service in those days. I would bring him his supper. He was a huge man and he never combed his hair as far as I could see. And I'd serve him a nice supper and this man with McLean — whoever he was — would give me a 100-dollar bill. That was my tip.

Then he asked me who the lady was in charge of Room Service. I told him Mrs. Regan. He said, "I'd like to see this lady." Then when he got in the elevator with me to take him down to the main floor to the kitchens where Mrs. Regan's office was, we met a man named Solvey. He was a cripple and he had seven children and Mr. McLean gave him a 100-dollar bill, too. And that was the same night that he was throwing money out of the windows. Yes, he was sober.

And then when we got down to Room Service and he met Mrs. Regan he gave her a 100-dollar bill. And then he said, "I want to meet the chef." There was a war on then, you know, in 1940 and we were at war with Italy. So he asked me the chef's name and I said, "This is Mr. Scaravelli." McLean grabbed a big frying pan and threw it at the chef and nearly knocked his head off. And then he turned around and gave him a 100-dollar bill, too.

The next time I met Mr. McLean was when I was bringing supper up to Billy Bishop and his family on the fifth-floor suite. And along comes Harry McLean and says, "Who are you bringing that up for?" And I said, "For Billy Bishop, the Victoria Cross man." And McLean says, "Come here with me," and he leads me over to a window and he opens it and he throws Billy Bishop's dinner out the window and down onto the street below. I didn't know what to do. I was nearly crying. So I went downstairs and I said to Mrs. Regan, "Mr. McLean just threw Billy Bishop's food out the window!" Nobody could believe it.

Yes, when we knew Harry McLean was coming to the Chateau we were all on our toes from the bellhop down. He sure commanded respect there.

Ernie Semier calling. I used to be the chief of police in Merrickville in 1957, '58, '59 and '60. I don't think anybody ever really knew Harry McLean. He never got close enough to anyone so they could get to know him. Of course, he was always drinking — I doubt if he ever got really drunk — but he was always at the drink. Anyway, when I first went there I was told to be prepared because he always tested the new policeman that went into the town. So, the first I was in town he called me up to the house. I asked if there was any trouble and he said, "No, I just want to meet you."

I thought I might as well get the first meeting over with, so I went up to the Big House. He had this old wooden cane and when I went in he came towards me just as though he were going to strike me right in the face with it. He wielded it above my head. I stood up to him. He was six-foot-four and weighed about 265 pounds at that time. But I was about the same size as he. So I said to McLean, "If you're going to strike me with that, are you ready to take what's coming back at you?" He looked at me to see if I would shake or bend. He was trying me out and I knew it. So I said, "Go ahead. Finish your swing." "No," he says, "I'll not. I'm glad to meet you. I thought you were going to run away. I've had a few of you guys run away from here."

He was a very generous man and for the town of Merrickville he couldn't do enough. If he would turn against you, though, that was it. He was quick to turn. I remember one time he called me up to the Big House. He was well under the influence and I felt he was wasting my time, so I said to him, "Look, I'm busy and I'm not going to come back here when you're like this. I haven't got time to just sit and talk to you." So he said, "You're going to sit down here right now." And I said, "No, I'm going and that's it." This was about two weeks before Christmas and he kept phoning my house and I had my wife answering the phone. "Tell him I'm busy and I'm not available unless it's really urgent." So anyway, Christmas morning this delivery truck pulls up to the door and there is a rap at the door. I went to the door and there was a great big cardboard box about four feet high on the doorstep. And I said to my wife, "Somebody must be playing a joke on us or something." And inside there's a great big tropical plant compliments of "You Know Who."

I remember he had a car and it was very low and every time he got into it he hit his head because he was so big. So he said to the driver. "We'll let the train look after it." And there were railway tracks at the back of his property and that's where they took the car, and the train did look after it.

No, I never charged him with anything, but he could have been charged many times over. If he wanted some money out of the bank on Sunday morning, for instance, he'd go in front of the bank and take a big stone and fire it through the bank window. The burglar alarm would ring all over town and he'd stand there until the bank manager came. And when the bank manager came, he'd say, "Oh, you're the guy I'm waiting for. Give me 1,000 dollars and here's 200 for your window, and if you need more, call me."

You know, you could never figure him out. You'd try to figure out his next move. And you'd try to study him. Was he laughing at you? Was he testing you all the time? Did he want to see how scared you'd be of him? He loved to laugh at people who were scared. And he only had respect for people he didn't scare. Yes, I knew that he had made a lot of money on the tunnel that he had built and on railroading. But they said he was a very, very hard man on his men. He wanted a full day's work out of them and, if he didn't get it, he would whip them. And this was his idea of getting the thing done on time. And I remember him telling me how he'd made an awful bundle of money on the tunnel because there was a clause in his contract which said that if he could build it in six months, he'd get so much bonus. And if he didn't build it in six months, he'd have to pay the company so much. So he built it in about three and a half months.

Oh, I remember something he did to prove he was a man. And at his age, too![2] He'd go and dig a big hole in the snow in the middle of winter and he'd strip down naked and he'd sleep in there with just a candle all night. He had married his second wife and she'd be phoning me all night long saying, "Oh, he's going to die in there. He's going to die in there!" And we'd say, "Ah, never mind. He'll come out. He'll come out." And sure enough around, eight o'clock in the morning he'd come back out of his hole in the snow with his bottle in his hand, stark naked.

I live in Spencerville and Mr. McLean was a pretty good friend of the local doctor, Dr. McIntosh. In 1947 or 1948 when I was seven years old, Mr. McLean drove into the town of Spencerville in his great big huge car — it was supposed to be a Packard or something like that — with his chauffeur. And he got out at the hotel corner and he was dressed in his pyjamas and his bathrobe and he started throwing money around. It was Saturday night. It's a farming community here and all the people in those days came into town to shop on Saturday night. So the town was crowded with people. When he started throwing the money around, the people crowded around him, but they didn't believe it at first. They were afraid to touch the money. "Go on. Go on," McLean yelled at them. "Take it. It's yours." So after a while bedlam broke loose and they crawled around on the street on their hands and knees, and they scratched for it, and they fought for it. And they picked it all up. I remember the kids running home to their parents yelling, "Come quick! There's a crazy man up the street and he's throwing money all around." And everybody came out of their houses. And McLean threw some more money around and laughed while they scratched for it. And then he went over to Dr. McIntosh's. I never got any, but I'll never forget that night in Spencerville.

My father, he used to drive Dr. McIntosh, and one time he drove him to Merrickville on a Sunday to visit McLean. And they had supper and, I suppose, a few drinks. Mr. McLean had just got a new horse and he wanted to show them the horse. They were going to go out to see it, but he said, "No, no. I'll have it brought in." So they brought the horse into the house. There was a huge winding

staircase in the house and he brought the new horse up the stairs. But they had a hell of a time getting the horse back down again.

I had a brother in the air force during the Second World War — I was pretty young then — but one time he came home on leave, and after his visit I took him down to Union Station where all the soldiers were going out, back to their stations and bases. And I remember Harry McLean there that night. He had climbed up into the girders above Union Station and he was throwing dollar bills all over the place. He climbed up into those girders by himself! And I'm telling you, I never saw anything like that in my life.

And I can tell you a bear story. My brother in the air force came home one time in an air force truck and he brought a young bear with him — a mascot bear. And he brought it up to our farm and we kept it there. And there used to be people around that knew Harry McLean real well. So one day they came down and they said to us, "How about selling us your bear and letting us take it up to the hunt camp?" So we did.

They took the bear up to the hunt camp and Harry McLean was hunting with them there. They tied the bear outside one night, but it began making a terrible noise and they couldn't sleep. So Harry McLean got up and put the bear in his new car. And when they went outside in the morning, the bear had torn it clean apart, cleaned it right out down to the metal.

But Harry decided to keep the bear. They say he used to take that bear to his bedroom at night with him in the Big House. But one night he got into a real row with the bear and was pretty well bitten up. So he decided to have bear meat. Mackenzie King was prime minister then. Harry took the bear down to the Chateau Laurier and had the cook cook up a big supper and the bear was on the menu. Yes, McLean and Mackenzie King and a whole gang of big politicians had the bear meat for their supper.

The lumberman's raft coming down the Ottawa River was very much like a "floating village", with men, provisions, cookery and sleeping cabin all on board. There were usually fifty cribs in a raft so it did indeed cover a large area. The Ottawa River had sufficient current in most places to bring the raft down. At rapids, slides or canals, the raft was taken apart into its cribs and later reassembled. In Memories of Bytown, W. H. Cluff writes that the raft 'was a pretty sight, a small flag on each sleeping cabin, a flag with the owner's trade mark floating from a tall pole on the cookery, every man at his post with his 24-foot oar duly posed so it could be brought into operation at a motion from the foreman, who was in the centre of the raft.' This photo was taken on the Ottawa River in 1895.

15

The recipe for toe whisky, the opening of the Burnstown General Store, May Day Rites

A MISCELLANY OF TRUE AND ORIGINAL STORIES GATHERED FROM ALL OVER THE VALLEY

Anson A. Gard was an Ohio American who, in his later years at the turn of this century came to Canada and was so taken with the "unknown land" that he decided to write about it. As he says in his introduction to one of his books, "I came to Canada and found a land so full of beauty and resources so vast, that I felt a desire to let my people and the world know of this great Northland." With this purpose in mind, Gard wrote a number of books, including The Hub and the Spokes *(Ottawa, 1904), probably the best-known of his works.* The Hub and the Spokes *is a meandering collection of brief travelogues in the Ottawa Valley, descriptions of geography, anecdotes, vignettes, "Ottawanettes", and sometimes amusing dialogues between the Colonel and Rube, a Boswellian device in which Gard plays Rube, the diarist or raconteur, and the Colonel the American foil.*

Rube describes a day-trip he and the Colonel took up the Ottawa River over Deschênes Lake to Fitzroy Harbour, Ontario, and Quyon, Quebec. They boarded a streetcar from Ottawa to Queen's Park in Aylmer, Quebec, where they caught the steamer, the George B. Greene, run then by Captain Chartier. The boat was filled with both Canadian and American excursionists and tourists enjoying half a day on the Ottawa for half a dollar. A man named Kedy who owned the Grand View Hotel at Fitzroy Harbour was chosen as the guide for the trip and, on the way upriver, Kedey tells the legend of Constance Bay, "a beautiful sheet of water."

In the early French days, the voyageurs' only means of reaching the far West was by Ottawa. On one occasion a large number of these voyageurs were coming up the river from Montreal for furs.

They would have run into an Indian ambush at this point but for a warning given them by a friendly Indian. He pointed out the camp where the Iroquois were entrenched, waiting for them. The voyageurs turned and made a wide detour, coming up Buckham's Bay behind the camp of the savages. After a short sharp battle, they killed all the Indians and went on their way up the Ottawa towards the West.

"Say, Kedey?" Rube asked, "Suppose the Indians had made that wide detour and, after a short sharp battle, had killed all the voyageurs, would it have been called a battle?"

"Oh, no, indeed," Kedy replied, "It would, in that case, have been called a wicked massacre."

Gard gives a brief description of landmarks along their route, Berry's Wharf, Pinhey's Point, Smith's Point, Armitage's Wharf, the Dominican Cottage, Twelve-Mile Island, Basken's Wharf, Mohr's Island, McLaren's Wharf, Fitzroy Harbour, Quyon. Of Quyon he writes, "The only considerable town on the way is reached shortly before coming to the Chats (Shaw) Falls. It is a summer resort for many Ottawans." He tells an amusing event which occurs at this point.

"Oh, look!" exclaimed an American lady passenger on board, shortly after passing Quyon. "There comes a town down the lake! Drawn by a steamboat! Say, Mr. Kedey, it that the way you move your towns up here in Canada?"

"My dear lady", Kedey returned. "That is not a town. That is a timber raft."

"A timber raft!" she exclaimed. "Why it looks like a Lilliputian town with all those tiny houses on it! Oh, isn't it just too funny!"

Pembroke, it would appear, was Anson Gard's favourite Valley town. This opinion seemed to have been based on its superior hospitality and its very scenic setting overlooking river and mountains. He was also partial to Pembroke because, even in those days, Pembroke story-tellers seemed to be capable of creating the wildest Tall Tales in the Valley. In a preamble Gard says the story was "one that had been told me only a few days before" (in Algonquin Park). It was one I would not have believed myself had I not had each part of it verified to my own eyes. It is but a sample story often repeated in this land of greater fishers and hunters."

"We had not been having very good luck fishing that morning" said the Pembroker. "But we moved the canoe down about one hundred yards and started in to 'whip'. Well, sir, you never saw trout snap the fly like them trout snapped it at that new hole! In less than ten minutes we had thirty as fine five-pounders as you ever saw. Here's one of them I had mounted."

There on the walls of his dining-room he showed me one of the fish mounted, as fine a specimen as I ever saw.

The Pembroker took another drink — of water

A timber crib with oarsman descending a timber slide, probably the Chaudiere at Hull, Quebec. The cribs, containing about twenty pieces of timber each, were formed by placing two round logs called 'floats' about 24 feet apart and then placing the squared timber between them. Poles called 'traverses' were then laid over the top of the timbers and pinned at each end of the floats. 'Loading timbers' were dragged on top of the traverses to keep the huge squared timbers from moving backwards and forwards. The river drivers would incorporate this crib once again at the bottom of the slide into the 'village' raft of timbers to make the journey to market in Montreal or Quebec.

TIMBER SLIDE

The image of the bear is firmly implanted in the Canadian psyche. Marian Engel was right when she wrote her award-winning novel, Bear. From my experience in oral history, I would say that in the Ottawa Valley there are as many if not more tall tales about bears as there are about fish. According to the tall-tale tellers, the bear in this photograph was one of the largest ever shot in Pontiac County!

— and continued as he started towards the parlour. "By this time I had grown tired of fishing and paddled the canoe out to the bank. We had just started up the bank when I saw two fine bucks in exact range. I am very quick and up went my gun like a flash. I fired and brought them both down, shooting both through the heads. And here are the heads."

And there were the heads, one on each side of the large hall.

"But a strange thing occurred when I fired that shot. There were two partridges sitting on a limb almost in exact range with the bucks. Well, sir, you may imagine my surprise when I saw both of them drop. I picked them up, put them into my game bag, and went on to the bucks. I did not think about the birds any more until I reached home, when I found both alive, they only having been stunned by the passing bullet. Here are the two birds. Now, honest, ain't they fine?"

I had to admit they were beauties. The Pembroker continued with his story.

"Well, after we had hung up the two bucks,

the old guide said, 'Say, I have a bear trap set over here to the left near a little creek. Let's go over and see what may be in it.' We went over, and bless you, there was as fine a bear as you ever saw, fat and full of fight. But I soon fixed him. I was by this time tired out with good luck. But the old guide said, 'I have another bear-trap down by the big pine. Let's go over and see what's in it.' We went over and sure enough, there was another bear, and here are the two skins. I had them both tanned for parlour rugs."

And there, sure enough, were the two bear rugs on his large parlour floor. It was very hard for me to believe his story. But what was I to do when, as I said before, he verified each part of it, by proof to my very eyes?

This story, almost as I have told it, was related to me in Pembroke as true, and the man had not been drinking anything but water, either.

As far as I can ascertain from my research so far, Anson Gard, an American, was the first oral historian in Canada. He probably was unaware of it, but he did pass from oral to written tradition many stories about people in The Hub (Ottawa) and the Spokes (the towns surrounding the city). In particular, he recorded a number of good stories about outstanding figures of the day including Sir John A. MacDonald, Sir Charles Tupper, Sir Sanford Fleming, Sir James A. Grant, M.D., George Johnson (then Dominion Statistician), Benjamin Sulte, historian and then President of the Royal Society of Canada, even William Wilfred Campbell, the poet.

Three-quarters of a century was to elapse before anyone, and least of all a Canadian, began again to translate the stories of the people from the oral to the written tradition. Some of the following stories were told by the people about the people on various openline programs on Ottawa radio in the last few years. I have translated them onto the record.

I've got a story that goes back to 1920 about the French faction of the Riopelle family. It was told to me by my uncle, who is in his late seventies and has a million stories. His name is Riopelle. My great-grandfather got his eye taken out by one of the Riopelles with a pike-pole when they were logging and the fights were just bloody. My grandfather's family and the Riopelle family used to meet every New Year's Day for a fight. My uncle says they would meet, and they would battle it out, and then the women would dress the wounds when they came home. One side would win one year, the other the next. It went on for twenty years in the Roaring Twenties.

Anyway, Riopelle lived here and when I was a young boy, he was an old caretaker at the school. Mr. Riopelle was a French faction of the Riopelles and he was one heck of a ball player and he used to barnstorm as a pitcher all around the Valley, all over the place. What my uncle says about this man was that one time he was playing for St. Gerard's Church. You know, everybody played on Saturday afternoon and they would have maybe two thousand people come out and watch the game. Riopelle was such a heck of a ball player that everybody wanted him to play for them. Anyhow, he was on the mound pitching this one Saturday. And he let a fast ball go. And in those days nobody wore any equipment. The batter swung at the ball,

tipped it and it flew back and hit the catcher in the groin. He jumped up and down with the pain. In fact he was in so much pain that, within two seconds, he dropped his pants and had a bowel movement. In front of two thousand men, women and children!

Ed Freel was in charge of Lansdowne Park for years until Montreal stole him away from us. Back when Stan Lewis was the Mayor of Ottawa, one year the Ottawa Exhibition was coming up and Stan went over to Lansdowne to look things over.

"Say, Ed", he said to Ed Freel, "The grass is awful brown."

And Ed says, "Well you know, Stan, that we got no water this year."

And Stan says, "Oh! You're going to have to get some fast because there's a bunch of trout that we put in Patterson's Creek and they've been there for three months and don't even know how to swim yet."

And this one goes back to the days when Ray Boucher[1] was actively refereeing in the CFL. This was twenty-five, thirty years ago, and Teddy Mc-Claritidy, a family friend of ours, was playing for the Rough Riders at the time. And he was called for an infraction. I believe it was holding, and Teddy didn't think too much of the call from Boucher. He put his hands on his hips and fumed and did a slow burn and finally burst out, "Boucher, you stink!" Whereupon Ray, after marking off the roughing infraction, trooped off another ten yards against the Rough Riders. He turned around smartly, put the ball down and said, "OK, McClartidy, how do I smell from here?"

The following groups of stories, many of them told on the open line programmes, have been gathered together from the little towns surrounding Ottawa that provide "the Spokes" for "the Hub and the Spokes" image: Aylmer, Rockland, Manotick Station, Ingleside, South March, Cumberland, Dunrobin, Lanark, Arnprior.

The Battle of Foran's Grove

My forefathers were Forans and they settled on the Aylmer Road and the Eardley Road. The first one settled across from the racetrack — it's still there— in that big stone house — it's still there — and the other one about four and a half miles the other side of Aylmer towards Luskville. And when the

This postcard dated June 23, 1913, was sent from Mabel Denison to her relatives in Eganville, Ontario with the usual message, "We're coming on up. Meet the train." In the background is the famous Cattle Barn still standing today at Landsdowne Park. In the old days, according to one anonymous story-teller, the Cattle Barn was used for more than livestock shows. "My grandfather used to tell me about two strongmen from Metcalfe, Ontario, Horace and Gibb MacGregor. One time when the roads weren't ploughed too well around Metcalfe, their old car ran off the road and into a ditch. They were so angry about it getting stuck on them,

that they just picked it up themselves and lifted it right back onto the road. My father also told me that they used to have boxing and wrestling competitions at the Ottawa Exhibition in the old Cattle Castle. They used to taunt Horace until he would actually climb into the ring with some of the world's best. And one time there was this lad who was a world contender and Horace beat him. So the men who put on the world competitions wanted Horace to go on the international circuit with them. But Horace wouldn't. He stayed at home on the farm."

railroad was going through — I don't know the real name of it because we always called it the PPJ (Push, Pull and Jerk), it was to cross the land that the Forans owned which ran right down to the Ottawa River. And one of my Foran forefathers went to the fence — his fence — just as the railroad construction crew was coming up, and he sat there with a shotgun and he said, "You're not crossing my land. My cattle aren't going to cross over a railroad track to get to water."

So this was a stand-off for quite some time because they didn't want to push it towards a showdown and they didn't want to get shot, and they

knew he meant business.

They came back the next day and Foran was still sitting on guard with his shotgun. The foreman told him that it was going to be war if he came back again and found him still there. Well, the construction crew came back again and they found Foran still there with his shotgun. Only this time he had with him a notorious wild fighting crew from the Gatineau called the Mountain Men. There were no shots fired but Foran won in the end. He got the only two culverts that you could actually drive a train through on that line.

Years ago when King George and Queen Elizabeth came here to visit, oh, way back long years ago, when they came down our road at Aylmer near the Conroy cemetery, there was just my sister and I there when they appeared. But within ten minutes there must have been 150 there at our gate while the King and Queen strolled down the road. We had been intending to go to Ottawa the very next day for the unveiling of the War Memorial and try to see them then. But there they were right at our place! And my son, then aged seven, was in the maple bush picking mayflowers — and he gave them to the Queen — and she patted his dog. He was so excited he couldn't go to school for a week. And for months everybody was at our door wanting to buy our dog because the Queen had patted it!

This young couple by the name of Slavinsky moved into an old farmhouse near Rockland, Ontario, just south of Ottawa. They were the only English-speaking people in an area that was about 90 percent French-speaking. One day Mrs. Slavinsky looked out her kitchen windows and saw that the fields were on fire. Quickly she telephoned her neighbour adjacent to warn her about the fire, which was spreading even as she dialled.

"Mrs. Dubois! Mrs. Dubois!" Mrs. Slavinsky cried out, "Did you know that there is a fire out in our fields?"

"Oui, oui," said Mrs. Dubois, "I saw the fire an hour ago. But it is in your fields, not ours."

Mrs. Slavinsky slammed down the receiver and dialled the number for the Rockland Fire Department.

"This is Mrs. Slavinsky speaking. Will you please come quickly. There is a fire spreading in the fields."

"Sorry. Very sorry, Madame," the voice on the other end responded. "We cannot come today. This is a holy day."

In the meantime, Mr. Slavinsky was frantically trying to dig ditches, shovel dirt onto the grass fire, while the neighbours — all Canadians of French descent — stood around and watched him. Only when one of these spectators thought that the fire was spreading towards his place did Mr. Slavinsky get any help at all. The neighbour worked for a while beating at the flames and then, when he was sure they were not headed for his place, he rejoined the spectators.

Back in the house, Mrs. Slavinsky frantically dialled the Plantagenet Fire Department.

"Sorry. Very sorry, Madame," the voice came back. "We can only go out on call in your area

when the Rockland Fire Department asks us to go."

Finally in desperation, Mrs. Slavinsky phoned the OPP and told them the problem. "There's a fire spreading in our fields here," she cried out, "And it's fast approaching the Larose reforestation area!"[7]

Within a few seconds the police and fire alarms were sounding in the area, helicopters were approaching and water bombs were dropped.

"Yes, thank God for the English in Canada!" Mrs. Slavinsky said later then telling the whole story to the reporters from Ottawa.

Back in 1930 a lad from Arnprior walked to Ottawa to buy some bedroom furniture. When asked why he replied, "I needed to sleep."

My roots in the Ottawa Valley go back to the early 1800s. My parents both were born in South March in the early 1870s. Around 1890 my father was working as a bartender in the old Klondike Inn at South March and he told dozens of stories about the area. But the one he seemed to like telling the most — he lived to be eighty-four — was about the time his Protestant neighbour, a member of the Loyal Orange Lodge for years, became King Billy for the Twelfth of July parade. Oh, that was as high up as you could go! We were Catholics, of course, and on the eve of July 11 my father and another R.C. friend stole into the neighbour's barn and painted King Billy's white horse — he always rode a white horse in the Twelfth of July parade — painted his white horse with green stripes. The neighbour who was King Billy found out the next day who did it, and chased my father and his friend, the two of them, all the way into Ottawa and, according to my father's story, they had to hide out there with relatives for about a week. That was a long trip into Ottawa in those days and a very long run.

Another time, my father told me, one of the farmers from South March had a serious illness in the family and nothing would do but he go fetch the priest from St. Patrick's Church in Ottawa. This was in the 1900s and the priest's name was Father Whalen. So the farmer drove in the long distance to Ottawa with his horse and buggy and picked up Father Whalen, who had a reputation for being real crotchety. On the way back to South March, Father Whalen got impatient with the long drive and said to the farmer, "Get going. Get that horse moving." And the farmer from South March was just about the same type as Father Whalen, so he says, "Whoa, there," to his horse and pulls him over to the side of the road.

"I might as well be walking as this!" says Father

Whalen.

And the farmer says, "Yes, and that is just about as dry a spot as any to get out. You can walk from here."

My father had dozens of stories like that one. He used to tell one about the farmer back in the days when sons were an asset on the farm and it was the custom that at least one son would stay on the farm and work it — and probably inherit it. So one day one of these sons of one of my father's neighbours said to his father, "Pa, I'd like to get more of an allowance for working the farm. As a matter of fact, if you don't give me more of an allowance, I'm going to pack up and leave."

And the old farmer pointed to the road and said to his son, "There you are. It's sixty-six feet wide and as long as you want to take it!"

There are two sayings you still hear often out in South March: "to go out and feed the hay" and "setting the tea."[8]

Anyhow, there's lots of Armitages out in South March and they have made a lot of money and very often they go down south to Florida. This happened about ten years ago and I know it's true. Some of the Armitage lads from South March were down there and they got involved in a very big card game. There were real VIPs at the table. One guy was a senator. There were about six sitting around the table, most of them very impressive people. So this guy from South March says to himself, "What am I going to say I do when they ask me? What am I going to say my profession is?" So finally one of them asked him, "Armitage, what the hell do you do for a living up there in Canada?"

And he said, "Well, amongst other things I happen to be the mayor of South March, Ontario, Canada."

And one of the VIPs turns to him and says, "In that case then your name must be Foley."

These are a couple of shanty stories that my uncle Downey from Manatick Station used to tell. He's been dead a long time and it happened long before I was born. Anyhow, when we were all kids he'd be telling us these stories and he'd tell us about how he'd go out to the bush to work for the lumbermen, and how hard, hard, hard the shantymen had to work. It would still be dark when they'd start out in the morning and they'd still be working in the dark at night, and walking back to camp in the dark, too. Every day of the week. And one day he was the last one leaving the bush to go into the shanty for supper, and somehow or other he got lost, got mixed up on the roads in the bush,

and he couldn't find his way back to camp. So he came to this big ram pike and he crawled up on it. We'd always ask him, "What's a ram pike, Uncle John?" And he'd say, "Well, that's a big high stump of a tree that was cut off when the snow was deep."

So anyhow, Uncle John crawled up on this big ram pike to see if he could see the lights of the camp and here, by golly, the thing was hollow and he fell down inside it, right to the bottom. He couldn't get out, so he thought he'd stay there for the night and when daylight would come he'd start shouting and somebody would hear him. But during the night he heard something climbing up on the outside of the ram pike. And what was it coming down inside the hollow stump towards him but a big black bear! Now, a bear always backs down into a hollow tree or stump and Uncle Johnny knew that. So he waited until the bear got close enough to him and he caught hold of its tail. The bear let out a roar and took off upwards in flight. "By golly," said Uncle Johnny, "in no time at all we both were sailing right out of that stump!"

Uncle Johnny also used to go shantying out West on those harvest excursions and he was always telling us about these little poisonous snakes they had out there. They were even worse than a rattlesnake and they'd call them hoop snakes and the reason they were called hoop snakes was because they caught their tails in their mouths and they'd roll along like a wheel. So one day Uncle Johnny was hoeing potatoes and he saw a hoop snake coming up the row that he was hoeing on. So he stepped over into the next row to let the snake go by. And as the snake passed him, it happened to touch the hoe handle. And Uncle Johnny said, "Would you believe it? It wasn't a minute until the hoe handle was swelled up so big I couldn't hold it in my hand."

Uncle Johnny had two sayings I remember well: "You'll live until you die, if you don't get your feet wet," and, "The cows are down in the field beyonst the bush."

My grandfather was Dick Muldoon from Dunrobin. He had a brother who lived up in Eardley at Quyon. He weighed 460 pounds. I don't remember him, but I do remember Grandpa, Dick Muldoon. He was a small fellow. Only about 340 pounds. He was almost totally deaf, but he always said he could hear what he wanted to hear. So he used to go down and bring a bunch of produce to the market on Saturdays — to the Ottawa market. Now he always was a soft touch. Everybody knew him

This bear photograph was taken in the 1930s some place north of Sudbury at a diamond-drilling site. Bored, lonely, macho men might befriend a cub like this one to tease and play with. The relationship changed when the bear was full-grown. Even today in the Province of Quebec there are men who make their living hunting bears.

because of his size; they also knew him because he always had a buck or two in his pocket. Anyhow, one day after the market was over, they all went, as usual, to the old Commercial Hotel to have a few. A friend of Grandpa Muldoon's came along — a sort of sponger lad — and he tapped Grandpa on the shoulder and said, "Could you lend me a dollar, Dick?" So Grandpa put his hand up to his ear and cocked his head and said, "What did you say?" And the sponger said, "Could you lend me five dollars, Dick?" And Grandpa said, "I heard you the first time."

Grandpa Muldoon always had his farm well equipped. He was the only one in the area that had the newfangled machinery and, naturally, people up and down the road — his neighbours — would come to borrow some of it, eh? And it would come back broken sometimes. Or they wouldn't return it and Grandpa would have to go and fetch it back again. Well, anyhow, one day Grandpa Muldoon and my uncle went to an auction sale. There was an old manure spreader up for sale there and the wheels were broken and the conveyor was broken and the tongue was gone out of it. When the auctioneer came to the manure spreader, Grandpa bid fifteen dollars on it and got it. So my uncle said to him, "Good Lord, Dad, you just bought a new manure spreader this spring! What did you buy this piece of junk for?"

And Grandpa said, "That's the lender."

Here's one from Lanark County. There was an old fellow by the name of Paddy Vaughan in Carleton Place. He was a blacksmith. There was a fellow came in there one day to his blacksmith's shop and was boasting about how far back he remembered. Paddy listened for a while and then he said,

"Oh hell! I can remember back to the time in Carleton Place when the Mississippi River only ran as far as the bridge on Main Street."

Mick Burns of Perth was one of the great characters of Lanark County. He was a great, great lad and a Roman Catholic. Now, one time the Presbyterian church in Perth had a fire, a bad fire, and they wanted to hire someone to take the remains down and level it off. They asked Mick Burns what he'd charge for the job and he said, "I'll take that damn Presbyterian thing down for nothing."

Mayo is a small, remote, obviously Irish community in the Gatineau situated on the Blanche River, a tributary of the Ottawa River. The teller of this collection of stories has his ancestry in the Mayo country, but the Chief Sharbot of whom he speaks was an Algonquin whose tribes held the original lands around Sharbot Lake and after whom Sharbot Lake was named. Tommy Sharbot of Calabogie, one of the most renowned fiddlers of the Valley, also belongs to this family of native people. One of his most outstanding assignments was as the fiddler in the screenplay, The Best Damn Fiddler from Calabogie to Kaladar.

My grandfather was James Haley from up at Mayo. My other grandfather, who used to get into all the fighting in the shanty, was Red Tom Daly. Red Tom Daly was the grandfather that set fire to Paddy Egan's paper on his doorstep. He's been dead about twenty years now. When him and his short brother, Pat, would come into a dance, everybody would sort of go along the walls. Like, they're here and what's going to happen now? He was called Red Tom because his hair was red. Then there was Black Tom Daly and there was Fighting Tom Daly, and all the other ones. My mother was a very humorous person, too, and she'd often say when the newcomers would come in, "Well, well! We'll have to go over and neighborize with them people." And my grandfather used to say, "Well, he was always a good-looking lad — until he got that bottle in the face."

Grandpa Daly, he used to get kind of wound up. And there was this old lad — one of his best friends down the street — and he used to borrow the paper from him every day. And the old lad used to say to my grandfather, "You can borrey it. But bring that paper back. I want that paper back this evening."

So one time Grandpa Daly got real mad and he brought the paper back all right, but he set fire to it on the damn steps. He said to the old lad — Paddy Egan — his best friend down the street — "You want your paper back? Well here it is." And he put a match to it.

My other grandfather, Grandfather Haley, he used to have all kinds of tricks when he'd be up hunting in the bush. He used to have the lads from the Ottawa police force up to his place. This was during the Dirty Thirties. He used to carve up plug tobacco to make it look like deer droppings. And then he'd go out in the bush with the lads from the police force and one of his neighbours, Mr. Preston.

And they'd be marching along the trail and he'd come across some droppings on the trail and he'd reach down and take a bite. "Here, Preston," he'd say to his neighbour, who was in on the whole thing, "What do you think of this? It tastes pretty fresh to me." And Mr. Preston, he'd take it, too, and he'd say, "Yes, Daly, it is pretty fresh." And the green-horn policemen would be standing there all agog, thinking they were hot on the trail of the deer, and my grandfather would say to them, "Yes, you've come to the right place. There are real hunters up here."

My father used to go out hunting, too. And they often used to have along with them on their hunting gang this French lad who told tall tales. He was always saying he'd been here and there, done everything, seen everything. One time my father shot this deer, but they couldn't locate it. He fortunately had this Indian chief with him in the gang, a Mr. Sharbot. So my father said to the gang, "Why do we need to tramp through the bush looking for the deer when we have this Indian here who can smell deer a mile away?" And the French guy who told the tall tales said, "What the hell do you mean? Nobody can smell deer!" Now, my father and this Indian chief Sharbot were not only in cahoots but they had already figured out where the deer was. So they winked at one another and started to put this French guy on. So then Chief Sharbot says to the French guy, "Stand back there. You're throwing my nose off."

"Yes," my father yells out, "stand back and give Chief Sharbot room."

So the French guy stands back and so does everybody else. And Chief Sharbot starts sniffing. He sniffs all around. He goes to the left and sniffs. "No," he says, "I can't smell deer here." Then he goes to the right. "Ah," he says, "there it is. Right this way."

So my father turns to the French guy and he says, "Now you saw that. This Indian smelt deer."

And the funny part about it was that, about a year later, my father was in a bar and he hears this guy in the other room saying in a loud voice, "I was right there! I seen it. This Indian could smell out the deer — where it was."

He's having a terribly hard time proving this to his friends and listeners. They all think he is into the BS, the tall tales. So the guy spies my father in the bar and he goes and brings my father into his side of the bar and says, "This man was right there. He saw the Indian smell the deer. Isn't that right? You were right there when that Indian, that Chief Sharbot, smelt out the deer, eh?"

And my father couldn't say anything but yes.

The following group of stories arise from the Renfrew area and the towns and country around there, Springtown, Eganville, Douglas, Killaloe, Barry's Bay, Clontarf, Rockingham.

These two lads a long time ago were working · together on the railway when it was going through Renfrew. One was holding a big spike, the other one the sledge-hammer. And the lad holding the spike said to the other lad, "When I nod my head, hit it." So he did.

These two lads from Renfrew were working on the roof of a building in town. And one lad said to the other, "Are you holding tight to the eaves-troughing?" And the other lad said, "Yes. Why?" "Because I'm taking the ladder away now," came the reply.

This MP from Renfrew County used to always like to take some of the rough redneck greenhorn Renfrew lads to wine and dine with him in the Royal York in Toronto. It was a sort of reward system for the help he got in his political campaigns. So one time this MP from Renfrew County was in the Royal York in the main dining room with some of the lads from Renfrew, one of whom was busily engaged in eating his peas off his knife. Gradually the MP from Renfrew County realized that all the dining room guests at the surrounding tables were watching in a mixture of horror and amusement the lad eating his peas with his knife. So finally the MP from Renfrew County turned to them all and said in a loud voice, "Don't worry. He won't stab himself. He's used to it."

One time this Cavanagh lad from back of Rockingham went down for his first visit to the big town of Renfrew. When he got back home, quite naturally the folks there all gathered round to hear his impressions. "How'd you like it, Tommy?" they asked.

"Oh, the town's fine, fine," said Cavanagh, "but the people there are very dirty."

"How come?" the folks asked him.

"Begorra, now, they all go to the bathroom inside, so they do."

Sophie and Emery Harper of Clontarf had been married a long, long time indeed, had celebrated their Diamond Anniversary. During all that time, it had been noted in Clontarf, Emery had never once opened his mouth without that Sophie had interrupted him or corrected him or criticized him.

So this one evening Emery is trying to tell a story to some friends in Clontarf and, sure enough, Sohie interrupts him and tells him how to tell the story.

Emery looked around at the circle and burst out, "There now! Can you see how hen-picked I am?"

"Hen-pecked," Sophie corrected.

"Hen-pecked."

This is a story about my uncle, Tom Murray of Barry's Bay. I used to enjoy sitting down talking with him and, of course, he did most of the talking. He could go back to picnics in Arnprior in 1895 and he lost most of us. But one afternoon my brother and I were up visiting and this nephew of Tom's was sitting there, too. And the nephew was then sixty-eight and Tom was ninety-six or ninety-seven. Tom was going on about how he had never had a drink until he was seventy years old. Then the doctor told him he should put on some weight — he only weighed 140 pounds — so he started drinking, on the doctor's advice, two pints of porter a day. So that was fine. But then Tom graduated from porter to Red Cap. So throughout our visit that afternoon, Tom would say, "It's getting a little thirsty. I think maybe I should have a beer. Would you all like a beer?" So we all agreed that we would. So out of the room Tom went to get the beer and I said to his son, M.J., who was sitting there at the time as well, "How has your father been lately healthwise?"

"You should know. You've been talking to him for the last three hours," said M.J.

"Well, yes", I said. "He seems great but after all a man of his age ——"

"The only thing I can tell," said M.J., "I think he drinks too much for his age."

"Well!" I said. "What do you tell a man of ninety-seven? That it's bad for his health?"

Well, anyhow, I had friends who lived between Renfrew and Admaston and their son Joe got pneumonia and Dr. Murphy from Renfrew would come out in his horse and buggy and prescribe medicine for him. So Joe seemed to be getting a bit better and, on his next call, Dr. Murphy said to Joe's mother, "Cook chicken and just give him the chicken broth." So that's fine. That's what Joe's mother did. But Joe got up in the middle of the night and got the chicken out of the icebox and ate the whole thing. His mother was frantic; Joe was supposed to eat the chicken broth but not the chicken. She phoned Dr. Murphy very early in the morning — you know how early farmers get up — and Dr. Murphy came out and brought an emetic so that Joe would bring up the chicken. But Joe wasn't going to take any of the damn emetic, so he gave it to the cat. The cat died, but Joe got better.

This very elderly gentleman of Eganville was painfully discovering his potency waning. Whenever he found himself ready for love-making he let his wife know about it immediately. However, they slept in separate rooms and almost always by the time he found her and/or she managed to get to

Jean Beaudry, Delore Belanger and a lad named Arkinson pouring 'one for their own health' in the old Rosemount Hotel in Mattawa at the turn of the century.

him — she had slowed down in her own way as well — his love-making apparatus had faded away to a mere waterworks. Finally in desperation the elderly gentleman from Eganville went to his doctor and complained about his problem.

"I have a good idea," said the sympathetic doctor. "Keep a gun at your side at all times, and when you find yourself ready, fire an immediate shot."

The elderly gentleman from Eganville thought this a good idea and promised to try it out.

Several months later the doctor met the elderly gentleman from Eganville on the street in town. "How did your plan work out?" the doctor enquired.

"Oh, it backfired something turrible," said the elderly gentleman from Eganville.

"How come?" the doctor asked.

"Well, we forgot that it was hunting season and she wore herself out."

I live out along the St. Lawrence River at Ingleside. It used to be called Altsville and years ago we used to have an old doctor here by the name of Brown. I used to have a milk run there and a Mr. Hart told me this story. Over on the island there used to be a number of farmers and when one of these farmer's wives was expecting a baby, Dr. Brown would be called in from Altsville. The doctor would come down to Hart's place on the shoreline and leave his horse there. In the summertime Hart would row Dr. Brown across the river and in the wintertime he'd take him across the ice by horse and sleigh. One day they were in the boat and Hart was rowing Dr. Brown back from the island. And Hart said to the doctor: "Do those people over there ever pay you?"

And Dr. Brown said, "How much do they pay you for bringing me back and forth?"

And Hart said, "Nothing."

"Well," said Dr. Brown, "we're in the same boat."

Along with Leslie Hanson, Johnny Campbell of White Lake is one of the few living people who can still speak with authenticity in the oral tradition about his memories, observations, and feelings surrounding the feudal system that the Last Laird Archibald MacNab maintained for twenty years in the White Lake district. But he also had stored in his memory a fund of amusing stories about the characters, customs and politics of his community.

The infamous Laird Archibald MacNab of Arnprior and White Lake, Ontario,[10] always used to carry a C-bill[11] to pay for his lodgings wherever he went in the Ottawa Valley. He thought it very funny that no one could change it, and so he always got off without having to pay.

I can tell you some stories about a relative of mine, Lame Jimmy McLaughlin.

Lame Jimmy got lame because there was once a teacher in Renfrew who used to make the children sit on a damp rock outside the school with their legs crossed as punishment for wrongdoings. And that's what happened to Lame Jimmy. He got crippled from the damp rock. And I knew of a man who went to school there in Renfrew and he swore afterwards if he ever met up with that teacher, he'd shoot him. He met him later but by then, he said, the teacher was too old to beat up. Lame Jimmy taught school. He taught my father. He was quite a man to drink, and he was very clever. He was a man to be reckoned with around election times because he was a very great speaker. So the Tories bought him a printing press and set him up in Arnprior. Most of the McLaughlins, you know, had always been Liberal. But when the Tories bought Lame Jimmy the printing press, he — and a lot of other McLaughlins — turned Tory.

So Lame Jimmy was publishing this Conservative paper in Arnprior and as publisher, of course, used to attend all the political meetings. Now I remember in my time being at this nomination meeting in Renfrew about 1910 or 1911. And one of these

Stewarts from down here — not the Churchfield Stewarts but the lumbermen Stewarts, very prominent Liberals and great speakers — one of those Stewarts was giving a great long speech. And he went on and on. And Lame Jimmy was sitting up front listening to this Liberal Stewart. And he went on and on. And finally Lame Jimmy couldn't take it any longer and he jumped up, took a few steps onto the platform and gave a great pull on Liberal Stewart's whiskers. It was the talk of the country. For years and years. The time Lame Jimmy pulled Liberal Stewart's whiskers.

There was an arsonist in town burning down places and he burnt down Lame Jimmy's printing press. So that was the end of that business. So Lame Jimmy went to Montreal, where he was a reporter for years for the old *Family Herald*. And then he became a Parliamentary reporter in Ottawa. The time the Prince of Wales toured Canada Lame Jimmy was, of course, covering the whole journey. That was the time they ran the Prince of Wales from Arnprior to Ottawa on the lumberman's raft. There was a big reception and press party afterwards. And Lame Jimmy and the Prince of Wales were the only two at the party who got drunk. They got so drunk together they both had to be helped out.

When I was a young boy growing up here people used to often say, "Why, that's as crazy as Vance Miller's will." That was a big newspaper story when I was young, about 1910 or 1911. Vance Miller was that really, really rich Toronto lawyer who started the Stork Derby. A bachelor, he was going to leave all his money to the Sick Children's Hospital in Toronto. And he made an appointment with Administrator Ross and Ross didn't keep it. So Miller made out a new will that went like this:

1. He left his money to the woman who would give birth to the most children in seven years, and started the Stork Derby.

2. He left his Bahama estates to three of his bitterest enemies.

3. He left a bunch of Masses for the Freemasons.

4. He left a brewery share to every ordained minister in Ontario. Except one. During the Prohibition Days down in Windsor these bootleggers were all there. And this Methodist minister went to the police and went at them for not cleaning it up. And they said to him if he knew so much, let him clean it up. And they put him in charge. Well, the first thing he did was he raided a hotel. He made a mistake and went in through a window. And the owner was there and the minister shot him. He was dead. He claimed it was in self-defence and

all that. But he wasn't too popular with a lot of people after that. So Vance didn't leave *him* a brewery share.

I can tell you a funny story about the blazing of the Opeongo Line. Everybody will tell you that it was so crooked because it was blazed by Drunken Dan McCauley. But that's not true at all. There was this blind Indian from Golden Lake and he had an uncanny knack for finding roads through the bush. He worked for the Carswell Lumber Company of Renfrew. And he blazed the Madawaska Hill for the Chief MacNab. Yes, sir. It was no Drunken Dan McCauley but a blind Indian from the Golden Lake Reserve that blazed out the Opeongo Trail.

This land, which belongs to my family and has for generations, was taken up in 1845 by Alexander Stewart, known as Snappy Sandy. The Stewarts around here were divided into two groups: the Churchfield Stewarts — they were teetotallers and they built the first church in Renfrew County and then there were the Drinking Stewarts. Well, one time, Churchfield John Stewart decided he wanted to build a cedar-log barn, thirty-five by fifty. Well, the local builders said it couldn't be done and they stood around and laughed while Churchfield John Stewart erected his barn. It's there to this day.

Burnstown got its name from the creek that ran through there. When I went to school there sixty-five years ago that creek ran year round. But it's nearly dried up now. Burnstown was known first as Johnston's Rock. And I remember the Johnstons. They were so big they could never keep a buggy.

This conglomerate of stories is set in the Springtown – Ashdad – Calabogie – Mount St. Patrick area.

I immigrated to Springtown from Germany and this is a story I brought over with me. In the old country, Germany, the preacher is usually given a house and a plot of land in which to grow his vegetables. So this old relative of mine had a pair of oxen and the preacher asked him if he could come over and plough his garden plot for him. So the old relative did that. A few months later the old relative's mother died and he, believing one good turn deserves another, asked the preacher if he would conduct the funeral service for him. The preacher did that. A few days later the old man got a bill from the preacher for twenty-five marks. He went to the preacher and asked him what the bill was for. The

The story is told that the great river boss Joseph Montferrand always marched his men off to mass whenever they were 'stoppin' over' on The Drive. There can be little doubt that he and his men were blessed for the hazardous journey in this old church at Springtown on the Madawaska River. The ancient burying-ground at the site contains the graves of many of the first settlers in the area.

---

preacher replied, "Well, it takes a lot of headwork to figure out what I'm going to say at a funeral and that bill is for the use of my head." So the old man went quietly home and made out a bill for the preacher. It said: "Please remit fifty marks for the headwork of two oxen."

As Pat was walking to the pub every night in Dublin, he would pass this huge billboard advertising a famous soft drink from Canada. Every night he passed it, going and coming. (It showed a famous soft drink with the competition ads beside it.)

Well, about three months passed and Pat hadn't been into the pub in Dublin even once. So one of the regulars said to the barman, "Have you not seen Pat lately?"

"No," says the barman, "and I don't think we'll be seeing him any more here either."

"Oh," says the regular, "did something terrible happen to him?"

"Well," says the barman, "it did and it didn't."

"What do you mean?" asks the regular.

"Well, he decided to take the advice on the billboard," the barman explains. "You see, he kept reading this sign which said, 'Come over to us. Drink Canada Dry.' So he emigrated."

This is an old Irish expression I heard a girl use one day that I worked with. I've never heard it before or since, but I never forgot it. She happened to come over to say something to me at my desk and she accidentally passed a little bit of gas. And before I could say anything at all, she said,

"Oh! Excuse me, but as my grandmother used to say, 'It's better to have an empty house than a bad boarder'."

One time this man from Calabogie died in the middle of the night. His widow was hysterical and phoned the undertaker in Renfrew. "You must come right away," she said, "I am going crazy alone in this house with the children and this dead body."

The undertaker said he would come, got up, put his pants on over his pyjamas and threw a coat on. In his haste he forgot his false teeth, his glass eye and his toupée.

When he arrived at the house of the bereaved in Calabogie, a little boy answered the door. When he saw the undertaker at the door he yelled out to his mother, "Mummy, Mummy, come quick! Frankenstein is at the door!"

Now, anyone worth his plate of beans in the Ottawa Valley knows that it is a network of valley clans, that the Armstrongs came from around South March; the Dicksons from Pakenham; the MacKechnies from the Pontiac; the Culhanes from

The largest Canada Dry bottle tops in the whole Ottawa Valley

Across the road from the Springtown church, on the river side, is McCrea's stopping-place on the Madawaska, one of the most important heritage resources in the area, and one of the largest log buildings in the country. It was once used as a summer place by McCreas from Toronto and Montreal. It has recently been bought by a developer. It is haunted by the ghosts of all the great rivermen like Chain-Lightning Stewart, Cockeye George McNee, John Henry McHugh, Wild Bob Ferguson, Ned McLaughlin, Lal Box and Gentleman Paddy Dillon, 'King of the Madawaska'. We also know that the giants of the lumbering saga passed through here as well: Joseph Montferrand, the seven Frost Brothers, the Hennesseys from Fort Coulogne, the Coltons from Pembroke, timber barons Carswell, MacKay, Barnett, Pottinger, O'Brien and Booth.

Ferguslea; the Pinks and Whites from Pembroke; and the McNultys from around Ashdad. This is an old story about Ed McNulty from around there.

It seems that, when Ed was one hundred years old, he decided to better celebrate his birthday by climbing on top of a fence-post on the old homestead and doing a step-dance for all the folks who were celebrating with him.

Then, when Ed was one hundred and four and celebrating his birthday once more, the folks in the Ashdad area asked him, "Ed, do you think you can do it again?"

And Ed replied, "You're damn right. But this time I think I might need a chair."

The Opening of the Burnstown General Store

Oh, it was a big day! All sorts of groovy people from Toronto, Montreal, Ottawa, the sophisticates come in from the big cities for a little touch of country class, to "ooh" and "aw" at the square-timbers of our forefathers. We were serving wine and cheese and we had the place all gussied up with crafts from the local artisans and new gingham curtains and all that. And I was doing the lah-de-dah, giving little tours of the premises, pointing out the old oaken counters and the counter stools and the woodwork painted to look like marble, and over here, look see, we have these special drawers for the raw spices and the spool-cupboard — and all of a sudden we all hear this terrible screeching of tires and laying of rubber at the front of the store, and it was a terrible domestic quarrel coming down the hill from Calabogie. This husband and wife were fighting and the husband got out of the car right in front of all our eyes and he was beating on the front windshield with a tire-iron. And she was backing up and running forward trying to run him over. And we're all standing gaping. But then he begins smashing at the windows with the tire-iron and suddenly there are all these people, these groovy people from Toronto, Montreal and Ottawa, backing up to the back of my store, sort of falling over each other as they fall back to the rear.

The domestic quarrel is sort of classic Calabogie. So even although I am a relative newcomer, I realize this and I try to ease the crowd.

"Geeze," I said, "we're having a domestic quarrel here."

I try to keep them together. And I lock the front door.

By this time the guy is looking for a bit of shelter and where better than my high up front porch? So he leaps up onto the store porch and she side-swipes him with the car full tilt as he leaps. She damn near takes a piece out of the front porch. The people in the store all duck down. She voom-vooms again and turns around in a cloud of dust and smoke. He gets down again off the porch and waves the tire-iron at her, yelling, "Come on, you bitch! Come on!" She tries to run him over again. Everyone is mesmerized. But freaked out. Finally she hits him right in the thigh with the front bumper. Oh, you can see he is in pain! You can see it. He crawls up to the front door of the store.

"Let me in. Let me in," he cries in a drunken moan.

"No, no," I say, shaking my head at him.

"No, no," comes the chorus of voices behind me.

"No, no," I say again. "We're closed. The store is closed.

"No, no," comes the chorus of voices behind me. "We're closed. The store is closed."

Finally the police showed up. I had called the police from Renfrew. The husband is sitting on the front porch with the tire-iron in his hand and she's disappeared.

And that's how we opened the Burnstown General Store!

Amongst critics, reviewers, people generally at large, there seems to be a commonly held misconception that the humour of the Ottawa Valley is principally distinguished by the Tall Tale. In actual fact, both Laughing All the Way Home *and* Legacies, Legends and Lies *demonstrate a rich variety of types ranging from the on-going spoonerisms of G. A. Howard to the original wit of Dinny O'Brien of the Burnt Lands of Huntley. The stories extend from sappy slapstick situational comedy to incestuous black humour, from raunchy irreverent to original indigenous, from pithy repartée to amusing legend.*

However, there does appear to be some basis for the misconception that the humour of the Ottawa Valley is principally distinguished by the Tall Tale. Although the humour of the Valley manifests itself in many different forms, still the humour of exaggeration, no question about it, is a predominant thread. Ed Hubert of Pembroke and Bernie Bedore of Arnprior are two Valley story-tellers who prefer this vein, and certainly Carl Jennings of Sheenboro has contributed to it in a major way.

Perhaps to the population at large the most famous examples of humour-of-exaggeration stories are still those which surround the American lumbercamp hero, Paul Bunyan. In actual fact there is a good case to be documented to demonstrate that Paul Bunyan was originally a Canadian lumberjack of French descent who went to the New England woods to lumber and there was adopted by the Americans. There is evidence of Bunyania on both sides of the border. Carl Jennings told Bunyan stories in Laughing All the Way Home *and here the late Ken Hodgins (see* Some of the Stories I Told You Were True*) originally from Shawville, Quebec, then of Noranda and Renfrew, contributes further to the Canadian collection of Bunyan stories.*

After the winter spent on my grandfather's timber limit at Kazubazua, I spent the summer at home as there was plenty of work on the farm in the summertime. In the fall of 1915 I took a team of horses and went up the Coulonge River for the Gillies Brothers, and skidded or hauled logs all winter. It was that year in the Gillies lumber camps on the Coulonge I first heard stories about Paul Bunyan's lumber camp, and I think they are true stories. The first one I remember went like this:

Paul had a camp one winter in by Powasson in the Muskoka Lake District. At that time it was all square-timber. The country was very hilly although there was fine big white pine for just the kind of square-timber that was in demand for ship masts in England. When the main roads were cut they started hauling out the timber to the river. Paul found that the turns in the road were so short and so sharp that, when Babe, the Blue Ox, pulled a long stick of timber, they nearly all broke in the middle going around the bends. This was no good at all for the value of the timber. It had to be sound and full length to sell well. So Paul Bunyan and Johnny Inkslinger sat down to figure out some way to save the big pine. They talked and planned all night and then (just to prove that there were smart people at that time, too), Johnny had a good idea. They sent a letter to Gillies Brothers at Braeside and asked for boom-chains. When they arrived from the Gillies Brothers, Paul and Johnny fastened one end of the road to a big pine stump and hitched Babe, the Blue Ox, to the other end of the road with the boom-chains. When they gave the order Babe, the Blue Ox, pulled with all her strength. And

they not only straightened out the tote-road completely but they had two miles of road left over.

Another Paul Bunyan story I heard, and this time did not believe, was that they had to use chicken-wire for screens to keep the mosquitoes out of the Bunyan sleep-camp and cookery. When I was in Wisconsin in 1966 I passed by a sign on the road that said, "Three Miles to Paul Bunyan's Logging Camp". We didn't waste any time covering that three miles! When we got there, the first thing I noticed was the chicken-wire netting across the front of the camps. So I asked the attendant if he knew why they had the chicken-wire there. And right away he said, "To keep the mosquitos out." Then he went on to explain further: "Of course everything was big around Paul's camp. Even the mosquitos. And when the men came out of the camp they had not protection from these huge mosquitos. So Paul Bunyan and Johnny Inkslinger went into a huddle. They had heard there was a certain type of bumble-bee in Australia that liked to feed on large mosquitos. So they sent for a boatload of these Australian bumble-bees. When the bees arrived they turned them loose in the camp.

Opeongo Line.

155

Unfortunately, the bumble-bees were all males. So they married the mosquitos and, after that, the mosquitos all had stingers on both ends."

There is a famous refrain that comes often from shantymen talking about their times in the camps and it goes something like this: "There were some lumber companies that fed the horses and starved the men. And there were the others that fed the men and starved the horses." This folk-poem or song, "The Jolly Drovers of West Meath," is about a camp where the horses got "the short end of the stick." It takes place up on the Schyan River and Schyan Bay, as the chorus conveys. But the Schyan River is translated phonetically in the same manner that Des Joachims has come down to us as "The Swisha" or "Swishaw." Phonetically on tape it translates something like "Schwhyo." I cannot remember who gave me this folk-poem. It is signed at the bottom "Code" and I assume that

Code was the author. Many of the men who brought teams to work in the lumber camps cared greatly for their animals and hated to see them abused and ill fed. Johnny McCosh, the foreman in this lumber camp on the "Schwyo," seems to have taken a perverse pleasure in telling the good teamsters that "their horses were getting fat." The Jolly Drovers of West Meath is an example of black humour.

Come all you Jolly Drovers, a story I will tell
Never go up Black River, or there you will catch hell;
Never go up Black River, or you will rue the day
You ever went to draw saw-logs on the Suyo, whyo bay.
The morning we left Westmeath, Westmeath village fair,
Our horses in good order, our sleighs in good repair.
We climbed those rocky mountains, o'er hills and dales we'd go,

'Tis said that some lumber companies starved the horses and fed the men, while others fed the men and starved the horses. It is to be hoped that some fed both!

Until we reached that cursed cove called Suyo,
whyo.

When we reached the shanty our bunks and
chains we rigged;
Our orders are to doubling, be the logs be
small or big;
We need not tell our hardships, but of this to
you we'll sing,
We'd oft times pray, both night and day, we
soon would see the spring.

Now Johnny McCosh was our foreman's name,
as you can plainly see
For killing and murdering horses, it's hanged
he'll surely be;
And when you meet him on the road, he'd
smile and tip his hat
And the first thing that you knew he'd say,
"Your horses are getting fat!"

When we would come in at nine o'clock or
ten
Supper being over, 'twas then the chat would
begin;
Jack he'd sit up 'round beside, listening at the
fun
To hear the teamsters tell about all the trips
they'd run.

Some'd be mixing up the medicine the lame-
ness for to cure;
Others saying, "I must go down. My horses
are getting poor."
And Jack he'd sit up round them, out of them
he'd pick some chat,
And the first thing that you know he'd say,
"Your horses are getting fat!"

There was one young man from Aylmer. We
did not know his name,
We always called him Tuesday. 'Twas on that
day he came;
He stayed until his team broke down. He
thought he'd never get back,
But the foreman still kept telling him, "Your
horses are getting fat!"

'Tis now the winter's over and homeward we
are bound
To see our wives and sweethearts we'd left
alone at home,
To see our wives and sweethearts, and tell
others not to go
To that Godforsaken country called the Suyo,
whyo.

The recipe for "toe whiskey"[4] originated in the
Ottawa Valley through the adventures of a lad
named O'Kelly from Beechgrove. Seems that O'Kelly
went up to Fort MacMurray to work during the
big boom there. One pay day in the coldest part of
winter he went on a drunk and found himself out
in the wilderness with night a-falling. No sleeping
bag, not enough clothes to protect him against the
forty-degree-below and falling temperature, no
matches or fire-making apparatuses. All he had,
indeed, with him was a forty-ouncer of good scotch
whiskey. He decided that it might save his life if
he sipped it slowly all night long. He hoped that he
would keep his body temperature up sufficiently to
survive with alcohol content.

Alas, and however, his fingers and toes started
to freeze anyhow. Finally, one toe froze completely
and broke off in his hand when he was trying to
massage it. Hoping to save it for the time when
he would be rescued and taken to hospital, he put
the toe in the remainder of his whiskey bottle.

At dawn rescuers did indeed find him. but at
the hospital the doctor told him the toe could not be
sewed back on. It was too far gone. The O'Kelly
lad from Beechgrove was a very hardy lad and the
very next night, surgery having been performed,
he was back in the Fort MacMurray Hotel telling
the boys in the bar about his all-night freeze-up
and showing them his toe in his bottle of whiskey.
Everyone was so taken with his story that they
ordered up a new bottle of whiskey for him and filled
up his bottle with his toe in it. This bottle was
solemnly passed around the bar and toasts were drunk
to the lad from Beechgrove and his true Ottawa
Valley toughness and survival spirit. From that time
on, the bottle was never allowed to go empty, and
any time you go to the Fort MacMurray Hotel,
if you wish, you can ask for a drink of toe whiskey
from the bottle still containing the toe of the great
O'Kelly from Beechgrove.

Stories from Cobden and Mud Lake

*When the country bumpkin, the greenhorn and the
ingenue goes to the Big City, the situation creates a
sure-fire formula for humour. The converse is also true.
When the Big City sophisticate moves to the country
or goes back to the land, the scene is also set for laughs.
Dorothy and Bob Turner, a couple in their forties now,
moved to the Valley about sixteen years ago, he to teach
in Pembroke and she to open the Village Pantry in
Cobden. They restored a beautiful log house in the Mud
Lake area. In their adjustment to life in the Ottawa
Valley they made some very perceptive observations and*

experienced some shockingly novel habits and attitudes of the natives.

When Bob and I first moved to the Mud Lake district the one thing we found absolutely incredible was the locals' attitude towards dynamite and dynamiting.

Like our neighbours, Gordon and Pansy Prang. Somebody told Gordon that, if you were having trouble with your well, if you would drop a stick of dynamite down the well, it would loosen it all up and start the water flowing again. So Gordon dropped three sticks of dynamite down his well and his wife Pansy didn't know anything at all about it until she saw the pumphouse going bar-ooooom up into the air! And it landed about twelve feet away from her on the other side of the garden. The explosion broke all the windows in the back of their house, smashed the pumphouse to smithereens. But no water came up from the well.

And this is another dynamite story from the Mud Lake area. This couple had just bought an old house out in the country. It was their first house and a brick house and it was in very poor repair. All the plaster on the walls was cracked and it was so bad they had to do something about the plaster before they could move in. So they were talking to some old people from the neighbourhood and they said the easiest way to solve the plaster problem was to put one stick of dynamite in a pail in the living room and let it off. The old folks said that was not enough dynamite to do any harm, just enough to shake all the old plaster off the walls. Just hang the stick of dynamite on a rope, they said, over the side of the pail. And let it go off.

Well, the young husband didn't want to waste too much time on this short-cut. So he left his wife sitting in the car on the road near the house while he went into the house alone. And he thought to himself, "Well, I'm going to make damn sure this works!" So he put fourteen sticks of dynamite into the pail and he let it off. The roof went straight off and up and the walls straight out in four directions while the wife was sitting in the car watching.

Alvan and Sylvia, other neighbours in the Mud Lake area, had an old log house. It was covered with brick. It had been built without a basement, only a kind of crawl space underneath, and one part of the crawl space was a bit deeper than the other. They couldn't make it any bigger because it was all built on rock. So someone told Alvan, "Hell, Alvan! You can dynamite that all out, make a bigger crawl space if you want." So one day, without telling anybody, Alvan went into the crawl

space and set up all the dynamite and when Sylvia was walking across the living room floor, right before her very eyes, it all rose six inches higher. Yes, Alvan blasted a new basement out, just like that, without ever telling anybody.

These local lads were doing a job somewhere in the Mud Lake district. They did all kinds of manual labour, from framing to masonry, every sort of thing. When they were on the job the only entertainment they had was this battery-operated radio and the only station they could get on it was CHOB in Pembroke. Don Sutherland had a programme on that station and they hated him because he moralized, and they just couldn't stand him for that. Anyway, they had gone through eight or ten jobs listening to this Don Sutherland and they decided together that, at the end of this particular job, they couldn't stand him anymore and they were going to blow him up. So at the end of the job, they dynamited the radio. The radio went whaaam and went straight up into the air, made some circles in the sky, and fell down again. Don Sutherland was still talking.

When we first moved here from the city, the other incredible thing was the party line. Oh, my God! The party line! I was so angry all the time with people listening all the time. When Bob's parents used to phone from Calgary, they'd always say, 'Hello, hellooooo to all the folks at Mud Lake! Because they're all listening!" And they were!

Our neighbours down the road, the Hawkinses, they were on a party line. And they didn't want people to know what they were talking about, so they used to talk to each other in Pig Latin. Soon the story went around that they were talking in strange tongues because one of them had "got religion" and was going daft.

New people moved in down the road, the Willises. Ted Willis had a very salty way of talking. He massages everything he says with a frequent sprinkling of four-letter words. They had just moved into their new house and he was talking on his party line one night to one of his friends, and he wasn't watching what he was saying or anything else. And he hung up after the conversation and, just as soon as he hung up, his phone rang and it was the neighbour down the road and she said to him, "Mr. Willis, I wish you'd watch your language on the phone because there are children listening in, you know."

And another neighbour of ours had this party line he shared with a woman, Big Myrtle, who listened all the time. One time he went to phone

Renfrew and he knew Big Myrtle was on the line so he said, "Myrtle, get off the line. I want to phone Renfrew." "Sure, I'm not listening." she said.

Years later we finally got a private line and we were talking to our neighbours, the Prangs, about how happy we were. They couldn't quite figure that out. And Gordon said, "Well, if I hear the phone ring. I think there is something wrong and I just have to listen and see. What if there was fire in the middle of the night? And what if you needed help? What if someone was stealing your cattle? You'd need help. You wouldn't want me NOT to listen, now would you?" He really believed that! It was his neighbourly duty. And it had nothing to do with the invasion of privacy!

These friends of ours, Jim and Cathy, bought a log house to restore and live in. They bought it because they particularly liked the colour of the old logs, golden reddy-brown. Between the time they bought it from the old farmer and the time they went to move in, he painted it all blue because he wanted it "to look nice for them." It took months and many, many man-hours to get all that blue paint off those logs!

A friend of ours, a sculptress, Joanne Pratt, from Toronto, bought a charming old house in Forrester's Falls. And oh, the locals, they cut her off there! A stranger in town and not only that, but a lady who was an artist! She couldn't even find someone to hire to plough out her driveway! Then the Pembroke paper did a story on her and they found out she was famous. After that, they were lined up to do the driveway.

In the days of Prohibition in the country back of Shawville, Quebec, there was a busy network of stills making potcheen, screech and alcool. Yes, all around Charteris, Yarm, Ladysmith and Otter Lake. The still-keepers always made sure that one still was more obvious so that, when the authorities came in to crack down on the illegal doings, they would always find the one inferior, rather small and more obvious still. When that one was closed down by the police or the RCMP, the other hidden and infinitely superior stills would immediately be turned up to full speed.

A long, long time away from the first of May in Pembroke! This is the Louis Montreuil camp, somewhere in Renfrew County in 1915; teamster, Long Joe Montreuil with loaders Gilbert Montreuil, Leo Doucette and Michele Rail.

My name is Lacey Roach. I'm from Pembroke and I've done the genealogy of the Roach family. I have an amusing ancestral story to tell. The Indians used to cut wood on my grandfather's farm all the time. But finally one of my uncles got possessive about the land and the woodlot and he said to the Indians, "No more cutting on this land." Whereupon Grandfather Roach, hearing of this, rose up in rage and said, "For the first fifteen years we were here on this land, the Indians helped up. We could not have survived without them. So long as I live, they will continue to cut wood here. Amen."

I won't tell you my name but this is a Pembroke story. One time I was working for this old lady as her companion — I was down on my luck then — and she was one of the upper class there. Wealthy, refined, butter wouldn't melt in her mouth most of the time. Well, anyway, along came the first of May and she is going around the house — she was into her nineties then but still dressing for breakfast every morning, having her hair done once a week, and entertaining at teas in the afternoons — she is going around the house chanting, "Hurrah! Hurrah! It's the First Day of May!" Finally I said to her, "What's this fuss all about? What's this about the First Day of May?" And after some coaxing she gave me all of the rhyme:

> "Hurrah! Hurrah!
> It's the First Day of May!
> Fucking in the grass
> Begins today!"

Shortly after the publication of Laughing All the Way Home in November, 1984, to honour one of the great characters and great story-tellers of the Valley, I took the first autographed copy of my book to give to Carl Jennings of Sheenboro. He had more stories to tell at the time. Indeed, I think it was that very day he was talking about some women he didn't like who was noted for her loose reputation in the community and he ended up his dissertation on her characters and morals by saying, "Sure, the truth to tell was that that woman had given most of it away — before she found out she could sell it!" Over the past year or so there have been further stories from that venerable "wit, sage, and master of imagery" as a Maclean's book reviewer so aptly described him.

It was one of the last times I was at church, maybe the last time. Who knows? And it was at the Sheen church and Father Harrington had a full house and he had gone on and on for about two hours. Half the congregation, including myself, had gone to sleep. Well, when it was all over and we

A 1910 photograph of a surprisingly angelic-looking Carl Jennings as a young schoolboy in Ottawa. He had been shipped off to attend St. Patrick's School there.

were filing out past Father Harrington headed for Keon's stable, I shook his hand and said to him rather loudly, "Father Harrington, you should always try to remember that — AFTER FIFTEEN MINUTES YOU'RE ALWAYS LOSING GROUND!"

This old Irish bachelor from Sheen whose name I won't tell you because all his relatives were made a fool of and some of them are still alive to know it. Anyhow, this old bachelor from Sheen was reputed to have great amounts of money stashed away in his safe. He lived on and on up until about ninety-seven or so, and all his relatives were dancing attention on him all the time in anticipation of his dying day when they would inherit his money. He assured them all that all of it was carefully stored away in his safe. Well, he did finally die, and right after the funeral his expectant heirs rushed to the safe. But, alas, no one had the combination to the safe! So they brought in experts from Ottawa,

Montreal, Toronto to crack the combination. Finally an expert from Renfrew named Gravelle — he was famous for opening anything — he opened the safe and all the anxious relatives, expecting piles of money, crowded around and peered in. And there inside, neatly stashed, were three straw hats!

Now, I've told you stories before about my uncle, A. P. Jennings of Chichester, a wonderful blacksmith and one of my favourite uncles. A. P. Jennings lived a long time and had a number of careers. After he sold his blacksmith's shop in Chichester he went to Pembroke to work on pointer boats for Cockburn and Archer. When that finished he went to work in Petawawa at the base as an inspector of small artillery. When he was older someone asked him one time what he had learned from all his experience. "Well," A. P. replied in that slow, easy drawl of his, "I do believe the most

important thing I learned was I learned to hold me tongue."

Danny Morris of Sheenboro had a terrible horse he was very fond of that used to lie down on him all the time whenever it took the fancy to do it. And poor Danny was always breaking his back trying to heave up this horse from wherever she fancied to lie herself down. Often he would have to get help from friends, neighbours, passers-by.

Well, finally he got fed up with the game and sold the horse — although he was really very fond of her. He got a new horse and, after he had had the new horse a little while, all the friends, neighbours, passers-by who had helped him heave up his old horse, well, they all began to ask him about his new horse.

"Come on, Danny. Tell us. Is she any better than the last one?"

An interior shot of a heritage blacksmith's shop at Richmond, Ontario. It is still owned by the Reillys, original settlers in the area.

And poor Danny Morris had to tell the truth.

"Yes, yes," he would say, "She's better in some ways. She's easier to lift."

The Hanrahans were famous in Sheen for, amongst many other things selling the hides off of everything that ever died on their farm. Why, they even tried to sell the hide of an old cat or rooster, it was said. And some of the other farmers in the area really looked down on this practice. Yes, they all sold the hides of animals off their farms, too. But not the hides of everything!

So one time Mike Hanrahan died on the farm and they were going to bury him in the Sheen churchyard. And these two old wags, long-time friends, Clemmie Hayes and Laura Meehan of Sheen were sitting there in front of Keon's bar watching the funeral procession go by. And Clemmie Hayes turned to Laura Meeham and he said, "But god, Laura, I do believe that that is the first time anything ever left Hanrahans with the hide on!"

One time a long time ago in the lumbering days of the Ottawa Valley a shantyman from Chapeau was crossing the ice at the junction of the Pickanock and the Ottawa Rivers. He was crossing over with a favourite horse and sleigh when the ice cracked and the water opened. The old shantyman saved himself but his horse and sleigh disappeared into the cold depths.

The following spring, curious about what might be left around the scene of the accident, he returned to the junction of the Pickanock and the Ottawa and looked down into the clear fresh waters. At first he saw only his own reflection. But then, to his amazement, he beheld below him the biggest fish he had ever seen in his life, swimming along through the water, complete in a horse's harness, collar, hames, and with the reins trailing out behind him.

And for years and years afterwards the American tourists used to come to see that fish swimming in the Pickanock.

Photo Credits

Page xiv, Joan Finnigan collection; p. 3, Irwin
Haggerty collection; p. 6, Finnigan; p. 8, Haggerty;
p. 14, Dr. Jonathan MacKenzie collection; p. 16,
Finnigan; p. 18, Finnigan; p. 22, Finnigan; p. 24,
Finnigan; p. 25, Finnigan; p. 27, Finnigan; p. 28,
Finnigan; p. 31, Finnigan; p. 32, MacKenzie; p. 34,
Finnigan; p. 36, Finnigan; p. 37, Finnigan; p. 39,
Finnigan; p. 41, Finnigan; p. 43, Finnigan; p. 44,
Finnigan; p. 45, Finnigan; p. 46, Finnigan; p. 51,
Finnigan; p. 52, Finnigan; p. 56, Finnigan; p. 58,
Finnigan; p. 59, Mrs. J. E. Green collection; p. 63,
Finnigan; p. 65, Finnigan; p. 68, Finnigan; p. 71,
Finnigan; p. 74, Finnigan; p. 78, Finnigan; p. 80,
Finnigan; p. 82, Finnigan; p. 84, Vic Doucette
collection; p. 92, Finnigan; p. 95, Finnigan;
p. 101, Finnigan; p. 102, Finnigan; p. 108, (both
pictures) Finnigan; p. 112, Finnigan; p. 115,
Finnigan; p. 116, Finnigan; p. 118, Eva Andai
collection; p. 121, Finnigan; p. 122, Finnigan;
p. 127, Finnigan; p. 127, Finnigan; p. 132,
Finnigan; p. 138, Notman collection; p. 140,
Arnprior Museum collection; p. 141, Finnigan;
p. 143, Finnigan; p. 146, Finnigan; p. 148,
Finnigan; p. 149, Finnigan; p. 151, Finnigan;
p. 152, Finnigan; p. 153, Finnigan; p. 155,
Finnigan; p. 156, Finnigan; p. 159, Finnigan;
p. 160, Finnigan; p. 161, MacKenzie.